Fodor's InFocus

FLORIDA KEYS

1st Edition

Where to Stay and Eat
for All Budgets

Must-See Sights
and Local Secrets

Ratings You Can Trust

Excerpted from *Fodor's Florida*

Fodor's Travel Publications New York, Toronto, London, Sydney, Auckland

www.fodors.com

FODOR'S IN FOCUS FLORIDA KEYS

Series Editor: Douglas Stallings

Editors: Mark Sullivan, Douglas Stallings

Writers: Chelle Koster-Walton (primary writer), Julia Neyman

Editorial Production: Carolyn Roth
Maps & Illustrations: David Lindroth, *cartographer*; William Wu and Rebecca Baer, *map editors*
Design: Fabrizio LaRocca, *creative director*; Guido Caroti, *art director*; Ann McBride, *designer*; Melanie Marin, *senior picture editor*
Cover Photo (Key West Lighthouse): Mark Lewis/Digital Vision/Getty Images
Production/Manufacturing: Matthew Struble

COPYRIGHT

1st Edition

ISBN 978-1-4000-0757-8

ISSN 1942-7328

SPECIAL SALES

This book is available for special discounts for bulk purchases for sales promotions or premiums. Special editions, including personalized covers, excerpts of existing books, and corporate imprints, can be created in large quantities for special needs. For more information, write to Special Markets/Premium Sales, 1745 Broadway, MD 6-2, New York, NY 10019, or e-mail specialmarkets@randomhouse.com.

AN IMPORTANT TIP & AN INVITATION

Although all prices, opening times, and other details in this book are based on information supplied to us at press time, changes occur all the time in the travel world, and Fodor's cannot accept responsibility for facts that become outdated or for inadvertent errors or omissions. **So always confirm information when it matters,** especially if you're making a detour to visit a specific place. Your experiences—positive and negative—matter to us. If we have missed or misstated something, **please write to us.** We follow up on all suggestions. Contact the Florida Keys editor at editors@fodors.com or c/o Fodor's at 1745 Broadway, New York, NY 10019.

PRINTED IN THE UNITED STATES OF AMERICA

10 9 8 7 6 5 4 3 2

Be a Fodor's Correspondent

Your opinion matters. It matters to us. It matters to your fellow Fodor's travelers, too. And we'd like to hear it. In fact, we *need* to hear it. When you share your experiences and opinions, you become an active member of the Fodor's community. Here's how you can help improve Fodor's for all of us.

Tell us when we're right. We rely on local writers to give you an insider's perspective. But our writers and staff editors also depend on you. Your positive feedback is a vote to renew our recommendations for the next edition.

Tell us when we're wrong. We update most of our guides every year. But things change. If any of our descriptions are inaccurate or inadequate, we'll incorporate your changes in the next edition and will correct factual errors at fodors.com *immediately*.

Tell us what to include. You probably have had fantastic travel experiences that aren't yet in Fodor's. Why not share them with a community of like-minded travelers? Share your discoveries and experiences with everyone directly at fodors.com. Your input may lead us to add a new listing or a higher recommendation.

Give us your opinion instantly at our feedback center at www.fodors.com/feedback. You may also e-mail editors@fodors.com with the subject line "Florida Keys Editor." Or send your nominations, comments, and complaints by mail to Florida Keys Editor, Fodor's, 1745 Broadway, New York, NY 10019.

Happy Traveling!

Tim Jarrell, Publisher

CONTENTS

MAPS

ABOUT THIS BOOK

Our Ratings

We wouldn't recommend a place that wasn't worth your time, but sometimes a place is so experiential that superlatives don't do it justice: you just have to be there to know. These sights, properties, and experiences get our highest rating, **Fodor's Choice**, indicated by orange stars throughout this book. Black stars highlight sights and properties we deem **Highly Recommended**, places that our writers, editors, and readers praise again and again for consistency and excellence.

Credit Cards

Want to pay with plastic? **AE, D, DC, MC, V** after restaurant and hotel listings indicate whether American Express, Discover, Diners Club, MasterCard, and Visa are accepted.

Restaurants

Unless we state otherwise, restaurants are open for lunch and dinner daily. We mention dress only when there's a specific requirement and reservations only when they're essential or not accepted—it's always best to book ahead.

Hotels

Unless we tell you otherwise, you can assume that the hotels have private bath, phone, TV, and air-conditioning. We always list facilities but not whether you'll be charged an extra fee to use them, so when pricing accommodations, find out what's included.

Many Listings

- ★ Fodor's Choice
- ★ Highly recommended
- ⊠ Physical address
- ✣ Directions
- Mailing address
- Telephone
- Fax
- On the Web
- E-mail
- Admission fee
- Open/closed times
- Ⓜ Metro stations
- Credit cards

Hotels & Restaurants

- Hotel
- Number of rooms
- Facilities
- Meal plans
- ✕ Restaurant
- Reservations
- Smoking
- BYOB
- ✕ Hotel with restaurant that warrants a visit

Outdoors

- Golf
- Camping

Other

- Family-friendly
- ⇨ See also
- Branch address
- ☞ Take note

WHEN TO GO

High season in the Keys is mid-December through Easter, and traffic on the Overseas Highway is inevitably heavy. From November to the middle of December, crowds are thinner, the weather is superlative, and hotels and shops drastically reduce their prices. Summer, which is hot and humid, is becoming a second high season, especially among families, Europeans, bargain-seekers, and lobster divers. (Rooms are scarce the first few weekends of lobster season, which starts in early August and runs through March.) There's also a two-day sport season in late July. Key West's annual Fantasy Fest is the last week in October; if you plan to attend this wildly popular event (emphasis on wild), reserve at least six months in advance. In Key Largo, room availability and rates are often affected by races at the Miami Homestead Speedway.

Climate

Florida is rightly called the Sunshine State. (Areas like Tampa Bay report 361 days of sunshine a year!) But it could also be dubbed the Humid State. From June through September, 90% humidity levels are not uncommon. Thankfully, the weather in the Keys is more moderate than in mainland Florida. Temperatures can be 10°F cooler during the summer and up to 10°F warmer during the winter. The Keys also get substantially less rain than mainland Florida—around 30 inches annually, compared with an average 55 to 60 inches in Miami and the Everglades. Most rain falls in quick downpours on summer afternoons, except in June, September, and October, when tropical storms can dump rain for two to four days. Winter cold fronts occasionally stall over the Keys, dragging overnight temperatures down to the high 40s. The hurricane season, which runs from June through November, can put a crimp on a summer or fall vacation. The Keys get their fair share of watches, warnings, and evacuation notices. Pay heed and evacuate earlier rather than later, when flights and automobile traffic get backed up.

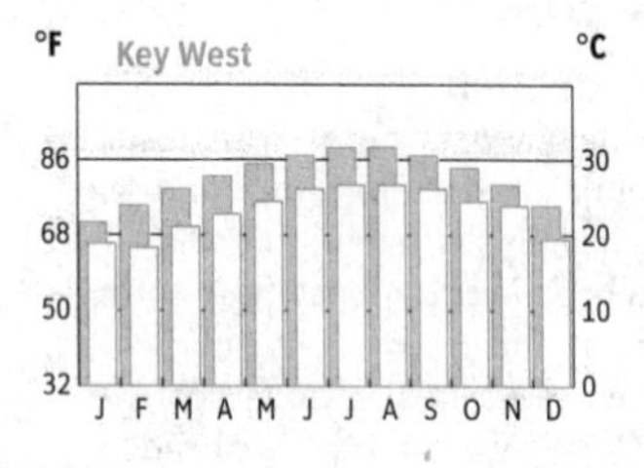

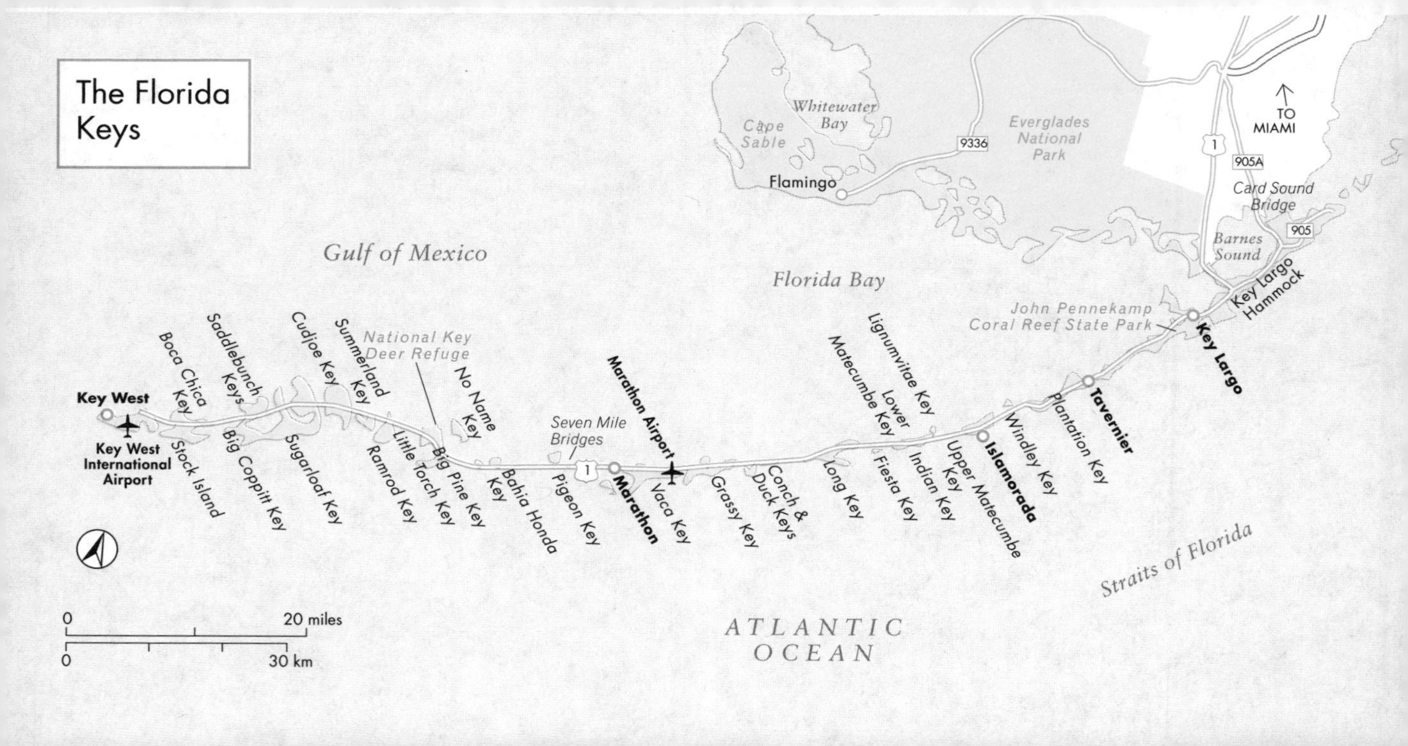

The Florida Keys
Gulf of Mexico
Florida Bay
Whitewater Bay
Cape Sable
Flamingo
9336
Everglades National Park
1
905A
TO MIAMI
Card Sound Bridge
905
Barnes Sound
Key Largo Hammock
John Pennekamp Coral Reef State Park
Key Largo
Tavernier
Plantation Key
Windley Key
Islamorada
Upper Matecumbe Key
Lignumvitae Key
Lower Matecumbe Key
Indian Key
Fiesta Key
Long Key
Conch & Duck Keys
Grassy Key
Vaca Key
Marathon Airport
Marathon
Seven Mile Bridges
Pigeon Key
Bahia Honda Key
No Name Key
National Key Deer Refuge
Big Pine Key
Little Torch Key
Ramrod Key
Summerland Key
Cudjoe Key
Sugarloaf Key
Saddlebunch Keys
Big Coppitt Key
Boca Chica Key
Stock Island
Key West
Key West International Airport
Straits of Florida
ATLANTIC OCEAN
0
20 miles
0
30 km

Welcome to the Florida Keys

WORD OF MOUTH

"Most people drive to the Keys because it is nice to have a car there. If that doesn't work for you, there is a Keys Shuttle. I know it picks up at the Ft. Lauderdale airport (search "Florida Keys shuttle"). There is a boat that goes from Miami to Key West. "

—keymom

www.fodors.com/forums

By Chelle Koster-Walton

BEING A CONCH is a condition of the heart, and foreclosure on the soul. Many throughout the Florida Keys wear that label proudly, yet there is anything but a shared lifestyle here. To the south, Key West has a Mardi Gras mood with Fantasy Festivals, Hemingway look-alike contests, and the occasional threat to secede from the Union. It's an island whose melting-pot character allows crusty natives to mingle (more or less peacefully) with eccentrics and escape artists who lovingly call this 4-mi sandbar "Paradise." Although life elsewhere in the island chain isn't quite as offbeat, it's nearly as diverse.

Flowering jungles, shimmering seas, and mangrove-lined islands are also, conversely, overburdened. A river of tourist traffic gushes along U.S. 1 (also called the Overseas Highway), the 110-mi artery linking the inhabited islands. Residents of Monroe County live by diverting the river's flow of dollars to their own pockets. In the process, the fragile beauty of the Keys—or at least the 45 that are inhabited and linked to the mainland by 43 bridges—is paying an environmental price.

At the top, nearest the mainland, is Key Largo, becoming more congested as it evolves into a bedroom community and weekend hideaway for residents of Miami and Fort Lauderdale. At the bottom, 106 mi southwest, is Key West, where hundreds of passengers from multiple cruise ships swarm the narrow streets. Offshore is the Florida Keys National Marine Sanctuary, established by Congress in 1990, a wondrous but fragile environment of sea-grass meadows, mangrove islands, and living coral reefs.

The expansion of U.S. 1 to the mainland to four lanes will open the floodgates to increased traffic, population, and tourism. Observers wonder if the four-laning of the rest of U.S. 1 throughout the Keys can be far away. For now, however, take pleasure as you drive down U.S. 1 along the islands. Gaze over the silvery blue-and-green Atlantic and its still-living reef, with Florida Bay, the Gulf of Mexico, and the backcountry on your right (the Keys extend east–west from the mainland).

At a few points the ocean and gulf are as much as 10 mi apart. In most places, however, they are from 1 to 4 mi apart, and on the narrowest landfill islands, they are separated only by the road. Try to get off the highway. Once you do, rent a boat, anchor, and then fish, swim, or marvel at the sun, sea, and sky. In the Atlantic, dive spectacular coral

CLOSE UP

Is Florida Bay in Trouble?

The years and man's encroachment have taken their toll on Florida Bay, Everglades National Park's shallow waterfront is home to myriad creatures. A multimillion-dollar Everglades restoration effort has been underway for several years, but some think it's too little too late. A 2008 study by scientists from Audubon of Florida, the state chapter of the National Audubon Society, reported that dropping numbers of roseate spoonbill nests indicate the bay's failing health. The nest census dropped 37% in one year and is at its lowest since the 1960s. Coupled with algae blooms in the bay, the drop in nests shows, Audubon says, that the restoration needs to be sped up to save the bay.

reefs or pursue grouper, blue marlin, and other deepwater game fish. Along Florida Bay's coastline, kayak and canoe to secluded islands and bays or seek out the bonefish, snapper, snook, and tarpon that lurk in the grass flats and in the shallow, winding channels of the backcountry.

HISTORY OF THE KEYS

One thing persists throughout the history of the Florida Keys: change. Of course, every destination evolves and matures, but the mood swings in the Keys seem singularly drastic. Except for Key West, an important shipping way station since Florida's earliest days, the Keys were only sparsely populated until the early 20th century.

The first residents were the Calusa and the Tequesta tribes, whose parched skeletons earned Key West its original Spanish name, Cayo Hueso (Bone Key). Ponce de León led the Spanish invasion after discovering the Keys on his first voyage in 1513, labeling the chain Les Martires because from the distance they appeared as men in distress, perhaps martyrs.

Despite their strategic shipping position, the Keys did indeed make martyrs of many ships that collided with the tricky barrier reef. Thus began one the most lucrative industries in the history of the Keys, salvaging shipwrecks. The occupation brought the first influx of white Bahamians—descendants of Loyalists who had fled to the islands after the American Revolution. Wrecking turned Key West into the richest city in the Americas (and largest in Florida), but that changed suddenly and drastically with the building of lighthouses.

Once the Keys became part of the United States and the Navy moved into Key West, an end came to another under-the-radar occupation, namely pirating. From feast to famine, islanders found new ways to scrape out a living. Next on the less-than-legal agenda was poaching birds for their feathers, until their decimation led to outcry, legislation, and enforcement. Rum-running and later drug smuggling continued the Keys' reputation for renegade lawlessness. Other islanders turned to fishing, sponging, and farming to eke out a meager existence.

In Key West, Cuban dissidents brought cigar-making to the economy in the 1860s, but aside from that, jobs were otherwise scarce until 1905. That was the year railroad magnate Henry Flagler began building the extension of his Florida railroad south from Homestead to Key West, despite ridicule and against all odds. His goal was to establish a Miami–Key West rail link for his steamships that sailed between Key West and Havana, just 90 mi across the Straits of Florida.

The monumental undertaking required tons of manpower, especially because the work was so intense and conditions so unhealthy that many lost their lives in the endeavor. Flagler bulked his work force with Bahamian immigrants and drifters from the South, and the town of Marathon swelled into an unruly, liquor-lubricated town, fueled by one of the largest payrolls in Florida at the time. The railroad arrived at Key West in 1912 and remained a lifeline of commerce until the Labor Day hurricane of 1935 washed out much of its roadbed. Along with it, the hurricane wiped out pineapple farming, and once again residents found themselves destitute. The Overseas Highway, built over the railroad's old roadbeds and bridges, was completed in 1938. With it came a pipeline bringing water and modern conveniences for the Navy and inhabitants.

The new highway brought tourists eager to view the Keys' pristine coral reefs and pull fish from the great schools that gathered around them. The dedication of Everglades National Park, John Pennekamp Coral Reef State Park, and National Key Deer Refuge increased environmental awareness. Hurricanes continued to impede prosperity, however. Only in modern times has tourism grown to fully

CLOSE UP

Going Buggy over Lobster

They call them "bug-hunters," and they descend in swarms. Lobster divers come in quest of the coveted Florida lobster, aka "bug," each year during sport season, the last consecutive Wednesday and Thursday in July, and regular season (August through March), when they must compete against commercial operations. The clawless spiny lobster is taken for its tail meat, which some proclaim sweeter than Maine lobster meat. Harvesting regulations are strict, and all divers must carry a special gauge to make sure their catch has a carapace longer than 3 inches and a tail no longer that 5½ inches. Bag limit is six legal lobsters per harvester per day. Diving for lobster at night (one hour after official sunset and one hour before sunrise) is prohibited. Harvesting in John Pennekamp Coral Reef State Park and other designated areas is also prohibited.

sustain the Keys, but this sweet story has its own bitter side as scientists see the effect of car fumes and runoff killing the very environment that attracts visitors. As the federal government works to restore destruction in neighboring Everglades National Park, local agencies push for reef relief. Hopefully heightened awareness will save the Keys from further irreparable environmental damage.

NATURE IN THE KEYS

More than 600 varieties of fish populate the reefs and islands of the Florida Keys. Diminutive Key deer and skinny raccoons, related to but distinct from their mainland cousins, inhabit the Lower Keys. And throughout the islands you'll find such exotic West Indian plants as Jamaican dogwood, pigeon plum, poisonwood, satin leaf, and silver-and-thatch palms, as well as tropical birds, including the great white heron, mangrove cuckoo, roseate spoonbill, and white-crowned pigeon. Mangroves, with their gracefully bowed prop roots, appear to march out to sea. Day by day they busily add more keys to the archipelago.

With virtually no distracting air pollution or obstructive high-rises, sunsets are a pure, unadulterated spectacle that each evening attracts thousands to waterfront parks, piers, restaurants, bars, and resorts throughout the Keys. Weather is another attraction: winter is typically 10°F warmer than on the mainland; summer is usually 10°F cooler. The Keys also get substantially less rain, around 30 inches annually, compared with an average 55 to 60 inches in Miami and the Everglades. Most rain falls in quick downpours on summer afternoons, except in June, September, and October, when tropical storms can dump rain for two to four days. Winter cold fronts occasionally stall over the Keys, dragging overnight temperatures down to the high 40s.

While the living reef surrounding the Keys has been in decline since the early 1980s, scientists have recognized that the larger ecosystem must be preserved in order to ensure the reef's continued health. In 1990, Congress established the Florida Keys National Marine Sanctuary, to protect the wondrous but fragile environment of sea-grass meadows, mangrove islands, and living coral reefs that surrounds the Keys. Its primary purpose is to put enforce a comprehensive program to protect the ecosystem, which is being compromised by pollution, overuse, and rising sea temperatures.

IF YOU LIKE

BOATING

If it floats, local marinas rent it. For up-close exploration of the mangroves and near-shore islands in Florida Bay, nothing beats a kayak or canoe. Paddle within a few feet of a flock of birds without disturbing them. Visiting the backcountry islands and inlets of Everglades National Park requires a shallow-draft boat: a 14- to 17-foot skiff with a 40- to 50-horsepower outboard is sufficient. Rental companies prohibit smaller boats from going on the ocean side. For diving the reef or fishing on the open ocean, you'll need a larger boat with greater horsepower. Houseboats are ideal for cruising the Keys near shore. Only experienced sailors should attempt to navigate the shallow waters surrounding the Keys with deep-keeled sailboats. On the other hand, small shallow-draft, single-hull sailboats and catamarans are ideal. Those interested in experiencing the reef without getting wet can take a glass-bottom-boat trip.

FISHING

These sun-bathed waters have many species of game fish as well as lobster, shrimp, and crabs. Flats fishing and backcountry fishing are Keys specialties. In flats fishing, a guide poles a shallow-draft outboard boat through the skinny, sandy-bottom waters while sighting for bonefish and snook to be caught on light tackle, spin, and fly. Back-

CLOSE UP

Croc Territory

If you take Card Sound Road to get from mainland to Key Largo (rather than U.S. 1), you'll travel through off-the-beaten-path Florida, including **Crocodile Lake National Wildlife Refuge.** Home to North America's largest concentration of saltwater crocs, it has no public access except by water. These crocodiles are normally shy, but sometimes you can see them sunning on the shore, their mouths opened menacingly to keep cool. You can tell you're looking at a crocodile, not an alligator, if you can see its lower teeth protruding when its jaws are shut. Gators are much darker in color—a grayish black—compared with the lighter tan color of crocodiles. Alligators' snouts are also much broader than their long, thin crocodilian counterparts. Open to the public is an interpretive **butterfly garden** next to refuge headquarters at Mile Marker 106. Adjacent to it lies **Key Largo Hammocks State Botanical Garden** with a self-guided nature trail and similar species to Crocodile Lake NWR.

country fishing may include flats fishing or fishing in the channels and basins around islands in Florida Bay. Charter boats fish the reef and Gulf Stream for deep-sea fish. Party boats, which can be crowded, carry up to 50 people to fish the reefs for grouper, kingfish, and snapper. Some operators have a guarantee, or NO FISH, NO PAY policy. It's customary to tip the crew 15% to 20% of the trip price if they were helpful. The best places to station a fishing vacation are Islamorada and Big Pine Key.

SCUBA DIVING & SNORKELING

Diving in the Keys is spectacular. In shallow and deep water—with visibility up to 120 feet—you can explore sea canyons and mountains covered with waving sea plumes, brain and star coral, historic shipwrecks, and sunken submarines. The best coral reef diving is at John Pennekamp Coral Reef State Park, in Key Largo, and Looe Key Reef, off Ramrod Key. Avid wreck divers might consider tackling all or part of the **Keys Spanish Galleon Trail** (🌐 *www.flheritage.com/archaeology*).

There's no best season for diving, but occasional storms in June, September, and October cloud the waters and make seas rough. Explore the reefs with scuba, snuba (a cross between scuba and snorkeling), or snorkeling gear, using your own boat or a rented boat or by booking a tour with a dive shop. Tours depart two or three times a day, stopping at two sites on each trip. The first trip of the day is usually the best. It's less crowded—vacationers like to sleep in—and visibility is better before the wind picks up in the afternoon.

There's also night diving. If you want to scuba dive but are not certified, take an introductory resort course. Although it doesn't result in certification, it allows you to dive with an instructor in the afternoon after morning classroom and pool instruction. Nearly all the waters surrounding the Keys are part of the Florida Keys National Marine Sanctuary and are, thus, protected; the reef is fragile and shouldn't be touched.

BEACHES

If you're looking for endless stretches of sand beach, don't look in the Keys. Because coral reefs create barriers on the chain's Atlantic Ocean side, natural beaches are few. That said: Don't miss Bahia Honda Key State Park, not only the best beach in the Keys, but often rated among the best in Florida. There are three beaches, actually, but Sandspur is the clear favorite. Other beaches in the Keys are more like mudflats. Some have been humanly augmented with sand, and the best of those are Sombrero Beach in Marathon, Long Key State Park, and the beach at Fort Zachary Taylor State Park in Key West.

NIGHTLIFE

In two words: Key West. Duval Street has been compared to Las Vegas's strip and New Orleans' Bourbon Street for its all-day, all-night party. Locals, cruise-ship passengers, and other visitors do the Duval Crawl, hitting bar after bar known for their margaritas, live bands, and sometimes raunchy activities. Other keys boast a legendary night spot or two such as Lorelei's Cabana Bar in Islamorada and the Caribbean Club in Key Largo. Both are colorful in their own peculiar way.

CULTURE

The flip side to Key West's bawdy personality is the number of museums, historic sites, and art galleries it holds. Through the decades, the island has attracted writers and artists, who have bequeathed it a sort of lowdown highbrow legacy. Most of Old Town's buildings have a historical context. Some, such as the Ernest Hemingway's Home and the Harry S Truman Little House Museum, welcome

CLOSE UP

Which Key for Me?

Can't decide where to base your Florida Keys vacation? This guide to the different islands' specialties and reputations may help. Note, however, that you will find fishing, diving, kayaking, birding, and other outdoor pursuits everywhere you travel in the Keys.

- Diving & Snorkeling: Key Largo has a reputation as "Diving Capital of the World."
- Fishing: Islamorada is known as "Sportfishing Capital of the World." For fishing on a smaller scale, Big Pine Key is the place.
- Kayaking: Big Pine Key has the most natural attributes and reputable operations.
- Camping: Long Key State Park's campground sits on one of the Keys' best beaches. You'll find private campgrounds plentiful throughout the Keys.
- Beaching: Bahia Honda Key's state park is a real show-off.
- Birding: Key Largo's proximity to Everglades National Park means stunning populations.
- Celebrity-spotting: Stars and statesmen show up regularly in Islamorada to catch the big fish. Key West is another place you can often spot celebs hanging out.
- Dining: Key West takes top spot there, but Islamorada is no slouch either.
- Nightlife: No competition: Key West by a landslide.
- Museums & Culture: Again, Key West hands-down for its historic sites, museums, architecture, art galleries, and theater scene.
- Gay Vacations: Key West is famous for its tolerance and enlightened attitude. Gay clubs, resorts, and activities are easy to find.
- Fantasy Resorts: Key Largo is wealthy with destination resorts that provide it all. The most fantasy resort of all, however, occupies Little Palm Island, accessible only by boat.
- Guesthouses: More than 100 bed-and-breakfasts and small inns in Key West welcome guests as though they were family.

visitors. Others you can admire from the outside. Museums explore everything from pirates and sunken treasure to fine art and Cuban heritage. Museums thin out as you head north of Key West, but you'll find wildlife-inspired art galleries throughout the chain.

2 The Upper Keys

WORD OF MOUTH

"Pennekamp State Park in Key Largo was probably the best snorkeling trip, in terms of the quality of snorkeling, but the boat was a little more crowded."

–mdc8k

"Take your daughter to Jacobs Aquatic Center in Key Largo. It has a zero entry pool, pirate themed water playground. Heaven for the toddler set!"

–keymom

www.fodors.com/forums

UPPER KEYS TOP 5

■ **Snorkeling.** The best snorkeling spots in these parts are to be found around the awe-inspiring Christ of the Abyss off John Pennekamp Coral Reef State Park.

■ **Sunsets.** Find a comfortable place to watch the sunset, keeping an eye out for the elusive green flash.

■ **Aquatic Mammals.** Get up close and personal with a dolphin or sea lion at Theater of the Sea.

■ **Boating.** Start with a visit to Robbie's Marina on Lower Matecumbe Key in Islamorada, a salty spot to find everything from fishing charters to kayaking rentals.

■ **Nightlife.** It's not a disco, but you can dance the night away to music by local bands at Lorelei's Cabana Bar.

2

Updated by Chelle Koster Walton

DIVING AND SNORKELING RULE IN THE UPPER KEYS, thanks to the tropical coral reef that runs a few miles off the seaward coast. Divers of all skill levels benefit from accessible dive sites and an established tourism infrastructure. Fishing is another huge draw, especially around Islamorada, known for its sports fishing in both deep offshore waters and in the backcountry. Offshore islands accessible only by boat are popular destinations for kayakers. In short, if you don't like the water you might get bored here.

Other nature lovers won't feel shortchanged. Within 1½ mi of the bay coast lie the mangrove trees and sandy shores of Everglades National Park, where naturalists lead tours of one of the world's few saltwater forests. Here you'll see endangered manatees, curious dolphins, and other underwater creatures. Although the number of birds has dwindled since John James Audubon captured their beauty on canvas, bird-watchers will find plenty to see, including the rare Everglades snail kite, bald eagles, ospreys, and a colorful array of egrets and herons. At sunset flocks take to the skies as they gather to find their night's roost, adding a swirl of activity to an otherwise quiet time of day.

EXPLORING THE UPPER KEYS

The best way to explore this stretch, or any stretch, of the Florida Keys is by boat. As soon as possible you should jump on any seaworthy vessel to see the view of and from the water. And make sure you veer off the main drag of U.S.

1. Head toward the water, where you'll often find the kind of laid-back restaurants and hotels that define the Keys. John Pennekamp Coral Reef State Park is the region's most popular destination, but it's certainly not the only place to get in touch with nature.

ABOUT THE RESTAURANTS

The Upper Keys are full of low-key eateries where the owner is also the chef and the food is tasty and never too fussy. The one exception is Islamorada, where you'll find the more upscale restaurants. Restaurants may close for a two- to four-week vacation during the slow season between mid-September and mid-November.

ABOUT THE HOTELS

In the Upper Keys, the accommodations are as varied as they are plentiful. The majority of lodgings are in small waterfront complexes with efficiencies and one- or two-bedroom units. These places offer dockage and often arrange boating, diving, and fishing excursions. There are also larger resorts with every type of activity imaginable and smaller boutique hotels where the attraction is personalized service.

WHAT IT COSTS

¢	$	$$	$$$	$$$$
RESTAURANTS				
under $10	$10–$20	$20–$30	$30–$40	over $40
HOTELS				
under $100	$100–$150	$150–$200	$200–$250	over $250

Restaurant prices are per person for a main course at dinner. Hotel prices are for a standard double room, excluding 6% sales tax (more in some counties) and 1%–4% tourist tax.

Depending on which way the wind blows and how close the property is to the highway, there may be some noise from U.S. 1. If this is an annoyance for you, ask for a room as far from the traffic as possible. In high season, expect to pay $85 to $175 for an efficiency unit; in low season, rates drop to $65 to $155. Some properties require two- or three-day minimum stays during holiday and high-season weekends. Conversely, discounts apply for midweek,

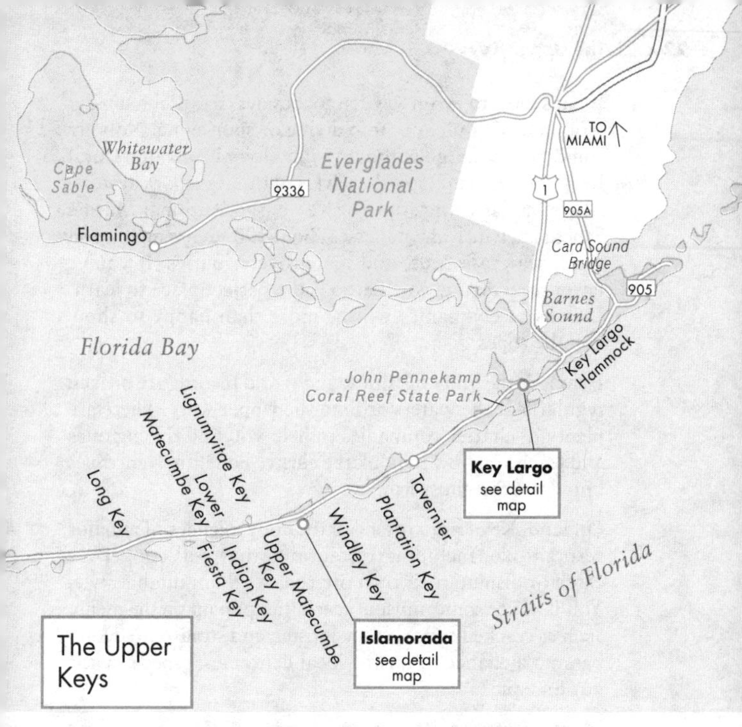

weekly, and monthly stays. Campgrounds and RV parks with full hookups charge $25 to $55.

KEY LARGO

56 mi south of Miami International Airport.

The first of the Upper Keys reachable by car, 30-mi-long Key Largo is also the largest island in the chain. Key Largo—named Cayo Largo ("Long Key") by the Spanish—makes a great introduction to the region. This is the gateway to the Keys, and an evening of fresh seafood and views of the sunset on the water will get you in the right state of mind.

The history of Largo reads similar to the rest of the Keys: a succession of native people, pirates, wreckers, and developers. The first settlement on Key Largo was named Planter, back in the days of pineapple and later key-lime plantations. For a time it was a convenient shipping port, but when the railroad arrived Planter died on the vine. Today three communities—North Key Largo, Key Largo, and Tavernier—make up the whole of Key Largo.

What's there to do on Key Largo, besides gaze at the sunset? Not much if you're not into diving or snorkeling. Nobody comes to Key Largo without visiting John Pennkamp Coral Reef State Park, one of the jewels of the state park system. Also popular is the adjacent Key Largo National Marine Sanctuary, which encompasses about 190 square mi of coral reefs, sea-grass beds, and mangrove estuaries. If you've never tried diving, Key Largo is the perfect place to learn. Dozens of companies will be more than happy to show you the ropes.

Fishing is the other big draw, and world records are broken regularly in the waters around the Upper Keys. There are plenty of charter companies to help you find the big ones and teach you how to hook the elusive bonefish, sometimes known as the ghost fish.

On land, Key Largo offers all the conveniences of a major resort town, including restaurants that will cook your catch or dish up their own offerings with inimitable style. You'll notice some unusual specialties pop up on the menu, such as cracked conch, spiny lobster, and stone crab. Don't pass up a chance to try the local delicacies, especially the key lime pie.

Most businesses are lined up along U.S. 1, the four-lane highway that runs down the middle of the island. Cars whiz past at all hours—something to remember when you're booking a room. Most lodgings are on the highway, so you'll want to be as far back as possible.

EXPLORING KEY LARGO

Key Largo runs northeast–southwest, with U.S. 1 running down the center. If the highway is your only glimpse of the island, you're likely to feel barraged by its tacky commercial side. Make a point of driving Route 905 in North Key Largo to get a better feel for the island.

MAKING MOVIES. **The 1948 film noir classic Key Largo, starring Humphrey Bogart and Lauren Bacall, was the most famous movie filmed in the Florida Keys, but not the only. Others have included Beneath the Twelve Mile Reef, PT 109, License to Kill, True Lies, Speed 2, and Red Dragon. Key Largo is also where Bogart and Katherine Hepburn filmed The African Queen. The steamboat used in the movie is on display at MM 100.**

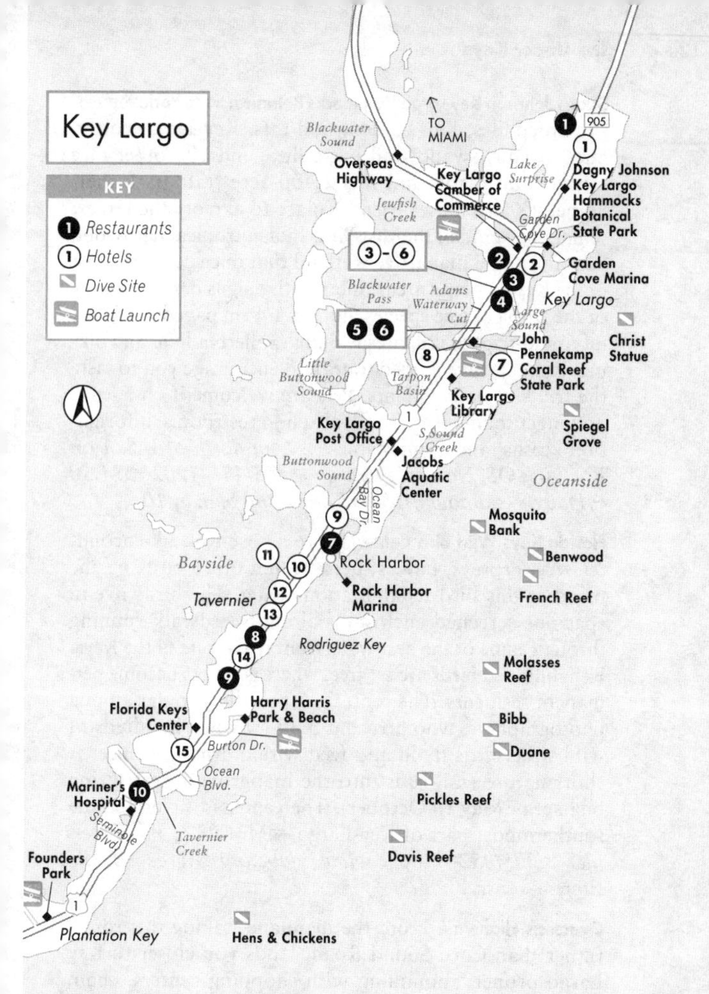

Restaurants

Alabama Jack's, **1**

Ballyhoo's, **7**

Chad's Deli & Bakery, **10**

The Fish House, **5**

The Fish House Encore, **4**

Harriette's Restaurant, **8**

Mrs. Mac's Kitchen, **2**

Rib Daddy's Steak & Seafood, **6**

Snapper's, **9**

Sundowners, **3**

Hotels

Amy Slate's Amoray Dive Resort, **3**

Azul Del Mar, **4**

Coconut Bay Resort & Bay Harbor Lodge, **11**

Coconut Palm Inn, **15**

Dove Creek Lodge, **14**

John Pennekamp Coral Reef State Park Campground, **8**

Jules' Undersea Lodge, **7**

Key Largo Grande Resort & Beach Club, **1**

Kings Campground, **2**

Kona Kai Resort, **12**

Largo Lodge, **6**

Marriott's Key Largo Bay Beach Resort, **5**

The Pelican, **9**

Popp's Motel, **13**

Seafarer Resort & Dive Center, **10**

Dagny Johnson Key Largo Hammocks Botanical State Park. American crocodiles, Key Largo wood rats, Key Largo cotton mice, Schaus swallowtail butterflies, and 100 other rare critters and plants call this 2,400-acre state park their home. It's also a user-friendly place to explore the largest remaining stand of the vast West Indian tropical hardwood hammock and mangrove wetland that once covered most of the Keys' upland areas. Interpretive signs describe many of the tropical tree species along a 1¼-mi paved road (2½ mi round-trip) that invites walking, rollerblading, and biking. Rangers give guided tours and encourage you to taste the fruits of native plants. Pets are welcome if on a leash no longer than 6 feet. You'll also find restrooms, information kiosks, and picnic tables. ✉ *1 mi north of U.S. 1 on Rte. 905, OS, North Key Largo* ☎ *305/451–1202* 🎫 *$1.50* ⏲ *Daily 8–sundown. Tours Thurs. and Sun. at 10.*

Florida Keys Wild Bird Center. Have a nose-to-beak encounter with ospreys, hawks, herons, and other birds on the mend at this bird rehabilitation center. The birds live in spacious screened enclosures along boardwalk running through some of the best waterfront real estate in the Keys. Rehabilitated birds are set free, whereas others become permanent residents. The center is especially popular among photographers, who arrive at 3:30 PM when hundreds of wild waterbirds fly in and feed within arm's distance. A short nature trail runs into the mangrove forest (bring bug spray May to October). The center is Tavernier, the southernmost part of Key Largo ✉ *MM 93.6, BS, Tavernier* ☎ *305/852–4486* 🌐 *www.fkwbc.org* 🎫 *Free* ⏲ *Daily sunrise–sunset.*

Overseas Highway. From the mainland, taking this route, rather than Card Sound Road, lands you closer to Key Largo proper, abounding with shopping centers, chain restaurants, and, of course, dive shops.

👶 **Jacobs Aquatic Center.** Take the plunge at one of three swimming pools: an eight-lane, 25-meter lap pool with a diving well; a 3- to 4-foot-deep pool accessible to people with mobility problems; and an interactive play pool with a waterslide, pirate ship, waterfall, and beachfront entry. ✉ *320 Laguna Ave., MM 99.6, OS* ☎ *305/453–7946* 🌐 *www.jacobsaquaticcenter.org* 🎫 *$8* ⏲ *Weekdays 11–6, weekends 10–7.*

★ Fodor's Choice **John Pennekamp Coral Reef State Park.** Where are 👶 the best diving and snorkeling sites in the Sunshine State?

This reef is on everyone's list of faves. This underwater gem encompasses 78 square mi of coral reefs, sea-grass beds, and mangrove swamps. Its reefs contain 40 of the 52 species of coral in the Atlantic Reef System and nearly 600 varieties of fish from the colorful stoplight parrotfish to the demure cocoa damselfish. The park's visitor center has a large floor-to-ceiling fish tank surrounded by smaller ones, so you can get a closer look at many of the underwater creatures. When you want to head out to sea, a concessionaire rents canoes and powerboats, as well as snorkeling and diving equipment. You can also sign up for snorkeling and diving trips ($29 and $50) and glass-bottom-boat rides to the reef ($22). One of the most popular excursions is the snorkeling trip to see Christ of the Deep, the 2-ton underwater statue of Jesus at Key Largo National Marine Sanctuary. The park also has short nature trails, two artificial beaches, picnic shelters, a snack bar, and a campground. ✉*MM 102.5, OS, Box 1560* ☎*305/451–1202* 🌐*www.floridastateparks.org/pennekamp* 🎟*$3.50 for 1 person, $6 for 2 people, 50¢ each additional person* ⏲*Daily 8–sunset.*

2

WHERE TO EAT

$ ✕ **Alabama Jack's.** Calories be damned—the conch fritters here are heaven on a plate. The crab cakes, made from local blue crabs, earn hallelujahs, too. Regulars at this weathered restaurant floating on two roadside barges in an old fishing community include weekend cyclists, relocated retirees, and boaters, who come to admire tropical birds in the nearby mangroves, the occasional crocodile in the canal, or the bands that play on weekend afternoons. Some locals say that Jack's has lost some of its biker-bar feel, but the food's still good and cheap. Jack's closes by 7 or 7:30, when the mosquitoes start biting. ✉*58000 Card Sound Rd., Key Largo* ☎*305/248–8741* ▭*MC, V.*

$ ✕ **Ballyhoo's.** "Eat. Drink. Fish" is the slogan on the back of the staff's T-shirts. What could better sum up a Keys attitude? Occupying a historic conch house with an outdoor patio, this place is all about the fish (including the nicely nautical decor). Yellowtail snapper, one of the moistest, most flavorful local fish, is served seven different ways, including jerked, stuffed with crab, and grilled with fresh spices. During stone crab season (mid-Oct. to mid-May), get in on the all-you-can-eat special. Typically Keys, the service is uneven at best, but the black beans and rice and the burgers settle the score. ✉*MM 97.8 median* ☎*305/852–0822* 🌐*www.ballyhoosrestaurant.com* ▭*AE, D, MC, V.*

$ ✕ **Chad's Deli & Bakery.** It's a deli! It's a bakery! It's a pasta place! By day, Chad's serves monster sandwiches in pita wraps or on freshly baked bread. At night durng the week and all day on weekends, there are also pizza (try the garlic chicken white pizza), pasta dishes (everyone loves the chicken parm), even vegetarian goulash. There's a good selection of beer and wine to wash it all down. Of course, you may bypass all this and make a meal out of one of Chad's white-chocolate macadamia nut or chocolate-chip cookies, approximately the size of your head. ✉*MM 92.3, BS* ☎*305/853–5566* ▭*MC, V.*

★ $$ ✕ **The Fish House.** The pan-sautéed black grouper will make you moan with pleasure, but it's just one of many headliners in this nautical eatery. On the fin side, the choices include mahimahi, swordfish, tuna, and yellowtail snapper that can be broiled, blackened, baked, or fried. Prefer shellfish or crustaceans? There are nearly as many choices on the shrimp, lobster, and (from mid-October to mid-May) stone-crab side of the menu. For a sweet ending, try the homemade key lime pie. To ease the long lines, the management added outdoor seating. ✉*MM 102.4, OS* ☎*305/451–4665 or 305/451–0650* 🌐*www.fishhouse.com* ▭*AE, D, MC, V* ⊙*Closed Sept.*

$$ ✕ **The Fish House Encore.** To accommodate the crowds that gather at the Fish House, the owners opened this place with similar but more refined cuisine ranging from sushi and steak. In the off-season, you can get your money's worth with $20 all-you-can-eat specials such as fried dolphin and peel 'n' eat shrimp. The favorite place to dine is in garden near the trickling fountain. Weekends bring live piano music. ✉*102.4 OS* ☎*305/451–4665 or 305/451–0650* 🌐*www.fishhouse.com* ▭*AE, D, MC, V* ⊙*No lunch. Closed Tues. Closed Oct., June–Aug.*

¢ ✕ **Harriette's Restaurant.** If you're looking for comfort food—like melt-in-your-mouth buttermilk biscuits—try this refreshing throwback. Little has changed over the years in this yellow-and-turquoise eatery. Owner Harriette Mattson personally greets guests who come for steak and eggs with hash browns or old-fashioned hotcakes with sausage or bacon. At lunchtime, Harriette's shines in the burger department, but there are also specials like meat loaf. ✉*MM 95.7, BS* ☎*305/852–8689* ▭*No credit cards* ⊙*No dinner.*

$ × **Mrs. Mac's Kitchen.** Townies pack the counters and booths at this tiny eatery, where license plates are stuck on the walls and folks talk fishing. Got a hankering for tuna casserole or crab cakes? You'll find it here, along with specials like grilled yellowfin tuna. Bring your appetite for the all-you-can-eat fish specials on Tuesday and Thursday. There's also an assortment of tasty burgers and sandwiches, and the chili wins raves. ⊠*MM 99.4, BS* ☎*305/451–3722* ▭*AE, D, MC, V* ⊗*Closed Sun.*

$ × **Rib Daddy's Steak & Seafood.** You'll swoon after tasting the Memphis-style mesquite-smoked prime rib, beef ribs, and pork baby back ribs flavored with specially formulated rubs and sauces. The menu extends beyond barbecue standards to include steak ad seafood. Must-try sides include grilled corn on the cob and sweet-potato casserole. Save room for key lime pie, mango pie, or coconut cake. The kids will love staring at the reef aquarium. ⊠*MM 102.2, BS* ☎*305/451–0900* ⊕*www.ribdaddysrestaurant.com* ✍*Reservations not accepted* ▭*MC, V.*

$$ × **Snapper's.** "You hook 'em, we cook 'em" is the motto here. Alas, "cleanin' 'em" is not part of the bargain. If you bring in your own ready-for-the-grill fish, dinner here will set you back $13.95 per person. Otherwise, they'll catch and cook you a yellowtail snapper, roasted on a cedar plank with a basil-cream sauce, a grilled tuna steak slathered with Asian barbecue sauce alongside a mound of chipotle mashed potatoes, or a little something from the raw bar. The aromatic steamed mussels are worth the hours of garlic breath, and the ceviche of yellowtail (merrily spiced) wins raves, too. Not for the weak of heart is the Nutty Lobster, a spiny lobster covered with mixed nuts and thrown into the deep fryer. All this is served up in a lively, mangrove-ringed waterfront setting with live music, killer rum drinks, and seating alongside the fishing dock. ⊠*139 Seaside Ave.* ☎*305/852–5956* ▭*AE, D, MC, V.*

★ $ × **Sundowners.** The name doesn't lie. If it's a clear night and you can snag a reservation, this restaurant will treat you to a sherbet-hued sunset over Florida Bay. If you're here in mild weather—anytime other than the dog days of summer or the rare winter cold snap—the best seats are on the patio. The food is excellent: try the key lime seafood, a happy combo of sautéed shrimp, lobster, and lump crab meat swimming in a sauce spiked with Tabasco. Wednesday and Saturday are all about prime rib, and Friday draws the crowds with an all-you-can-eat fish fry. ⊠*MM 104, BS* ☎*305/451–4502* ⊕*sundownerskeylargo.com* ▭*AE, D, MC, V.*

WHERE TO STAY

$–$$ **Amy Slate's Amoray Dive Resort.** The double-entendre in its name sums up this hotel's many charms. When read "a moray," it refers to the moray eels you'll encounter on the reef. Read "amore," Italian for love, it calls to mind the place's romance atmosphere. One- and two-story clapboard cottages huddle around the property's marina and sandy beach. A PADI-certified dive facility, it's a great place to rent equipment or take courses. Unlike many other resorts, single rooms are available. **Pros:** Top-notch dive operation, free use of kayaks and snorkel equipment. **Cons:** Noise from the highway. ✉*MM 104.2 BS 33070* ☎*305/451–3595 or 800/426–6729* 🌐*www.amoray.com* *14 room, 1 suite, 10 apartments* *In room: kitchens (some), refrigerator. In hotel: pool, beachfront, diving, laundry facilities, no-smoking rooms* 💳*AE, D, MC, V.*

$$$ **Azul Del Mar.** The dock points the way to many beautiful sunsets at this adults-only boutique hotel. Advertising executive Karol Marsden and her husband, Dominic, a commercial travel photographer, transformed a run-down mom-and-pop place into this waterfront gem. As you'd expect from innkeepers with a background in the image business, the property offers great visuals, from marble floors and granite countertops to yellow leather sofas and ice-blue bathroom tiles. The owners are crazy about the ocean, so kayaks and other water sports equipment are plentiful. If you mix business with pleasure, take advantage of the wireless Internet connection on the beach. **Pros:** Great garden, good location, sophisticated design. **Cons:** Smallish beach, not the place for families with young kids. ✉*MM 104.3, BS, 104300 Overseas Hwy., Key Largo* ☎*305/451–0337 or 888/253–2985* 🌐*www.azulkeylargo.com* *5 suites* *In-room: no phone, kitchen, refrigerator, VCR, Wi-Fi. In-hotel: beachfront, water sports, bicycles, no elevator, public Wi-Fi, no kids under age 16, no-smoking rooms* 💳*AE, MC, V.*

$–$$ **Coconut Bay Resort & Bay Harbor Lodge.** Some 200 feet of waterfront is the main attraction at this lodge. Coconut palms whisper in the breeze, and gumbo-limbo trees shade the 2½-acre grounds. Nice features abound, like well-placed lounge chairs for gazing out over the water, and kayaks and paddleboats (for when you want to get closer). Everybody shows up on the sundeck or the 30-foot dock to watch the sun slip into Davy Jones's Locker. Easter egg–hued cottages are simply furnished. Ask for Unit 25 and you'll have extra space and a water view. **Pros:** Lush gardens, walking distance to restaurants. **Cons:** A bit dated, no beach. ✉*MM 97.7, BS, 97770 Overseas Hwy.* ☎*305/852–1625 or 800/385–0986* 🌐*www.coconutbaykeylargo.com* *8 rooms, 5 efficiencies, 1 suite, 1 2-bedroom villa, 6 1-bedroom cottages* *In-room: kitchen (some), refrigerator, Wi-Fi (some). In-hotel: pool, beachfront, no elevator, public Wi-Fi, some pets allowed (fee)* *AE, D, MC, V.*

$$ **Coconut Palm Inn.** This low-key inn is set in a quiet residential neighborhood of towering gumbo-limbo and buttonwood trees. Built in the 1930s, the waterfront lodge draws repeat guests with its friendly, relaxed vibe. A 400-foot sandy beach is dotted with the requisite hammocks and swaying palm trees. Screened porches are a welcome touch, letting tropical breezes in and keeping mosquitoes out. Rooms, decorated in West Indies style, vary from one-room efficiencies to one- and two-bedroom suites. No two are alike, although seafoam green paint is used liberally. **Pros:** Lovely beach, tranquil location. **Cons:** Not much going on here. ✉*MM 92, BS, 198 Harborview Dr., Tavernier* ☎*305/852–3017* 🌐*www.coconutpalminn.com* *8 suites, 12 rooms* *In-room: kitchen (some), refrigerator, VCR (some), Wi-Fi. In-hotel: pool, beachfront, no elevator, laundry facilities, public Wi-Fi, no-smoking rooms* *AE, MC, V.*

$$ **Dove Creek Lodge.** Old-school anglers would likely be scandalized by this fishing camp's sherbet-hued paint and plantation-style furnishings. But when they got a load of the massive flat-screen TV, the comfy leather couch, and the stack of fishing magazines in the lobby, they would never want to leave. You can head out on a boat from the marina, chase billfish offshore or bonefish on the flats, and come to brag to your buddies about the one that got away. The surprisingly plush rooms range in size from simple lodge rooms to luxury suites. It's a lively scene—liveliest if you stay in Room 201 or 202, where you'll hear the music from the seafood restaurant next door. **Pros:** Great for fishing enthusiasts, luxurious rooms. **Cons:** Formica countertops in suites, loud music next door. ✉*147 Seaside Ave.33037* ☎*305/852–6200 or 800/401–0057* 🌐*www.dovecreeklodge.com* *14 rooms* *In-room: safe, kitchen (some), refrigerator, Ethernet. In hotel: pool, public Wi-Fi, airport shuttle, parking (no fee), no-smoking rooms* *AE, D, MC, V.*

$$$$ **Jules' Undersea Lodge.** You can truly sleep with the fishes at this underwater inn. This former research lab has two rooms that sit 5 fathoms (30 feet) below the surface,

letting you watch the undersea world through three 42-inch porthole windows. This isn't the place if you're claustrophobic (each of the two rooms is a very cozy 8 by 10 feet) or value your privacy (you share a kitchen and bathroom with the other guests). You also need to be a good swimmer, as the only way to gain access to the lodge is by strapping on scuba gear. You must either be a certified diver or take the hotel's three-hour introductory course (an additional $120). Rates include breakfast and dinner (delivered to your door) and the unlimited use of diving gear. Because of the length of time you'll spend underwater, you can't fly for 24 hours after checking out. The office is open 8 AM to 4 PM. **Pros:** One-of-a-kind experience, unbeatable views. **Cons:** Must be a certified diver or take the special course to stay here, potentially claustrophic accommodations. ✉ *MM 103.2, OS, 51 Shoreland Dr.* ☎ *305/451–2353* 🌐 *www.jul.com* *2 rooms* *In-room: kitchen, VCR. In-hotel: pool, diving, no elevator, no kids under 10, no-smoking rooms* *AE, D, MC, V* *MAP.*

$$$$ **Key Largo Grande Resort & Beach Club.** Nestled within a hardwood hammock near the southern border of Everglades National Park, this sprawling hotel got a $12 million makeover in 2008. Spacious guest rooms each have a private balcony; most rooms overlook the water or woods, but some face the parking lot. Lighted nature trails and boardwalks lead through the woods to a small beach. Two small pools are separated by a coral rock wall and waterfall. Both restaurants, one of which is very casual, have great views. **Pros:** Nice nature trail on bay side, pretty pools with waterfalls. **Cons:** Pools near the highway, hefty charge for parking. ✉ *MM 97, BS, 97000 Overseas Hwy.* ☎ *305/852–5553 or 866/597–5397* 🌐 *www.keylargogrande.com* *190 rooms, 10 suites* *In-room: safe, refrigerators (some). In-hotel: 2 restaurants, room service, bars, tennis courts, pools, gym, beachfront, water sports, bicycles, parking (fee), some pets allowed (fee), no-smoking rooms* *AE, D, DC, MC, V.*

★ Fodor's Choice **Kona Kai Resort.** Brilliantly colored bougain-**$$$$** villeas, coconut palms, and guava trees make this 2-acre hideaway one of the prettiest places to stay in the Keys. Each of the intimate cottages has furnishings that add to the tropical feel. Spacious studios and one- and two-bedroom suites—with full kitchens and original art—are filled with natural light. Outside, kick back in a lounge chair or hammock, soak in the hot tub, or contemplate sunset from the deck. The resort also has an art gallery and an orchid house with more than 225 plants. Maid service is every third day to prolong your privacy; however, fresh linens and towels are available at any time. At the pool, help yourself to free bottled water and fruit. **Pros:** Lush landscaping, free use of sports equipment, knowledgeable staff. **Cons:** Expensive rates, some rooms lack privacy. ✉*MM 97.8, BS, 97802 Overseas Hwy.* ☎*305/852–7200 or 800/365–7829* 🌐*www.konakairesort.com* *8 suites, 3 rooms* *In-room: no phone, kitchen (some), refrigerator, DVD. In-hotel: tennis court, pool, beachfront, no elevator, concierge, public Internet, public Wi-Fi, no kids under 16, no-smoking rooms* *AE, D, MC, V* *Closed Sept.*

★ $$ **Largo Lodge.** When you drive under the dense canopy of foliage at the entrance of Largo Lodge you'll feel like you've gone back in time. Vintage 1950s cottages are tucked amid 3 acres of palm trees, sea grapes, and orchids. Baby-boomer couples seem right at home here in rooms that might call to mind places they stayed as kids. (Young children aren't allowed here, however.) Accommodations—surprisingly spacious—feature small kitchen and dining areas and large screened porches. A lavish swath of bay frontage is perfect for communing with the friendly squirrels and ibises. For swimming, you'll need to drive about 1 mi to John Pennekamp Coral Reef State Park. Pros: Lush grounds, great sunset views, affordable rates. Cons: No pool, some traffic noise outdoors. ✉*MM 101.7, BS, 101740 Overseas Hwy.* ☎*305/451–0424 or 800/468–4378* 🌐*www.largolodge.com* *6 cottages* *In-room: no phone, kitchen. In-hotel: beachfront, no elevator, no kids under 16* *MC, V.*

★ $$$$ **Marriott's Key Largo Bay Beach Resort.** Park the car and toss the keys in the bottom of your bag; there's no need to go anywhere else (except maybe John Pennekamp Coral Reef State Park, just a half mile north). This 17-acre bayside resort has plenty of diversions, from tennis to parasailing to a day spa. Given all that, the pool still rules, so a stroll to the tiki bar could well be your most vigorous activity of the day. The resort's lemon-yellow facade exudes an air of warm, indolent days. This isn't the poshest chain hotel you've ever encountered, but it's fresh looking and suitably tropical in style. Some of the choicest rooms and suites offer sunset views. **Pros:** Lots of activities, lively atmosphere, lovely pool. **Cons:** Rooms facing highway can be noisy. ✉*MM 103.8, BS, 103800 Overseas Hwy.* ☎*305/453–0000 or 866/849–3753* 🌐*www.marriottkeylargo.com* *132 rooms, 20 2-bedroom suites, 1 penthouse suite* *In-room: safe, kitchen (some), Wi-Fi.*

In-hotel: 3 restaurants, room service, bars, tennis court, pool, gym, spa, beachfront, diving, water sports, bicycles, children's programs (ages 5–13), laundry facilities, laundry service, no-smoking rooms ▭*AE, D, DC, MC, V.*

¢–$ **The Pelican.** This 1950s throwback is reminiscent of the days when parents packed the kids into the station wagon and headed to no-frills seaside motels. This is the kind of place where you might see an old-timer fishing off the dock. The owners have spiffed things up and added a beach, but basically it's just a motel, not fancy but comfortable. Guests here don't mind skipping a bit of space and a few frills in favor of homey digs and a low price tag. **Pros:** Free use of kayaks and paddleboats, well-maintained dock, reasonable rates. **Cons:** Some small rooms, needs a little sprucing up. ⊠*99340 Overseas Hwy.* ☎*305/451–3576 or 877/451–3576* ⊕*www.hungrypelican.com* ⇨*13 rooms, 4 efficiencies, 4 suites* ♨*In-room: no phone, kitchen (some), refrigerator, DVD (some), VCR. In-hotel: beachfront, water sports, no-smoking rooms* ▭*AE, D, DC, MC, V* 🍽*CP.*

$ **Popp's Motel.** Stylized metal herons mark the entrance to this 50-year-old family-run motel. The third and fourth generation of Popps are currently at the helm, taking care of the basic-but-clean units. Room 9 is closest to the beach. Family-friendly as it seems, no kids under age 13 are welcome. **Pros:** Nice beach, budget prices. **Cons:** Rooms need updating, 2-night minimum stay required. ⊠*MM 95.5, BS, 95500 Overseas Hwy.* ☎*305/852–5201 or 877/852–5210* ⊕*www.popps.com* ⇨*10 units* ♨*In-room: kitchen. In-hotel: beachfront, water sports, no elevator* ▭*AE, MC, V.*

¢ **Seafarer Resort & Dive Center.** It's a budget lodging, but the Seafarer Resort is not without its charms. Outdoors, there's a pond and hammocks. Most rooms boast water views. Rooms 3 and 4 are spacious and best for families. Unit 6, a one-bedroom cottage called the "beach house," has a large picture window with an awesome view of the bay. Some units have private patios. Guests gather at the beachfront picnic table for alfresco dining and on the dock and lounge chairs for sunset watching. The dive shop offers scuba certification courses. **Pros:** On-site dive shop, sandy beach. **Cons:** Some rooms close to road noise, basic accommodations. ⊠*MM 97.6, BS, 97684 Overseas Hwy.* ☎*305/852–5349* 🖷*305/852–0474* ⊕*www.seafarerresort.com* ⇨*15 units, 7 rooms, 2 studios, 3 1-bedroom cottages, 1 2-bedroom cottage, 2 apartments* ♨*In-room: no phone, kitchen (some), refrigerator. In-hotel: beachfront,* *diving, water sports, bicycles, no elevator, public Internet, no-smoking rooms* ⊟*MC, V.*

CAMPGROUNDS

★ **John Pennekamp Coral Reef State Park.** Divers and snorkelers won't find a better location in the Upper Keys. Pennekamp's campsites are carved out of hardwood hammock, providing shade and privacy away from the heavy day-use areas. Water laps the shore, providing a soothing lullaby. Activities include boating, fishing, scuba diving and snorkeling, and hiking. There's no restaurant, but there are vending machines for late-night snack attacks. *Flush toilets, partial hookups (electric and water), dump station, drinking water, showers, fire pits, picnic tables, electricity, public telephone, general store, ranger station, swimming (ocean)* *47 partial hookups for RVs and tents* ⊠*MM 102.5, OS* ☎*305/451–1202 park, 800/326–3521 reservations* ⊕*www.reserveamerica.com* ⊟*AE, D, MC, V.*

Kings Kampground. Florida Bay breezes keep things cool at this campground, and the neighboring waterway gives boaters direct access to John Pennekamp Coral Reef State Park. The campground has a marina for storing boats ($10 per day). The park can accommodate RVs up to 40 feet long, and if you don't want to bring your own, you can rent one ($110–$125). This property also has a cottage ($195–$220), motel-style units ($55–$75), and tent sites ($50). *Partial hookups (electric and water), dump station, drinking water, picnic tables, electricity, public telephone, swimming (ocean)* *60 hookups for RVs and tents* ⊠*MM 103.5, BS* ☎*305/451–0010* ⊕*www.kingskamp.com* ⊟*MC, V.*

NIGHTLIFE

The semiweekly *Keynoter* (Wednesday and Saturday), weekly *Reporter* (Thursday), and Friday through Sunday editions of the *Miami Herald* are the best sources of information on entertainment and nightlife. Daiquiri bars, tiki huts, and seaside shacks pretty well summarize Key Largo's bar scene.

Mingle with locals over cocktails and sunsets at **Breezers Tiki Bar** (⊠*MM 103.8, BS* ☎*305/453–0000*), in Marriott's Key Largo Bay Beach Resort. Walls plastered with Bogart memorabilia remind customers that the classic 1948 Bogart-Bacall flick *Key Largo* has a connection with the **Caribbean Club** (⊠*MM 104, BS* ☎*305/451–4466*). It draws beard-and–baseball cap types, happiest while they're shooting the breeze or shooting pool. Postcard-perfect sunsets and live music draw revelers on weekends. **Coconuts** (✉*MM 100, OS, 528 Caribbean Dr.* ☎*305/453–9794*), next to Marina Del Mar Resort, has live music Wednesday to Sunday. The crowd is primarily thirty- and fortysomething, sprinkled with a few more-seasoned townies.

SPORTS & THE OUTDOORS

BIKING

Not as big a pursuit as on other islands, biking can be a little dangerous along Key Largo's main drag.

Tavernier Bicycle & Hobbies (✉*MM 91.9, BS, 91958 Overseas Hwy., Tavernier* ☎*305/852–2859*) rents single-speed adult bikes. Cruisers go for $15 a day, $75 a week. Helmets and locks are free with rental. Closed on Sunday and Monday.

DIVING & SNORKELING

Much of what makes the Upper Keys a singular dive destination is variety. Places like Molasses Reef, which begins 3 feet below the surface and descends to 55 feet, have something for everyone from novice snorkelers to experienced divers. The *Spiegel Grove,* a 510-foot vessel, lies in 130 feet of water, but its upper regions are only 60 feet below the surface. On rough days, Key Largo Undersea Park's Emerald Lagoon is a popular spot. Expect to pay about $75 for a two-tank, two-site dive trip with tanks and weights, or $35 to $40 for a two-site snorkel outing. Get big discounts by booking multiple trips.

Ocean Divers (✉*MM 105.5, BS, 522 Caribbean Dr.* ✉*MM 100, OS, 105800 Overseas Hwy.* ☎*305/451–0037 or 800/451–1113* 🌐*www.oceandivers.com*) operates two shops in Key Largo. Both are PADI five-star facilities and offer day and night dives, a range of courses, and dive-lodging packages. The cost is $80 for a two-tank reef dive with tank and weight rental. Snorkel trips cost $45 with snorkel, mask, and fins. **Amy Slate's Amoray Dive Resort** (✉*MM 104.2, BS* ☎*305/451–3595 or 800/426–6729* 🌐*www.amoray.com*) makes diving easy. Stroll down to the full-service dive shop (NAUI, PADI, TDI, and BSAC certified), then onto a 45-foot catamaran. The rate for a two-dive trip is $75.At ★ John Pennekamp Coral Reef State Park, **Coral Reef Park Co.** (✉*MM 102.5, OS* ☎*305/451–6322* 🌐*www.pennekamppark.com*) gives scuba ($29) and snorkeling ($50) tours of the park. Besides the great location and the dependability of this operation, it's suited for water adventurers of all levels. **Conch Republic Divers** (✉*MM 90.8, BS* ☎*305/852–1655 or 800/274–3483* 🌐*www.conchrepublicdivers.com*) offers instruction as well as scuba and snorkeling tours of the Pennekamp, Molasses, and other reefs. Two-location dives are $75 with tank and weights.**Quiescence Diving Service** (✉*MM 103.5, BS* ☎*305/451–2440* 🌐*www.quiescence.com*) sets itself apart in two ways: it limits groups to six to ensure personal attention and offers day and night dives, as well as twilight dives when sea creatures are most active. Two-dive trips start at $59.

DOLPHIN INTERACTION PROGRAMS

The educational program at **Dolphin Cove** (✉*MM 101.9, BS, 101900 Overseas Hwy., Key Largo* ☎*305/451–4060 or 877/365–2683* 🌐*www.dolphinscove.com*) begins during a 30-minute boat ride on adjoining Florida Bay. At the facility's lagoon you have a get-acquainted session from a platform. Finally, you slip into the water for some frolicking with your new dolphin pals. The cost is $165 to $185. For two- to four-year-olds there's a special program that costs $70.

Dolphins Plus (✉*MM 99, 31 Corrine Pl., Key Largo* ☎*305/451–1993 or 866/860–7946* 🌐*www.dolphinsplus.com*) programs emphasize education and conservation. Costing $125, the Natural Swim program begins with a one-hour briefing; then you enter the water to become totally immersed in the dolphins' world. No touching or interacting is allowed. For that, sign up for the $165 Structured Swim program.

FISHING

Private charters and big head boats (so-named because they charge "by the head") are great for anglers who don't have their own vessel.

Sailors Choice (✉*MM100, OS* ☎*305/451–1802 or 305/451–0041* 🌐*www.sailorschoicefishingboat.com*) has fishing excursions departing twice daily ($40 for half-day trips). The ultramodern 65-foot boat with air-conditioned cabin leaves from the Holiday Inn docks. Rods, bait, and license are included.

KAYAKING

The folks at **Florida Bay Outfitters** (☎*MM 104, BS, 104050 Overseas Hwy., Key Largo* ☎*305/451–3018* ⊕*www.kayak-floridakeys.com*) know Upper Keys and Everglades waters well. Take a full-moon paddle, or a one- to seven-day canoe or kayak tour to the Everglades, Lignumvitae, or Indian Key. Trips run $60 to $795.

WATER SPORTS

Sea kayaking is the fastest-growing water sport in the Keys, thanks in part to the many new outfitters offering tours. Advances in the equipment—such as foot pedals, rudders, and sails—make sea kayaking easier than ever. You can paddle for a few hours or the whole day, on your own or with a guide. Some outfitters even offer overnight trips. The 110-mi Florida Keys Overseas Paddling Trail, part of a statewide system, runs from Key Largo to Key West. You can paddle the entire distance, which takes approximately seven days.

At John Pennekamp Coral Reef State Park, **Coral Reef Park Co.** (✉*MM 102.5, OS* ☎*305/451–6325*) has a fleet of canoes and kayaks for gliding around the mangroves or along the coast. It also rents power boats. Rent canoes or sea kayaks from **Florida Bay Outfitters** (✉*MM 104, BS* ☎*305/451–3018* ⊕*www.kayakfloridakeys.com*). The company, which helps with trip planning and matches equipment to your skill level, sets up self-guided trips on the Florida Keys Overseas Paddling Trail. It also run myriad guided tours around Key Largo.

SHOPPING

For the most part, shopping is sporadic in Key Largo, with a couple of shopping centers and fewer galleries than you find on the other big islands. If you're looking to buy scuba or snorkel equipment, you'll have plenty of places from which to choose.

Pick up an old Hemingway novel or the latest tome from a local poet at **Cover to Cover Books** (✉*Tavernier Towne Shopping Center, MM 91.2, BS, 91272 Overseas Hwy.* ☎*305/853–2464*). The children's department is especially interesting. There's also a gourmet coffee bar with Internet access. Original works by major international artists—including American photographer Clyde Butcher, sea captain–turned-painter Dirk Verdoorn, local artist John David Hawver, and French sculptor Polles—are shown at the **Gallery at Kona Kai** (✉*MM 97.8, BS, 97802 Overseas Hwy.* ☎*305/852–7200*), in the Kona Kai Resort. Go into olfactory overload—you'll find yourself sniffing every single bar of soap and scented candle—at **Key Lime Products** (✉*MM 95.2, BS, 95200 Overseas Hwy.* ☎*305/853–0378 or 800/870–1780* 🌐*keylimeproducts.com*). Take home some key lime juice and bake a pie; the super-easy directions are right on the bottle. You can find lots of shops in the Keys that sell cheesy souvenirs—snow globes, alligator hats, and shell-encrusted anything. **Shellworld** (✉*MM 97.5* ☎*305/852–8245*) is the granddaddy of them all. The sprawling building is stuffed with clothing, jewelry, and, yes, delightfully tacky souvenirs.

ISLAMORADA

MM 90.5–70.

True story: Early settlers named this key after their schooner, *Island Home,* but to make it sound more romantic they translated it into Spanish: *Isla Morada*. The chamber of commerce prefers to use its literal translation "Purple Island," which refers either to a purple-shelled snail that once inhabited these shores or to the brilliantly colored orchids and bougainvilleas.

Early maps show Islamorada as encompassing only Upper Matecumbe Key. But the incorporated "Village of Islands" is made up of a string of islands islands crossed by the Overseas Highway, including Plantation Key, Windley Key, Upper Matecumbe Key, Lower Matecumbe Key, Craig Key, and Fiesta Key. In addition, two islands accessible only by boat—Indian Key and Lignumvitae Key—belong to the group.

Islamorada (locals pronounce it "*eye*-la-mor-*ah*-da") is one of the world's top fishing destinations. For nearly 100 years, seasoned anglers have fished these clear, warm waters teeming with trophy-worthy fish. There are numerous options for those in search of the big ones, including chartering a boat with its own crew or heading out on a vessel rented from one of the plethora of marinas along this 20-mi stretch of the Overseas Highway. More than 150 backcountry guides and 400 offshore captains are at your service.

Islamorada is one of the more affluent resort areas of the Keys. Sophisticated resorts and restaurants meet the needs

MIND YOUR P'S & CRACKERS

If you spend enough time in Florida, sooner or later you'll start hearing about Crackers. Depending on whom you ask, and in which part of the state, you might get a very different answer. Some folks are proud to identify themselves as Crackers; others consider it a racial epithet and a violation under the Florida Hate Crimes Act.

In the early 1500s the Spanish came to the Americas, bringing caballeros and horses. These early cowboys got the nickname "Crackers" for the cracking sound they made with their whips. This was also the name given to the small Spanish horses, which were agile and ideal for working with cattle. Florida Cracker horses are still an active breed in Florida and essential to the cattle industry. Another theory is that the term is derived from the practice of "corncracking," a way to grind dried corn kernels into grits and cornmeal. Often the term is used disparagingly about people who can't afford much to eat, especially those who live in the Panhandle. Call somebody a Cracker in these parts, and you might be adding hefty insult to injury.

Many Floridians will agree that "Cracker" refers to people who can claim native Floridian heritage. Crackers were frontiersmen and pioneers, mostly living off the land, hunting, raising their own meat, and building their own houses. Original Cracker houses were akin to log cabins but styled more like two cabins separated by a long hallway. These shotgun houses were built this way to make it possible to fire a gun through the front door and not hit any other wall in the house. Nowadays, a Cracker house is usually a clapboard home with a wraparound porch common in the northern and western part of the state.

of those in search of luxury, but there's also plenty for those looking for something more casual and affordable. Art galleries and boutiques make Islamorada's shopping scene the best in the Upper Keys.

EXPLORING ISLAMORADA

Anne's Beach. On Lower Matecumbe Key, this beach is a popular village park whose "beach" (really a typical Keys-style sand flat) is best enjoyed at low tide. The nicest feature here is a ½-mi elevated wooden boardwalk that meanders through a natural wetland hammock. Covered picnic areas

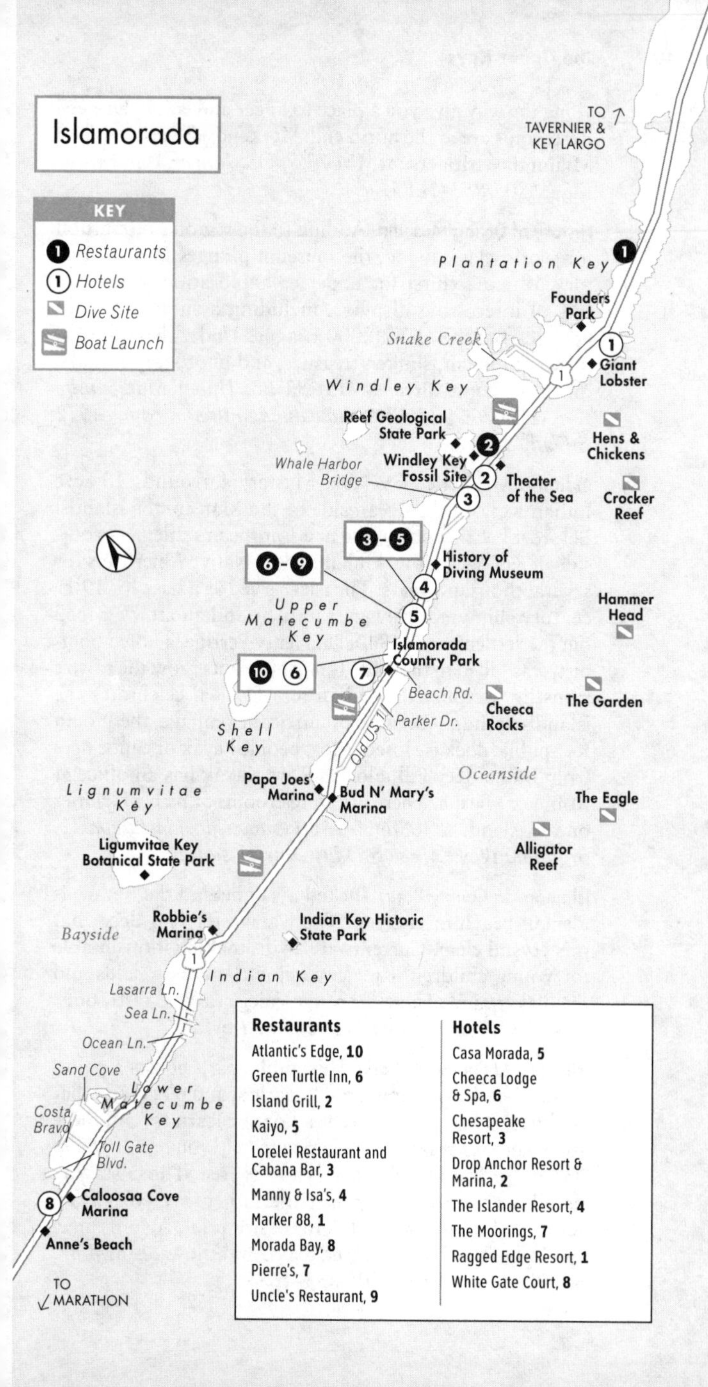
Islamorada
KEY
Restaurants
Hotels
Dive Site
Boat Launch
TO TAVERNIER & KEY LARGO
Plantation Key
Founders Park
Snake Creek
Giant Lobster
Windley Key
Reef Geological State Park
Hens & Chickens
Whale Harbor Bridge
Windley Key Fossil Site
Theater of the Sea
Crocker Reef
History of Diving Museum
Upper Matecumbe Key
Hammer Head
Islamorada Country Park
Beach Rd.
Parker Dr.
Old US 1
Cheeca Rocks
The Garden
Shell Key
Oceanside
Lignumvitae Key
Papa Joes' Marina
Bud N' Mary's Marina
The Eagle
Alligator Reef
Ligumvitae Key Botanical State Park
Bayside
Robbie's Marina
Indian Key Historic State Park
Indian Key
Lasarra Ln.
Sea Ln.
Ocean Ln.
Sand Cove
Lower Matecumbe Key
Costa Bravo
Toll Gate Blvd.
Caloosaa Cove Marina
Anne's Beach
TO MARATHON
Restaurants
Atlantic's Edge, 10
Green Turtle Inn, 6
Island Grill, 2
Kaiyo, 5
Lorelei Restaurant and Cabana Bar, 3
Manny & Isa's, 4
Marker 88, 1
Morada Bay, 8
Pierre's, 7
Uncle's Restaurant, 9
Hotels
Casa Morada, 5
Cheeca Lodge & Spa, 6
Chesapeake Resort, 3
Drop Anchor Resort & Marina, 2
The Islander Resort, 4
The Moorings, 7
Ragged Edge Resort, 1
White Gate Court, 8

along the way give you a place to linger and enjoy the view. Restrooms are at the north end. Weekends are packed with Miami day-trippers. ✉*MM 73.5, OS, Lower Matecumbe Key* ☎*305/853–1685.*

History of Diving Museum. Adding to the region's reputation for world-class diving, the museum plunges into the history of man's thirst for undersea exploration. There are lots of interesting displays, including a submarine and helmet from the film 20,000 Leagues Under the Sea. Historic equipment, sunken treasure, and photographs make the story come alive. ✉*MM 83 BS, Upper Matecumbe Key* ☎*305/664–9737* 🌐*www.divingmuseum.com* 🎟*$12* ⏲*Daily 10–5.*

Indian Key Historic State Park. Mystery surrounds 10-acre Indian Key, on the ocean side of the Matecumbe islands. Before it became one of the first European settlements outside of Key West, it was inhabited by Native Americans for several thousand years. The islet served as a base for 19th-century shipwreck salvagers until an Indian attack wiped out the settlement in 1840. Dr. Henry Perrine, a noted botanist, was killed in the raid. Today his plants grow the town's ruins. In October the Indian Key Festival celebrates the island's heritage. Because of hurricane damage, the Indian Key public dock is closed. Most people kayak or canoe here from Indian Key Fill. Florida Keys Kayak has an office at Robbie's Marina. There are no restrooms or picnic facilities on the island. ☎*305/664–2540* 🌐*www.floridastateparks.org/indiankey* 🎟*Free* ⏲*Daily sunrise–sunset.*

Islamorada County Park. Tucked away behind the library is a small beach on a creek. The water isn't very deep, but it is crystal clear. Currents are swift, making it unsuitable for young children. Kids can enjoy the grassy fields and the playground. There are also picnic areas and restrooms. ✉*MM 81.5, BS, Upper Matecumbe Key.*

Islamorada Founder's Park. This public park boasts a palm-shaded beach, swimming pool, marina, and plenty of other facilities. If you want to rent a boat or learn to sail, there are businesses here that are happy to help you out. If you're staying in Islamorada, admission is free. Those staying elsewhere pay $8 to enter the park. Either way, you pay an additional $3 to use the Olympic-size pool. A spiffy new amphitheater hosts concerts, plays, and shows. ✉*MM 87, BS, Plantation Key* ☎*305/853–1685.*

Lignumvitae Key Botanical State Park. On the National Register of Historic Places, this 280-acre bayside island is the site of a virgin hardwood forest and the 1919 home of chemical magnate William Matheson. His caretaker's cottage serves as the park's visitor center. Access is by boat—your own, a rented vessel, or a ferry operated by Robbie's Marina at 10 AM and 2 PM Thursday to Monday. (Paddling here from Indian Key Fill, at MM 78.5, is a popular pastime.) The only way to do the trails is by a guided ranger walk, offered Thursday through Monday at 10 and 2. Wear long sleeves and pants, and bring mosquito repellent. On the first weekend in December is the Lignumvitae Christmas Celebration. ☎*305/664–2540* *www.floridastateparks.org/lignumvitaekey* *Free; tour $1; ferry $20* *Thurs.–Mon. 8–5.*

Plantation Key. Between 1885 and 1915, settlers earned good livings growing pineapples here by using Bahamian workers to plant and harvest their crops. The plantations that gave the place its name are long gone, replaced by a dense concentration of homes, businesses, and a public park. ✉*MM 90.5–86.*

★ **Robbie's Marina.** Prehistoric-looking denizens of the not-so-deep, tarpons congregate around the docks at this marina on Lower Matecumbe Key. Children—and lots of adults—pay $3 to feed them or $1 just to watch. Spend some time hanging out at this authentic Keys community, where you can grab a bite to eat, do a little shopping, or charter a boat. ✉*MM 77.5, BS, Lower Matecumbe Key* ☎*305/664–9814 or 877/664–8498* *www.robbies.com* *Dock access $1* *Daily 8–5.*

Theater of the Sea. The second-oldest marine mammal center in the world doesn't attempt to compete with more modern, more expensive parks. Even so, it's among the better attractions north of Key West, especially if you have kids in tow. Like the pricier parks, there are dolphin, sea lion, and sting ray encounters ($55 to $175, including general admission) where you can get up close and personal with underwater creatures. These are popular, so reserve in advance. Ride a "bottomless" boat to see what's below the waves or take a guided tour of the marine life exhibits. Entertaining educational shows highlight conservation issues. You can stop for lunch at the grill, shop in the boutique, ot sunbathe at a lagoon-side beach. This easily could be an all-day attraction if you're so inclined. ✉*MM 84.5,*

OS, 84721 Overseas Hwy., Windley Key ☎305/664–2431 🌐www.theaterofthesea.com 💵$26 ⏲Daily 9:30–5; last ticket sold at 3:30.

Upper Matecumbe Key. One of the earliest of the Upper Keys to be permanently settled became an early pineapple-growing area. Early homesteaders were so successful at growing pineapples in the rocky soil that at one time the island yielded the country's largest annual crop. However, foreign competition and the hurricane of 1935 killed the industry. Today, life centers on fishing and tourism, and the island is filled with bait shops, marinas, and charter-fishing boats. ✉*MM 84–79.*

Windley Key. The highest point in the Keys is still only 16 feet above sea level, so it's not likely to give anyone altitude sickness. Originally two islets, this area was first inhabited by Native Americans, who left behind a few traces of their dwellings, and then by farmers fishermen who built their homes here in the mid-1800s. Henry Flagler bought the land from homesteaders in 1908 for his Florida East Coast Railway, filling in the inlet between what were then called the Umbrella Keys. His workers quarried coral rock for the rail bed and bridge approaches—the same rock used in many historic South Florida structures, including Miami's Vizcaya and the Hurricane Monument on Upper Matecumbe. Although the Quarry Station was destroyed by the 1935 hurricane, quarrying continued until the 1960s. Today a few resorts occupy the island. ✉*MM 86–84.*

Windley Key Fossil Reef Geological State Park. A fossilized coral reef dating back about 125,000 years shows that the Florida Keys were once beneath the ocean. Excavation of Windley Key's limestone bed by the Florida East Coast Railway exposed the petrified reef, full of beautifully fossilized brain coral and sea ferns. The park contains the **Alison Fahrer Environmental Education Center,** with historic, biological, and geological displays about the area. There also are guided and self-guided tours along trails that lead to the railway's old quarrying equipment and cutting pits, where you can make rubbings of the interesting quarry walls. The first Saturday in March is Windley Key Day, when the park sells native plants and hosts environmental exhibits. ✉*MM 85.5, BS, Windley Key ☎305/664–2540 🌐www.floridastateparks.org/windleykey 💵Education center free, quarry trails $1.50, ranger-guided tours $2.50 ⏲Education center Thurs.–Mon. 8–5; tours at 10 and 2.*

WHERE TO EAT

$$$ ✕ **Atlantic's Edge.** Taking advantage of its enviable location, Cheeca Lodge's restaurant faces the sea in all its glory. Whether your appetite is small or large, the inventive menu will have something to please you. A selection of small plates allow you to share the lobster dim sum, osso buco with blackberries, or goat cheese ravioli. Full-blown entrées concentrate on local seafood in dishes like black grouper with lobster potato hash and meat with the truffle-crusted bone-in beef tenderloin with roasted wild mushrooms. There's also a nice Mediterranean-style vegetable dish. ✉ *Cheeca Lodge, MM 82, OS, Box 527, Upper Matecumbe Key* ☎ *305/664–4651 or 800/327–2888* 🌐 *www.cheeca.com* *Reservations essential* ▭ *AE, D, DC, MC, V.*

$$ ✕ **Green Turtle Inn.** This landmark dating back to 1928 is a slice of Florida Keys history. Period photographs decorate the wood-paneled walls. Breakfast and lunch options include surprises like smoked salmon cheesecake with bagel chips and yellowfin tuna tartare. Award-winning Chef Andy Niedenthal relies heavily on Continental classics tossed with a few Latin touches for his dinner menu. Favorites include turtle chowder (don't gasp; it's made from farm-raised freshwater turtles), churassco steak with yucca hash, and rum-glazed duck with sweet plantain mash. He uses organic produce wherever possible. ✉ *MM 81.2 OC, 81219 Overseas Hwy., Upper Matecumbe Key* ☎ *305/664–2006* 🌐 *www.greenturtlekeys.com* *Reservations essential* ▭ *AE, D, MC, V.*

★ $ ✕ **Island Grill.** Don't be fooled by appearances, as this shack on the waterfront takes island cuisine up a notch. The eclectic menu tempts you with such dishes as guava barbecue shrimp with pineapple salsa and spicy lobster tacos. Southern-style shrimp and andouille sausage with grits joins island-style specialties such as grilled mahimahi with black bean and corn salsa on the list of entrées. There's air-conditioned dining room as well as outdoor seating under the trees. Two bars—one indoors and another outdoors—have live entertainment Wednesday to Sunday. ✉ *MM 85.5, OS, Windley Key* ☎ *305/664–8400* ▭ *AE, MC, V.*

★ $ ✕ **Kaiyo.** Kaiyo's decor—an inviting setting that includes colorful abstract mosaics, polished wood floors, and upholstered banquettes—almost steals the show. The menu, a fusion of East and West offers sushi and sashimi and rolls that combine local ingredients with traditional Japanese tastes. The key lime lobster roll is a blend of Florida lobster with hearts of palm and essence of key lime ($13.75). The baby conch roll surrounds tempura conch, ponzu mayo, and kimchee with sushi rice for an inside-out effect. Wash it down with an ice-cold Voss—naturally, hip water is served here—or a top-shelf sake. ✉*MM 82, OS, Upper Matecumbe Key* ☎*305/664–5556* 🌐*www.kaiyokeys.com* 💳*AE, MC, V* ⏲*Closed Sun.*

¢ ✕ **Lorelei Restaurant and Cabana Bar.** Local anglers gather here for breakfast. Lunch and dinner brings a mix of islanders and visitors for straightforward food and yucking good times. Live bands ensure a lively nighttime scene, and the menu staves off inebriation with burgers, guava-barbecued baby back ribs, and whole fried snapper. Sunday afternoon's pig roast gives you a choice of jerk pork, jerk chicken, or pulled pork. Key lime pie comes traditional, frozen, or on a stick. ✉*MM 82 BS, Upper Matecumbe Key* ☎*305/664–2692* 🌐*www.loreleifloridakeys.com* 💳*AE, MC, V.*

$ ✕ **Manny & Isa's.** Fans will be joyous to learn that this restaurant is back after being closed for several years, but is now in a new location. Manny still oversees the operation, and his award-winning recipes continue to please. Plan your meal around key lime pie, because you have to try this award-winning version. The all-day menu satisfies any appetite with killer conch chowder and chili con carne, Cuban sandwiches, lobster with enchilado[sic] sauce, and other specialties. ✉*MM 81.9 OS, Upper Matecumbe Key* ☎*305/664–4767* 🌐*www.mannyandisas.com* 💳*MC, V* ⏲*Closed Tues.*

★ $$ ✕ **Marker 88.** A few yards from Florida Bay, this seafood restaurant has been popular for more than 40 years. Large picture windows offer great sunset views, but the bay is lovely no matter what time of day you visit. Chef Sal Barrios serves such irresistible entrées as grilled yellowfin tuna with wasabi aioli and yellowtail snapper in a delicate meunière sauce. Landlubbers find dishes like Parmesan-crusted filet mignon. If you not that hungry, there's also a long list of sandwiches. The extensive wine list is an oenophile's delight. ✉*MM 88, BS, Plantation Key* ☎*305/852–9315* *Reservations essential* 💳*AE, MC, V.*

✕ **Morada Bay.** This bayfront restaurant wins high marks
$$ for its funky feel, tables planted in the sand, and tiki torches that bathe the evening in romance. "It's great bistro food—original and tasty," as one recent guest put it. Entrées feature alluring combinations like roasted mahimahi with vegetable couscous and caramelized jumbo sea scallops with wild mushroom risotto. Seafood takes center stage,

but you can always get chicken (flavored with lemon) or a steak. The dining room showcases renowned photographer Clyde Butcher's black-and-white photography of the region. Choose a table in the dining room hung with surfboards or outdoors overlooking a beach dotted with kids playing in the sand—as everywhere, they eat faster than their parents. There's nightly live music and a monthly full-moon party. ✉*MM 81, BS, Upper Matecumbe Key* ☎*305/664–0604* 🌐*www.moradabay-restaurant.com* ▭*AE, MC, V.*

★ **Fodor'sChoice** ✕ **Pierre's.** One of the Keys' most elegant restaurants, Pierre's marries British colonial style with South Florida trendiness. Full of Indian and Asian architectural artifacts, the place oozes style, especially the wicker chair–strewn veranda overlooking the bay. Put on your best "tropical chic" duds so you'll be as fabulous as your surroundings. The food, drawn from French and Floridian influences, is layered, brightly colored, and beautifully presented. Among the appetizer choices, few can resist the open-face lobster ravioli or shrimp bisque. The changing list of entrées might include shellfish risotto or pan-seared snapper with roasted corn and pepper hash. The downstairs bar is a perfect vantage point for sunset watching. ✉*MM 81.5, BS, Upper Matecumbe Key* ☎*305/664–3225* *Reservations essential* ▭*AE, MC, V* ⊙*Closed Mon.*

$$$

✕ **Uncle's Restaurant.** Former fishing guide Joe LePree adds flair to stand seafood dishes by expanding the usual grilled, broiled, or blackened options. Here you can also have them française (in a lemony sauce), milanese (breaded and fried), or LePree (with artichokes, mushrooms, and garden-grown spices). You also can feast on mussels or littleneck clams in a red or white sauce. Specials sometimes combine game (bison, caribou, or elk) with seafood. Portions are huge, so share dishes or take home a doggie bag. Weather permitting, sit outdoors in the garden; poor acoustics make dining indoors unusually noisy. ✉*MM 81, OS, Upper Matecumbe Key* ☎*305/664–4402* ▭*AE, D, DC, MC, V* ⊙*Closed Mon.*

$$

WHERE TO STAY

★ **Fodor'sChoice** **Casa Morada.** A trio of hoteliers brought their cumulative 50 years of New York and Miami Beach experience to the Keys. Using their transformative magic, the women turned this place into an all-suites resort worthy of the French Riviera. Lush landscaping, a pool surrounded by a sandy "beach," and lounge chairs at the water's edge are just the start. Complimentary yoga classes, a Zen

$$$$

garden, and a rock waterfall lend a spalike vibe. Cool tile-and-terrazzo floors invite you to kick off your shoes and step out to your private patio overlooking the gardens and the bay. Breakfast and lunch are served on the waterside terrace. **Pros:** Cool design, plenty of places to relax, complimentary use of bikes and kayaks. **Cons:** Trailer park across the street, not much of a beach. ✉*MM 82, BS, 136 Madeira Rd., Upper Matecumbe Key* ☎*305/664–0044 or 888/881–3030* 🌐*www.casamorada.com* *16 suites* *In-room: safe, DVD. In-hotel: restaurant, room service, bar, pool, bicycles, no elevator, concierge, laundry service, public Wi-Fi, no kids under 16, no-smoking rooms* *AE, MC, V* *CP.*

★ $$$$ **Cheeca Lodge & Spa.** Stretching across 27 oceanfront acres, this classic resort has luxurious beachfront bungalows. The West Indies–style furnishings (think mahogany and marble) are a nice contrast with the high-tech touches (42-inch plasma TVs). Rooms have views of ocean, garden, or golf course. Beckoning the grown-ups are the beach with its selection of water sports equipment and the spa with a wide range of massages, facials, and body treatments. For kids there's Camp Cheeca, a fun and educational program. High season tends to draw lots of families, so Cheeca is not the place to be if you're single or not fond of small fry. **Pros:** Beautifully landscaped grounds, lots of wildlife, plenty of activities. **Cons:** Expensive rates, hefty resort fee for activities, slow service in restaurants. ✉*MM 82, OS, Box 527, Upper Matecumbe Key* ☎*305/664–4651 or 800/327–2888* 🌐*www.cheeca.com* *135 rooms, 6 suites* *In-room: safe, refrigerator (some), DVD, Wi-Fi. In-hotel: 2 restaurants, room service, bar, golf course, tennis courts, pools, gym, spa, beachfront, diving, water sports, bicycles, concierge, children's programs (ages 5–12), laundry service, Wi-Fi, no-smoking rooms* *AE, D, DC, MC, V.*

$$$ **Chesapeake Resort.** A stem to stern renovation restores this boutique hotel's reputation for step-above-typical accommodations. High-tech gadgets like flat screen TVs, CD players, and MP3 players give the place an up-to-date feel. Coral stone and dark wood accent the rooms, each of which has a porch or a balcony. Most units are lined up along the long stretch of sand that all but encircles a lagoon; others overlook the tennis court. **Pros:** Oceanfront location, free use of water sports equipment. **Cons:** Dated exterior, mandatory resort fee. ✉*83409 Overseas Hwy., Upper Matecumbe Key* ☎*305/664–4662 or 800/338–3395* 🌐*www.chesapeake-resort.com* *57 rooms, 8 suites* *In*

room: kitchens, Wi-Fi. In hotel: tennis court, pools, beachfront, watersports, bicycles, laundry facilities, public Wi-Fi ▭AE, D, MC, V ⊚CP.

★ **Drop Anchor Resort & Marina.** It's easy to find your cottage here, as they are painted in an array of Crayola colors. Immaculately kept, this place has the feel of your college chum's beach house. Inside you'll find soothing West Indies–type furnishings and kitschy-cool, 1950s-era tile in the bathrooms. Welcoming as the rooms may be, you didn't come to the Keys to sit indoors: there's a luscious expanse of white sand awaiting, and you can catch ocean breezes from either your balcony, a comfy Adirondack chair, or a picnic table perched in the sand. There are a fishing pier and boat ramp to accommodate anglers. **Pros:** Colorful, attention to detail, laid-back charm. **Cons:** Noise from the highway, beach is better for fishing than swimming. *✉84959 Overseas Hwy., MM 85, OS, Windley Key, Box 22233036 ☎305/664–4863 or 888/664–4863 ⊕www.dropanchorresort.com 18 rooms In-room: kitchen (some), refrigerator. In-hotel: pool, beachfront, no elevator, laundry facilities, public Internet, public Wi-Fi ▭AE, D, DC, MC, V.*

$-$$

$$$ **The Islander Resort.** Although the vintage sign is straight out of a *Happy Days* rerun, this 1950s-era property has undergone a top-to-bottom transformation. The decor is strikingly modern, with white cottage-style furnishings and elegant fabrics. Sunny yellow bedrooms look like pages from a Pottery Barn catalog. Private screened porches lead to a coral-shell beach with palm trees bending in the breeze. Families snap up suites in the oceanfront Beach House; couples looking for a more privacy head to rooms set back from the beach. The pools—one saltwater, one freshwater—win raves, as do the full kitchens. A 200-foot dock, lighted at night, adds to the resort feel. **Pros:** Spacious rooms, nice kitchens, eye-popping views. **Cons:** Pricey for what you get, beach has rough sand. *✉MM 81.2, OS, Upper Matecumbe Key ☎305/664–2031 or 800/753–6002 ⊕www.islanderfloridakeys.com 114 rooms In-room: safe, kitchen, Wi-Fi. In-hotel: restaurant, bar, pools, gym, beachfront, water sports, bicycles, laundry facilities, laundry service, public Wi-Fi ▭AE, D, DC, MC, V ⊚CP.*

★ **The Moorings.** This tropical retreat has everything you've dreamed about, from hammocks swaying between towering trees to a sugar-white beach lapped by aqua-green waves. West Indies–style cottages with colorful shutters, private verandas, and wicker furniture are enveloped by a canopy

$$-$$$$

2

of coconut palms on a residential street off the highway. This is a high-end slice of Old Florida, so don't expect tacky tiki bars. The one-, two-, and three-bedroom cottages all have modern kitchens. Four date back to the 1930s; the others were built in the early '90s. A palm-lined walkway leads to the beach, where a swimming dock awaits. The spa offers massages and beauty treatments. There's a two-night minimum-stay requirement for one-bedroom cottages, a one-week minimum on other lodgings. Often compared to Cheeca Lodge, The Moorings has more of a feeling of privacy. **Pros:** Romantic setting, good dining options, beautiful beach. **Cons:** No room service, extra fee for housekeeping, daily resort fee for activities. ✉*MM 81.6, OS, 123 Beach Rd., Upper Matecumbe Key* ☎*305/664–4708* 🌐*www.themooringsvillage.com* *3 cottages, 15 houses* *In-room: kitchen, Wi-Fi. In-hotel: tennis court, pool, spa, beachfront, water sports, no elevator, laundry facilities* ▭*AE, MC, V.*

$–$$ **Ragged Edge Resort.** Tucked away in a residential area at the ocean's edge, this hotel is big on value but short on style. Ragged Edge draws returning guests who would rather fish off the dock and hoist a brew than loll around in Egyptian cotton sheets. Even those who turn their noses up at the cheap plastic deck furniture and pine paneling admit that the place has a million-dollar setting, with ocean views all around. There's no beach to speak of, but you can ride a bike across the street to Islamorada Founder's Park, where you'll find a nice little beach and water toys for rent. If a bit of partying puts you off, look elsewhere. Plain-Jane though they are, rooms are clean and fairly spacious. Ground-floor units have screened porches; upper units have large decks, more windows, and beam ceilings. **Pros:** Oceanfront location, quiet neighborhood, cheap rates. **Cons:** Dated decor. ✉*MM 86.5, OS, 243 Treasure Harbor Rd., Plantation Key* ☎*305/852–5389 or 800/436–2023* 🌐*www.ragged-edge.com* *10 units* *In-room: kitchen, Wi-Fi. In-hotel: pool, bicycles, no elevator, public Wi-Fi* ▭*AE, MC, V.*

$$ **White Gate Court.** This small inn is a dog lover's paradise, with plenty of open space for pooches to play. All the sunny yellow cottages have beamed ceilings and spacious floor plans. The backyard has a barbecue and an umbrella-shaded table under palm trees. Rates include use of bicycles, paddleboat, and snorkeling gear. Boaters will appreciate the free docks and ramp. **Pros:** Pet-friendly, homey feel, pretty trees. **Cons:** No pool, simple accomodations. ✉*MM 76, BS, 76010 Overseas Hwy., Upper Matecumbe Key*

☎305/664–4136 or 800/645–4283 ⊕www.whitegatecourt.com ⇨7 units ♨In-room: kitchen, dial-up. In-hotel: beachfront, water sports, bicycles, no elevator, laundry facilities, some pets allowed (fee) ▭MC, V.

NIGHTLIFE

Islamorada is not known for its raging nightlife, but for local fun, Lorelei's is legendary. Others cater to the town's sophisticated clientele and fishing fervor.

Hog Heaven (*✉MM 85.3, OS, Windley Key ☎305/664–9669*) is a lively sports bar with three satellite dishes broadcasting the big game. These give way on weekends to a ★ DJ or live bands.Behind a larger-than-life mermaid is the **Lorelei Cabana Bar** (*✉MM 82, BS, Upper Matecumbe Key ☎305/664–4656*). This is the kind of place you fantasize about during those long, cold winters up north. It's all about good drinks, tasty pub grub, and sherbet-hued sunsets set to music. Live bands play island tunes and light rock. **Zane Grey Long Key Lounge** (*✉MM 81.5, BS, Upper Matecumbe Key ☎305/664–4244*), above the World Wide Sportsman, was created to honor writer Zane Grey, one of the most famous members of the Long Key Fishing Club. The lounge displays the author's photographs, books, and memorabilia. Listen to live blues, jazz, and Motown on a wide veranda that invites sunset watching. **Ziggie & Mad Dog's**(*✉MM 83 BS, Upper Matecumbe Key ☎305/664–3391* the area's glam celebrity hangout, serves appetizers with its happy hour drink specials.

SPORTS & THE OUTDOORS

BOATING

Marinas pop up every mile or so in the Islamorada area, so finding a rental or tour is no problem. Robbie's Marina is a prime example of a salty spot where you can find it all—from fishing charters and kayaking rentals to lunch and tarpon feeding

Bump & Jump (*✉MM 81.2, OS,Upper Matecumbe Key ☎305/664–9404 or 877/453–9463 ⊕www.keysboatrental.com*) is a one-stop shop for windsurfing, sailboat, and powerboat rentals, sales, and lessons. This company delivers to your hotel, house, or drop it off right at the beach. **Founder's Park Watersports**(*✉MM 87 BS, Plantation Key ☎305/434–8984 ⊕www.the-helm.com*) operates out of Islamorada Founder's Park. Hobie Wave sailboats are available, as are pedal boats and kayaks. Lessons range from a one-hour classes to race coaching. See the islands from the comfort of your own boat (captain's cap optional) when you rent from **Houseboat Vacations of the Florida Keys** (✉*MM 85.9, BS, 85944 Overseas Hwy., Plantation Key* ☎*305/664–4009* 🌐*www.floridakeys.com/houseboats*). The company maintains a fleet of 42- to 55-foot boats that accommodate up to 10 people and come outfitted with everything you need besides food. (You provision yourself at a nearby grocery store.) The three-day minimum starts at $1,112; one week costs $1,950 and up. Kayaks, canoes, and skiffs suitable for the ocean are also available. Electric boats offer a noise-free, fume-free alternative. The earth-friendly **Islamorada Queen** (✉Robbie's Marina,*MM 77.5 BS, Lower Matecumbe Key* ☎*No phone*) offers two-hour backcountry and sunset excursions that start at $39 per person. Historical excursions to Lignumvitae Key State Park are also popular. Can't decide between a limo and a yacht? Do both aboard the **Nauti-Limo** (✉*Lorelei Restaurant & Yacht Club, MM 82 BS, Upper Matecumbe Key* ☎*305/942–3793* 🌐*www.nautilimo.com*). Captain Joe Fox has converted the design of a 1983 pink Caddy stretch limo into a less-than-luxurious but certainly curious watercraft. Two-hour tours start at $100 per couple. The seaworthy hybrid—complete with wheels—can sail topless if you're in the mood to let it all hang out. Only in the Keys! **Robbie's Boat Rentals & Charters** (✉*MM 77.5, BS, 77520 Overseas Hwy., Lower Matecumbe Key* ☎*305/664–9814 or 877/664–8498* 🌐*www.robbies.com*) does it all. The company will deliver your boat to your hotel and give you a crash course on how not to crash it. The rental fleet includes an 18-foot skiff with a 60-horsepower outboard for $135 for four hours and $185 for the day and a 23-foot deck boat with a 130-horsepower engine for $185 for the half day and $235 for eight hours. Robbie's also rents fishing and snorkeling gear (there's good snorkeling nearby) and sells bait, drinks and snacks, and gas. Want to hire a guide who knows the local waters and where the fish lurk? Robbie's offers offshore fishing trips, patch reef trips, and party-boat fishing. Backcountry flats trips are a specialty. Captains Pam and Pete Anderson of **Treasure Harbor Marine** (✉*MM 86.5, OS, 200 Treasure Harbor Dr., Plantation Key* ☎*305/852–2458 or 800/352–2628* 🌐*www.treasureharbor.com*) provide everything you'll need for a vacation at sea. Best of all, they have excellent advice on where to find the best anchorages, snorkeling spots, or lobstering sites. Vessels range from a 19-foot Cape Dory to a 41-foot Morgan Out Island. Rates start at $160 a day and $700 a week. Hire a captain for $175 to $200 a day. Marina facilities are basic—water, electric, ice machine, laundry, picnic tables, and restrooms with showers. A store sells snacks, beverages, and sundries.

DIVING & SNORKELING

About 1.25 nautical miles south of Indian Key is the **San Pedro Underwater Archaeological Preserve State Park,** which includes wreck of a Spanish treasure fleet ship that sunk in 1733. The State of Florida protects the site for divers; no spearfishing or souvenir-collecting is allowed. Resting in only 18 feet of water, it can be seen by snorkelers as well as divers and attracts a colorful array of fish.

Florida Keys Dive Center (✉*MM 90.5, OS, Plantation Key* ☎*305/852–4599 or 800/433–8946* 🌐*www.floridakeysdivectr.com*) organizes dives from John Pennekamp Coral Reef State Park to Alligator Light. The center has two 46-foot Coast Guard–approved dive boats, offers scuba training, and is one of the few Keys dive centers to offer Nitrox (mixed gas) diving.

With a resort, pool, restaurant, lessons, and twice-daily dive and snorkel trips, **Holiday Isle Dive Shop** (✉*MM 84, OS, 84001 Overseas Hwy.,, Windley Key* ☎*305/664–3483 or 800/327–7070* 🌐*www.diveholidayisle.com*) is a one-stop dive shop. Rates start at $75 for a two-tank dive.

FISHING

Here in the self-proclaimed Sportfishing Capital of the World, sailfish is the prime catch in the winter and dolphinfish in the summer. Buchanan Bank just south of Islamorada is a good spot to try for tarpon in the spring.

Captain Ted Wilson (✉*Bud n' Mary's Marina, MM 79.9 OS, Upper Matecumbe Key* ☎*305/942–5224 or 305/664–9463* 🌐*www.captaintedwilson.com)* takes you into the backcountry for bonefish, tarpon, redfish, snook, and shark aboard a 17-foot boat that accommodates up to three anglers. For two people, half-day trips run $350, full-day trips $500, and evening excursions $375. There's a $100 charge for an extra person. Long before fly-fishing became popular, Sandy Moret was fishing the Keys for bonefish, tarpon, and redfish. Now he attracts anglers from around the world with the **Florida Keys Outfitters** (✉*Green Turtle, MM 81.2, Upper Matecumbe Key* ☎*305/664–5423*

🌐*www.floridakeysoutfitters.com*). Weekend fly-fishing classes, which include classroom instruction, equipment, and daily breakfast and lunch, cost $985. Add $1,070 for two additional days of fishing. Guided fishing trips cost $395 for a half day, $535 for a full day. Packages combining fishing and accommodations at Cheeca Lodge are available. The 65-foot party boat **Miss Islamorada** (✉*Bud n' Mary's Marina, MM 79.8, OS,Upper Matecumbe Key* ☎*305/664–2461 or 800/742–7945* 🌐*www.budnmarys.com*) has full-day trips for $60. Bring your lunch or buy ★ one from the dockside deli. Captain Ken Knudsen of the *Hubba Hubba* (✉*MM 79.8, OS, Upper Matecumbe Key* ☎*305/664–9281*) quietly poles his flatboat through the shallow water, barely making a ripple. Then he points and his clients cast. Five seconds later there's a zing, and the excitement of bringing in a snook, redfish, trout, or tarpon begins. Knudsen has fished Keys waters for more than 40 years. Now a licensed backcountry guide, he's ranked among the top 10 by national fishing magazines. He offers four-hour sunset trips for tarpon ($400 to $425) and two-hour sunset trips for bonefish ($225), as well as half- ($375) and full-day ($500) outings. Prices are for one or two anglers, and tackle and bait are included. Like other top fly-fishing and light-tackle guides, Captain Geoff Colmes of **Fishabout Charters** (✉*105 Palm La., Upper Matecumbe Key* ☎*305/853–0741 or 800/741–5955* 🌐*www.floridakeysflyfish.com*) helps his clients land trophy fish in the waters around the Keys ($500 to $550). But unlike the others, he also heads across Florida Bay to fish the coastal Everglades on three- and four-day trips (from $695 per angler) off his 65-foot mother ship, the *Fishabout*. It has four staterooms, private baths, living room, kitchen, satellite TV, and separate crew quarters. It's ideal when cold, windy weather shuts out fishing around the Keys. Rates include captain, crew, guide fees, lodging, all meals, tackle, and use of canoes for getting deep into shallow Everglades inlets.

TENNIS

Not all Keys recreation is on the water. Play tennis year-round at the **Islamorada Tennis Club** (✉*MM 76.8, BS, Upper Matecumbe Key* ☎*305/664–5340* 🌐*www.islamoradatennisclub.com*). It's a well-run facility with four clay and two hard courts (all lighted), same-day racket stringing, ball machines, private lessons, and a full-service pro shop. Rates are from $25 a day.

WATER SPORTS

Florida Keys Kayak (*Robbie's Marina ✉MM 77.5, BS, 77522 Overseas Hwy., Lower Matecumbe Key ☎305/664–4878*) rents kayaks for trips to Indian and Lignumvitae keys, two favorite destinations for paddlers. Kayak rental rates are $20 per hour for a single, and $27.50 for a double. Half-day rates (and you'll need plenty of time to explore those mangrove canopies) are $40 for a single kayak and $55 for a double. The company also offers guided two- and three-hour tours ($39 and $49 per person).**Parasail Islamorada** (*✉Whale Harbor Marina, MM 83.5 OS, Upper Matecumbe Key ✉Holiday Isle Resort, MM 84 OSWindley Key ☎305/726–4608* ✍ parasailislamorada@yahoo.com) offers free-fall, tandem, get-wet, and stay-dry flights from two locations. An approximately 600-foot-high ride costs $60 per person. The length of the ride depends upon the number of people in your group. With two people, for instance, each gets about a 25-minute ride.

SHOPPING

Art galleries, upscale gift shops, and the mammoth World Wide Sportsman (if you want to look the part of a local fisherman, you must wear a shirt from here) make up the variety and superior style of Islamorada shopping.

BOOKS

Among the best buys in town are the used best-sellers at **Hooked on Books** (*✉MM 82.6, OS, 82681 Overseas Hwy., Upper Matecumbe Key ☎305/517–2602*). There are also new titles, audio books, and CDs.

GALLERIES

The go-to destination for one-of-a-kind gifts is **Gallery Morada** (*✉MM 81.6, OS, 81611 Old Hwy.,Upper Matecumbe Key ☎305/664–3650*), where blown-glass objects are beautifully displayed, as are the sculptures, original paintings and lithographs, and hand-painted scarves and earrings by top South Florida artists. The **Rain Barrel** (*✉MM 86.7, BS, Plantation Key ☎305/852–3084*) is a natural and unhurried shopping showplace. Set in a tropical garden of shady trees, native shrubs, and orchids, the crafts village has shops with works by local and national artists and eight resident artists in studios, including John Hawver, noted for Florida landscapes and seascapes. The **Redbone Gallery** (*✉MM 81.5, OS, 200 Industrial Dr., Upper Matecumbe Key ☎305/664–2002*), the largest sporting-art gallery in

Florida, stocks hand-stitched clothing and giftware, in addition to work by wood and bronze sculptors such as Kendall Van Sant; watercolorists Chet Reneson, Jeanne Dobie, and Kathleen Denis; and painters C. D. Clarke and Tim Borski. Proceeds benefit cystic fibrosis research.

GIFTS

★ At the **Banyan Tree** (✉*MM 81.2, OS, 81197 Overseas Hwy., Upper Matecumbe Key* ☎*305/664–3433*), a sharp-eyed husband-and-wife team successfully combines antiques and contemporary gifts for the home and garden with plants, pots, and trellises in a stylishly sophisticated indoor–outdoor setting. At **Down to Earth** (✉*MM 82.2, OS, 82205 Overseas Hwy.,Upper Matecumbe Key* ☎*305/664–9828*), indulge your passion for *objets* that are at once practical and fanciful, such as salad tongs carved from coconut shells or Indonesian furniture with intricate designs. The prices are reasonable, too.**Island Silver & Spice** (✉*MM 82, OS, Upper Matecumbe Key* ☎*305/664–2714*) has tropical-style furnishings, rugs and home accessories. The shop also stocks women's and men's resort wear and a large jewelry selection with high-end watches and marine-theme pieces.

SPORTING GOODS

★ Former U.S. presidents, celebrities, and record holders beam alongside their catches in black-and-white photos on the walls at **World Wide Sportsman** (✉*MM 81.5, BS, Upper Matecumbe Key* ☎*305/664–4615 or 800/327–2880*), a two-level retail center that sells upscale fishing equipment, resort clothing, and gifts.When you're tired of shopping, relax at the Zane Grey Long Key Lounge.

LONG KEY

MM 70–65.5.

Long Key isn't a tourist hot spot, making it a favorite destination for those looking to avoid the masses and enjoy some cultural and ecological history in the process. Offering both is **Long Key State Park**. On the ocean side, the Golden Orb Trail leads to a boardwalk that cuts through the mangroves and alongside a lagoon where waterfowl congregate. A canoe trail leads through a tidal lagoon, and a broad expanse of shallow grass flats are perfect for bonefishermen. Bring a mask and snorkel to observe the marine life in the shallow water. The park is particularly popular with campers who long to stake their tent at the campground on a beach. Repairs after four hurricanes have left the park with improved facilities, but with very little shade. Replanting efforts are ongoing. Good news: the park has added kayaks to its paddle craft rental fleet. Canoes rent for $5 per hour, while kayak rentals start at $17 for two hours.

Across the road from Long Key State Park, beginning at a marker partially obscured by foliage, is the free **Layton Nature Trail** (✉*MM 67.7, BS*). This 20- to 30-minute walk leads through tropical hardwood forest to a rocky Florida Bay shoreline overlooking shallow grass flats. A marker relates the history of the Long Key Viaduct, the first major bridge on the rail line, and the exclusive Long Key Fishing Camp, which Henry Flagler established nearby in 1906. The camp was washed away in the 1935 hurricane and never rebuilt. ✉*MM 67.5, OS, Box 776* ☎*305/664–4815* 🌐*www.floridastateparks.org/longkey* 🎫*$3.50 for 1 person, $6 for 2 people, and 50¢ for each additional person in the group* ⏲*Daily 8–sunset.*

WHERE TO STAY & EAT

$ ✕ **Little Italy.** It's your basic Italian joint that looks like it's been around forever. The menu offers no real surprises—except maybe conch parmigiana and mahimahi with sherry and mushroom sauce. The lunch and dinner menus offer plenty of variety, but few can resist the pull of the pasta. (Maybe it's the garlicky aroma that permeates the place.) The light-bites menu has smaller portions for calorie watchers. Reward those light bites with a slice of decadent chocolate pecan pie. ✉*MM 68.5, BS* ☎*305/664–4472* 💳*AE, MC, V* ⏲*Closed Wed.*

$ 🏨 **Lime Tree Bay Resort.** Easy on the eye and the wallet, this 2½-acre resort on Florida Bay is far from the hustle and bustle of the larger islands. You can get a good workout on the water or simply break a sweat lolling around on the beach or in a hammock in the pleasantly landscaped garden. Walls painted in lovely faux finishes and hung with tropical arts add a sophisticated look to the rooms. The five suites are the best places to stay because of the gulf views, followed by the cottages without gulf views. Four deluxe rooms upstairs have cathedral ceilings and skylights. The best bet for two couples traveling together is the upstairs Tree House. Most units have a shared balcony or porch. **Pros:** Great views, friendly staff, close to Long

Key State Park. **Cons:** Only one restaurant nearby. ✉*MM 68.5, BS* ⓑ*Box 839, Layton 33001* ☎*305/664–4740 or 800/723–4519* 🌐*www.limetreebayresort.com* ⇨*10 rooms, 11 studios, 8 suites, 5 apartments, 2 cottages.* ♁*In-room: kitchen (some), refrigerator, dial-up. In-hotel: tennis court, pool, beachfront, water sports, bicycles, no elevator, no-smoking rooms* ▭*AE, D, DC, MC, V.*

★ **Long Key State Park.** Each of these oceanfront tent and RV sites is right on the water, which is why they are booked so far in advance. You can—and should—reserve up to 11 months in advance, especially if you're planning a winter trip. By day you can try biking, hiking, boating, and fishing for bonefish, permit, and tarpon in the flats. By night there are seasonal campfire programs. All sites have water and electricity. A two-night minimum stay is required on holidays and weekends. ♁*Flush toilets, partial hookups (electric and water), dump station, drinking water, showers, picnic tables, electricity, public telephone, ranger station, swimming (ocean), some pets allowed* ⇨*60 partial hookups, 50 RV sites, 10 tent sites* ✉*MM 67.5, OS, Box 776* ☎*305/664–4815 or 800/326–3521* 🌐*www.reserveamerica.com* ▭*AE, D, MC, V.*

EN ROUTE. **As you cross Long Key Channel, look beside you at the old Long Key Viaduct. The second-longest bridge on the former rail line, this 2-mi-long structure has 222 reinforced-concrete arches. The old bridge is popular with anglers, who fish off the sides day and night.**

THE UPPER KEYS ESSENTIALS

For information on transportation, as well as contacts and resources to help you plan your trip to the Upper Keys, see
☞ *Florida Keys Essentials.*

To research prices, get advice from other travelers, and book travel arrangements, visit www.fodors.com.

TOUR OPTIONS

BOAT TOURS

Captain Sterling's Everglades Eco-Tours operates Everglades and Florida Bay ecology tours ($50 per person) and sunset cruises ($59 per person).

Key Largo Princess offers two-hour glass-bottom-boat trips ($25) and sunset cruises on a luxury 70-foot motor yacht with a 280-square-foot glass viewing area, departing from the Holiday Inn docks three times a day.

Contacts **Everglades Eco-Tours** (*✉Dolphin's Cove, MM 102, BS, Key Largo ☎305/853-5161 or 888/224-6044 🌐www.captainsterling.com*). **Key Largo Princess** (*✉MM 100, OS, 99701 Overseas Hwy., Key Largo ☎305/451-4655 or 877/648-8129 🌐www.keylargoprincess.com*).

VISITOR INFORMATION

Contacts **Islamorada Chamber of Commerce** (*✉MM 83.2, BS, Box 915, Upper Matecumbe Key, Islamorada ☎305/664-4503 or 800/322-5397 🌐www.islamoradachamber.com*). **Key Largo Chamber of Commerce** (*✉MM 106, BS, 106000 Overseas Hwy., Key Largo ☎305/451-14747 or 800/822-1088 🌐www.keylargochamber.org*).

The Middle Keys

3

WORD OF MOUTH

"If you have any interest in dolphins, stop at the Dolphin Research Center on Grassy Key. I could have spent the entire day there watching the dolphins."

–beth_fitz

"We lived in Florida years ago and thought Manny and Isa had the standard by which all key lime pie should be judged."

–T4TX

www.fodors.com/forums

Revised & Updated by Chelle Koster Walton

MOST OF THE ACTIVITY FOR THE MIDDLE KEYS centers around the town of Marathon, the region's third-largest metropolitan area. On either end of it, smaller keys hold resorts, wildlife research and rehab facilities, a historic village, and a state park. The Middle Keys make a fitting transition from the Upper Keys to the Lower Keys not only geographically, but mentally. Crossing Seven Mile Bridge prepares you for the slow pace and don't-give-a-damn attitude you'll find a little further down the highway. Fishing is one of the main attractions—in fact, the region's commercial fishing industry was founded here in the early 1800s. Diving is another popular pastime. There are many beaches and natural areas to enjoy in the Middle Keys, where mainland stress becomes an ever more distant memory.

EXPLORING THE MIDDLE KEYS

If you get bridge fever—the heebie-jeebies when driving over long stretches of water—you may need a pair of blinders (or a couple tranquilizers) before tackling the Middle Keys. Stretching from Conch Key to the far side of the Seven Mile Bridge, this zone is home to the region's two longest bridges: Long Key Viaduct and Seven Mile Bridge, both historic landmarks.

U.S. 1 takes you from one end of the region to the other in a direct line that takes in most of the sights, but you'll find some interesting resorts and restaurants off the main drag.

ABOUT THE RESTAURANTS

Hope you're not tired of seafood, because the run of fish houses continues in the Middle Keys. In fact, Marathon boasts some of the best. Several are not so easy to find, but worth the search because of their local color and ocean views. Expect casual and friendly service with a side of sass. Restaurants may close for two to four weeks during the slow season between mid-September and mid-November, so call ahead if you have a particular place in mind.

ABOUT THE HOTELS

From quaint old cottages to newly built town house communities, the Middle Keys have it all, often with prices that are more affordable than at the chain's extremes. Hawk's Cay has the region's best selection of lodgings.

WHAT IT COSTS				
¢	$	$$	$$$	$$$$
RESTAURANTS				
under $10	$10–$20	$20–$30	$30–$40	over $40
HOTELS				
under $100	$100–$150	$150–$200	$200–$250	over $250

Restaurant prices are per person for a main course at dinner. Hotel prices are for a standard double room, excluding 6% sales tax (more in some counties) and 1%–4% tourist tax.

CONCH & DUCK KEYS

MM 63–61.

This stretch of islands ranges from rustic fishing village to boating elite. Fishing dominates the economy, and many residents are descendants of immigrants from the mainland South. Across a causeway from the tiny fishing village of Conch Key is Duck Key, home to a more upscale community. There are a few lodging options here for those exploring Marathon or taking advantage of the water sports on Duck Key.

WHERE TO STAY

$$ **Conch Key Cottages.** Rescued from some years of neglect, this once-beloved property is getting a complete makeover. The pastel-hued cottages, each named for a shell or sea creature, are going boutique with Bali-style furnishings. Each room comes with a juicer and an unlimited supply of oranges. Continental breakfast is delivered to your doors. The best part of the lodging—its secluded setting and mangrove-framed beach—haven't changed. **Pros:** Far from the traffic noise, sandy beach, lots of sunny decks. **Cons:** Some dust from ongoing renovations, far from restaurants. ✉*MM 62.3 OS, Conch Key* ☎*305/289–1377 or 800/330–1577* 🌐*www.conchkeycottages.com* *9 cottages, 2 villas, 2 rooms* *In-room: kitchen, Wi-Fi (some). In-hotel: pool, beachfront, public Wi-Fi* *AE, D, MC, V* *CP.*

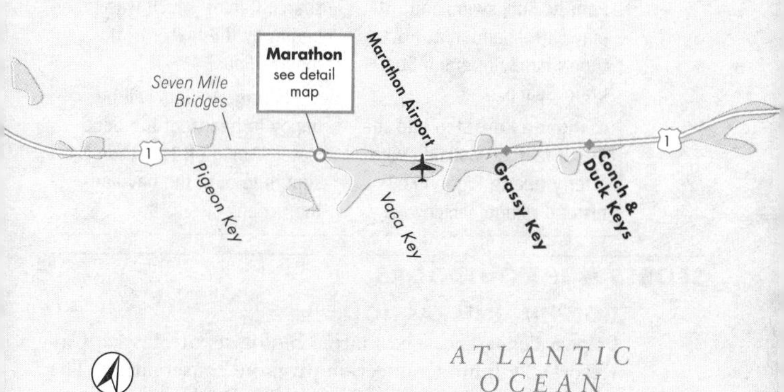

★ **Fodor'sChoice** **Hawk's Cay Resort.** An in-the-water program that lets you get up close and personal with dolphins makes this sprawling resort a family favorite. This Caribbean-style retreat has plenty to keep the kids occupied, such as a pirate ship with water cannons. When the older generation wants to head to the spa or out to dinner at one of the restaurants, there are supervised programs for kids and teens. The spacious rooms and villas sport a West Indies look, thanks to a $35 million renovation completed in 2008. The room rate does not include a $20 daily resort fee. **Pros:** Huge rooms, restful spa, full-service marina. **Cons:** No real beach, far from the action. ✉*MM 61, OS, 61 Hawk's Cay Blvd., Duck Key* ☎*305/743–7000 or 888/443–6393* ⊕*www.hawkscay.com* *177 rooms, 16 suites, 295 2-bedroom villas* *In-room: kitchen (some), refrigerator, Ethernet, Wi-Fi. In-hotel: 4 restaurants, room service, bars, tennis courts, pools, gym, spa, diving, water sports, children's programs (ages 5–17), laundry facilities, laundry service, concierge, public Wi-Fi, airport shuttle, no-smoking rooms* *AE, D, DC, MC, V.*

$$$$

MIDDLE KEYS TOP 5

- **Crane Point.** Visit 63-acre Crane Point Museum, Nature Center & Historic Site in Marathon for a primer on local natural and social history.
- **A Beach for the Whole Family.** Sun, swim, and play with abandon at Marathon's family-oriented Sombrero Beach.
- **Pigeon Key.** Step into the era of railroad building with a ferry ride to Pigeon Key's historic village, which was once a residential camp for workers on Henry M. Flagler's Overseas Railroad.
- **Dolphins.** Kiss a dolphin, and maybe even watch one paint, at Dolphin Research Center, which was begun by the maker of the movie *Flipper.*
- **Fishing.** Anglers will be happy to hear that the deep-water fishing off Marathon is superb in both the bay and the ocean.

SPORTS & THE OUTDOORS

DOLPHIN INTERACTION

Dolphin Connection. The marine biologists at Hawk's Cay Resort's Dolphin Connection promote conservation. The resort offers three programs, including Dockside Dolphins, a 30-minute encounter from the dry training docks ($50 for resort guests, $60 for nonguests); Dolphin Discovery, an in-water program that lasts about 45 minutes and lets you kiss, touch, and feed the dolphins ($135, $150); and Trainer for a Day, a three-hour session with the animal training team ($275, $285). ✉*MM 61, OS, 61 Hawks Cay Blvd., Duck Key* ☎*888/814–9154* 🌐*www.dolphinconnection.com.*

SCUBA & SNORKELING

Dive Duck Key (✉*MM 61, 61 Hawk's Key Blvd., Duck Key* ☎*305/289–4931 or 877/386–3483* 🌐*www.tildensscubacenter.com*) is a full-service dive shop offering rentals, charters, lessons, and certification courses. Snorkel trips cost $35 without gear, $45 with gear. Scuba trips are $60 without gear and $75 to $115 with gear. Basic open-water certification courses requires five days and $525. There's also Snuba, a snorkel-scuba hybrid where your tanks are on the surface rather than on your back. Excursions are $99.

WATER SPORTS

Sundance Watersports (✉*MM 61 OS, Duck Key* ☎*305/743–0145*) can take care of all your fun-on-the-water needs. Go on a one-hour guided Jet Ski tour ($149 for one or two people), soar on a parasail flight ($79 for single, $139 for tandem), take waterskiing or wakeboarding lessons (starting at $89 for a half-hour), or enjoy a glass-bottom boast trip or sunset cruise.

GRASSY KEY

MM 60–57.

Local lore has it that this sleepy little key was named not for its vegetation—mostly native trees and shrubs—but for an early settler by the name of Grassy. The key is primarily inhabited by a few families operating small fishing camps and roadside motels. There's no marked definition between it and Marathon, so it feels sort of like a suburb of its much larger neighbor to the south. Grassy Key's sights-to-see tend toward the natural, including a worthwhile dolphin attraction and a small state park.

★ The 1963 movie *Flipper* popularized the notion of humans interacting with dolphins. The film's creator, Milton Santini, also created the **Dolphin Research Center.** Home to a colony of dolphins and sea lions, the not-for-profit center has tours, narrated programs, and programs that allow you to greet the dolphins from dry land or play with them in their watery habitat. Programs range from a stay-dry Meet the Dolphin program for $25 to get-wet Dolphin Dip ($100), Dolphin Encounter ($180), and Trainer for a Day ($650) programs. You can even paint a T-shirt with a dolphin—you pick the paint, the dolphin "designs" your shirt ($55). The center also offers five-day programs for children and adults with disabilities. ✉*MM 59, BS* *Box 522875, Marathon Shores 33052* ☎*305/289–1121 or 305/289–0002* *www.dolphins.org* *Tours $19.50* *Daily 9–4:30*

Looking for a slice of the Keys that's far removed from tiki bars? On the ocean and bay sides of U.S. 1, **Curry Hammock State Park** covers 260 acres of upland hammock, wetlands, and mangroves. On the bay side, there's a trail through thick hardwoods to a rocky shoreline. The ocean side is more developed, with a sandy beach, a clean bathhouse, picnic tables, a playground, grills, and a 28-site campground open November to May. Locals consider the

CLOSE UP

Close Encounters of the Flipper Kind

Here in the Florida Keys, where Milton Santini made the 1963 movie *Flipper*, close encounters of the mammalian kind are an everyday occurrence. There are a handful of facilities that allow you to commune with trained dolphins. In-water programs, where you actually swim with these intelligent creatures, are extremely popular and require advance reservations. All of the programs begin with a course on dolphin physiology and behavior taught by a marine biologist. Afterward you learn a few important dos and don'ts (for example, don't wave your hands—you might, literally, send the wrong signal). Finally, you take the plunge.

For the in-water programs, the dolphins swim all around you. If you lie on your back with your feet out, they use their snouts to push you around. You can also grab a dorsal fin for an exciting ride. The in-water encounter lasts between 10 to 25 minutes, depending on the program. The entire experience takes about two hours. The best time to go is when it's warm, from March through December. You spend a lot of time in and out of the water, and you can feel your teeth chattering on a chilly day.

There's no need to get completely wet, however. Waterside programs let you feed, shake hands, and do tricks with dolphins from a submerged platform. These are great for people who aren't strong swimmers or for youngsters who don't meet a facilities minimum age requirements for in-water programs.

Possibilities include the Dolphin Connection in Duck Key, Dolphin Cove and Dolphins Plus in Key Largo (see ⇨ Chapter 2, "The Upper Keys"), and the Dolphin Research Center in Grassy Key.

paddling trails under canopies of arching mangroves one of the best kayaking spots in the Keys. Manatees frequent the area, and it's a great spot for bird-watching. Herons, egrets, ibis, plovers, and sanderlings are commonly spotted. Raptors are often seen in the park, especially during migration periods. ✉*MM 57, OS, 56200 Overseas Hwy., Crawl Key, Marathon* ☎*305/289–2690* 🌐*www.floridastateparks.org/curryhammock* 💵*$3.50 for 1 person, $6 for 2, 50¢ per additional passenger* ⏲*Daily 8–sunset.*

WHERE TO STAY & EAT

$$ ✕ **Hideaway Café.** The name says it all—**Hideaway Café is** tucked between Grassy Key and Marathon, easy to miss if you're barnstorming through the middle islands. When you find it (upstairs at Rainbow Bend Resort), you'll discover a favorite of locals who appreciate a well-planned menu, lovely ocean view, and quiet evening away from the crowds. For starters, dig into escargots à la Edison (sautéed with vegetables, pepper, cognac, and cream). Then feast on several specialties, such as a rarely-found chateaubriand, a belly-busting whole roasted duck, or the seafood special combining the catch of the day with scallops and shrimp in a savory sauce. ✉ *Rainbow Bend Resort, MM 58, OS, Grassy Key* ☎*305/289–1554* ⊕*www.hideawaycafe.com* ▭*AE, D, DC, MC, V* ⊘*No lunch.*

$ **Gulf View Waterfront Resort.** "Hey, baby!" may be your greeting at the easygoing Gulf View, but the comment is mostly likely coming from Coco, a white cockatiel. With a flock of 15 birds on property, this homey duplex is part resort, part aviary. Owner-occupied, the Gulf View is decorated with simple wicker furniture, tropical pastels, and ceiling fans. The only jarring design note is the green concrete ledge supporting the elevated swimming pool. Guests—mostly couples during the winter and families during holidays—appreciate the close proximity to the Dolphin Research Center, practically next door. (The resort offers discount passes.) Canoes, paddleboats, and kayaks are also available for guests for free. **Pros:** Parklike setting, sandy beach area with hammocks, close to restaurants. **Cons:** Ground-level units are dark, some traffic noise. ✉*MM 58.5, BS, 58743 Overseas Hwy.* ☎*305/289–1414* ⊕*www.gulfviewwaterfrontresort.com* *2 rooms, 6 suites, 3 efficiencies* *In-room: kitchen (some), refrigerator, Wi-Fi. In-hotel: pool, water sports, no elevator, laundry facilities, public Wi-Fi, parking, some pets allowed (fee), no-smoking rooms* ▭*AE, D, MC, V.*

¢–$ **Bonefish Resort.** Set on a skinny lot bedecked with palm trees, banana trees, and hibiscus plantings, this motel-style hideaway is the best choice among the island's back-to-basics properties. It's not fancy, but it's cheap, clean, and a good base for paddling a kayak, wading for bonefish, and watching the waves roll in from a lounge chair. Rooms are decorated with tropical motifs like the colorful metal lizards on the doors. A narrow gravel courtyard lined with umbrella-shaded tables leads to a small beach and a waterfront pool. The kayaks and paddleboats encourage exploration of the waterfront. The communal deck is scattered with hammocks and chaises. Check-in is at next-door sister property Yellowtail Inn, which has cottages and efficiencies. **Pros:** Decent price for the location, oceanside setting. **Cons:** Decks are small, simple decor. ✉*MM 58, OS, 58070 Overseas Hwy.* ☎*305/743–7107 or 800/274–9949* 🌐*www.bonefishresort.com* *3 rooms, 11 efficiencies* *In-room: kitchen (some), refrigerator, VCR. In-hotel: beachfront, bicycles, no elevator, laundry facilities, public Wi-Fi, some pets allowed (fee)* 💳*D, MC, V.*

MARATHON

MM 53–47.5.

New Englanders founded this former fishing village in the early 1800s. The community on Vaca Key subsequently served as a base for pirates, salvagers (also known as "wreckers"), spongers, and, later, Bahamian farmers who eked out a living growing cotton and other crops. More Bahamians arrived in hopes of finding work building of the railroad. According to local lore, Marathon was renamed when a worker commented that it was a marathon task to position the tracks across the 6-mi-long island.

During the building on the railroad, Marathon developed a reputation for lawlessness that rivaled that of the Old West. It is said that to keep the rowdy workers from descending on Key West for their off-hours endeavors, residents would send boatloads of liquor up to Marathon. Needless to say, things have quieted down considerably since then.

Marathon is a bustling town, at least compared to other communities in the Keys. As it leaves something to be desired in the charm department, Marathon will probably not be your first choice of places to stay. But there are a surprising number of good dining options, so you'll definitely want to stop for a bite even if you're just passing through on the way to Key West.

Outside of Key West, it has the most historic attractions that merit a visit. Fishing, diving, and boating are the main events here. Throughout the year, it throws tarpon tournaments in March and April, more fishing tournaments in June and September, a birding festival in September, and lighted boat parades around the holidays.

EXPLORING MARATHON

Grassy Key segues into Marathon with little more than a slight increase in traffic and higher concentration of commercial establishments. Marathon's roots are anchored to fishing and boating, so look for marinas to find local color, fishing charters, and good restaurants. At its north end, Key Colony Beach is an old-fashioned island neighborhood worth a visit for its shops and restaurants. Nature lovers shouldn't miss the attractions on Crane Point. Other good places to leave the main road are at Sombrero Beach Road (MM 50), which leads to the beach, and 35th Street (MM 49), which takes you to a funky little marina and restaurant. U.S. 1 hightails through Hog Key and Knight Key before the big leap over Florida Bay and Hawk's Channel via the Seven Mile Bridge.

★ **Crane Point Museum, Nature Center, & Historic Site.** Tucked away from the highway behind a stand of trees, Crane Point—part of a 63-acre tract that contains the last-known undisturbed thatch-palm hammock—is delightfully undeveloped. The facility includes the **Museum of Natural History of the Florida Keys,** which has displays about local wildlife, a seashell exhibit, and a marine life display that makes you feel you're at the bottom of the sea. Also here is the **Children's Activity Center,** with a replica of a 17th-century galleon and pirate dress-up room where youngsters can play swashbuckler. On the 1-mi indigenous loop trail, visit the **Wild Bird Center** and the remnants of a Bahamian village, site of the restored **George Adderly House.** It is the oldest surviving example of Bahamian tabby (a concrete-like material created from sand and seashells) construction outside of Key West. A newly recreated Cracker house demonstrates the vernacular housing of the early 1900s. A boardwalk crosses wetlands, rivers, and mangroves before ending at Adderly Village. From November to Easter, docent-led tours, are available; bring good walking shoes and bug repellent during warm weather. Events include a Bahamian Heritage Festival in January. ✉ *MM 50.5, BS, 5550 Overseas Hwy., Box 536* ☎ *305/743–9100* 🌐 *www.cranepoint.net* 🎟 *$8* ⏲ *Mon.–Sat. 9–5, Sun. noon–5; call to arrange trail tours.*

NEED A BREAK? **If you don't get a buzz from breathing in the robust aroma at Leigh Ann's (More Than Just A) Coffee House (** ✉ ***7537 Overseas Hwy.*** ☎ ***305/743–2001*****), order an espresso shot, Cuban or Italian, for a satisfying jolt. Pastries are baked fresh daily, but**

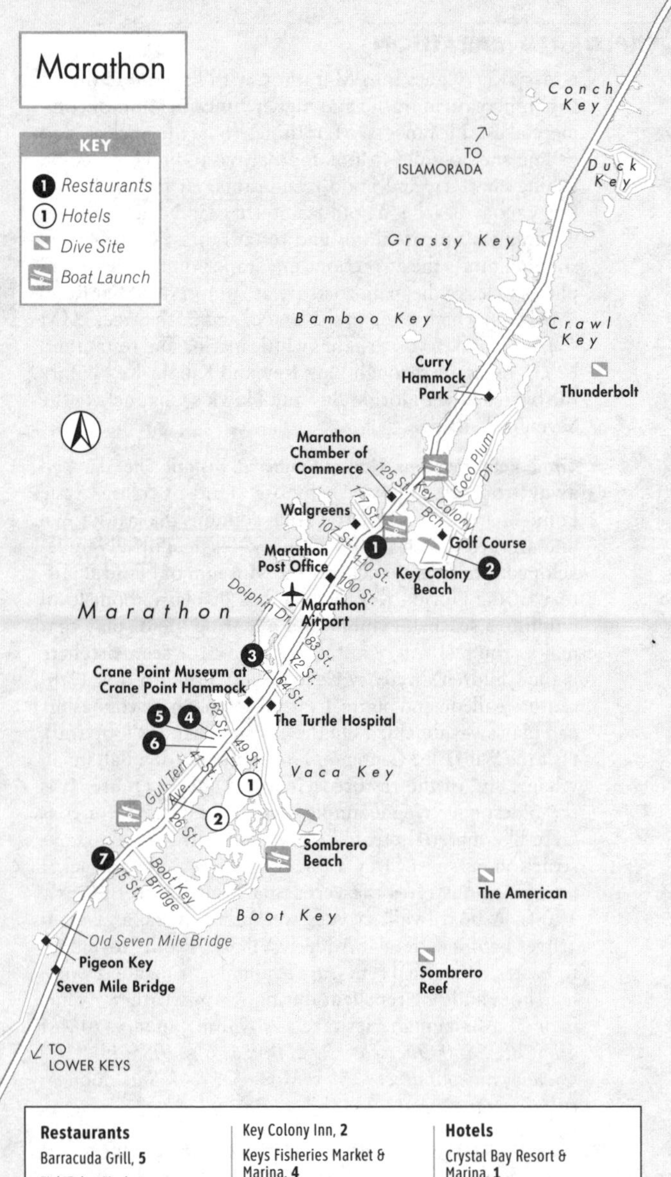

Restaurants

Barracuda Grill, **5**

Fish Tales Market and Eatery, **1**

Herbie's. **3**

Key Colony Inn, **2**

Keys Fisheries Market & Marina, **4**

7 Mile Grill, **7**

The Stuffed Pig, **6**

Hotels

Crystal Bay Resort & Marina, **1**

Tranquility Bay, **2**

the biscuits with sausage gravy and the Italian frittata cooked without added fat are among the big movers. Business has been so good that Leigh Ann's is now open for dinner. (Try the risotto, followed by the ultimate seven-layer brownie.) Dinner is served until 9 PM in season. It's closed on Sunday.

3

★ **Pigeon Key.** There's much to like about this 5-acre island under the Old Seven Mile Bridge. You can reach it by walking across a 2¼-mi section of the bridge or by ferry. Once there, tour the island on your own or join a guided tour. The tour explores the buildings that formed the early-20th-century work camp for the Overseas Railroad that linked the mainland to Key West. Later the island became a fish camp, a state park, and then government administration headquarters. Exhibits in a small museum recall the history of the Keys, the railroad, and railroad baron Henry M. Flagler. Pick up the ferry at the gift shop inside the railroad car on Knight's Key (MM 47, OS). ✉ *MM 45, OS, Box 500130, Pigeon Key* ☎ *305/289–0025 general information, 305/743–5999 tickets* 🎫 *$11* ⏲ *Daily 9:30–4:30; ferry boat departures at 10, 11:30, 1, 2:30.*

Seven Mile Bridge. One of the most-photographed images in the Keys actually measures slightly less than seven miles, despite its name. Connecting the Middle and Lower Keys, it is believed to be the world's longest segmental bridge. It has 39 expansion joints separating its various concrete sections. Each April, runners gather in Marathon for the annual Seven Mile Bridge Run. The expanse running parallel to Seven Mile Bridge is what remains of the **Old Seven Mile Bridge,** an engineering and architectural marvel in its day that's now on the National Register of Historic Places. It rested on a record 546 concrete piers. No cars are allowed on the old bridge today, but a 2-mi segment is open for biking, walking, and Rollerblading.

Sombrero Beach. Pleasant, shaded picnic areas overlook a coconut palm-lined grassy stretch and the Atlantic Ocean at this beach. Separate areas allow swimmers, boaters, and windsurfers to share the narrow cove. Facilities include barbecue grills, showers, and restrooms, as well as a baseball diamond, a large playground, and a volleyball court. Sunday afternoons draw lots of local families toting coolers. The park is accessible for those with disabilities and allows leashed pets. Turn east at the traffic light in Marathon and follow signs to the end. ✉ *MM 50, OS, Sombrero Beach Rd.* ☎ *305/743–0033* 🎫 *Free* ⏲ *Daily 8–sunset.*

TURTLE TIME

Five species of threatened and endangered sea turtles frequent the waters of the Florida Keys. The **Loggerhead**, the most common, is named for the shape of its noggin. It grows to a heft of 300 pounds. It is the only of the local turtles listed as threatened rather than endangered.

The vegetarian **Green Turtle** was once hunted for its meat, which has brought populations to their endangered stage. It can reach an impressive 500 pounds.

Named for the shape of its mouth, the **Hawksbill Turtle** is a relative lightweight at 150 pounds. It prefers rocks and reefs for habitat. The Keys are the only U.S. breeding site for the endangered critter.

The largest reptile alive, the **Leatherback Turtle** can weigh in at up to 2,000 pounds, attained from a diet of mainly jellyfish.

The rarest of local sea turtles, the **Kemps Ridley** is named after a Key West fisherman. A carnivore, it grows to 100 pounds.

The biggest threats to sea turtle survival include fibropapilloma tumors, monofilament fishing line (which can sever their flippers), entanglement in ropes and nets, boat propeller run-ins, oil spills, and other human and natural impact.

The Turtle Hospital. More than 70 injured sea turtles check in here every year. The guided tours takes you into recovery and surgical areas at this, the world's only state-certified veterinary hospital for sea turtles. If you're lucky, you can visit hatchlings. Call ahead, as tours are sometime cancelled due to medical emergencies. ✉ *MM 48.5 BS33050* ☎ *305/743–2552* 🌐 *www.turtlehospital.org* 🎫 *$15* ⏲ *Daily 9–5; tours at 10, 1, and 4.*

WHERE TO EAT

★ Fodor'sChoice ✕ **Barracuda Grill.** Sparsely decorated with fish
$ and bird art and filled with tables covered with butcher paper, this restaurant is not much to look at. But when it comes to the food, Barracuda Grill delivers. The sophisticated, eclectic menu capitalizes on local seafood (take a test drive with the mangrove snapper), but give equal treatment to aged Angus beef, rack of lamb, and braised pork shank. Smaller entrées such as mini-mahi and baby steak appeal to light appetites. Favorite main courses include

Francesca's spicy voodoo stew with scallops, shrimp, and vegetables in a tomato-saffron stock; a 22-ounce cowboy rib eye; and sashimi of yellowfin tuna accompanied by wasabi and tamari. For dessert, slices of oh-so-rich key lime cheesecake fly out of the kitchen. The well-thought-out wine list is heavily Californian. Call ahead, as the owners often close during the off-season. ✉*MM 49.5, BS, 4290 Overseas Hwy.* ☎*305/743–3314* *Reservations not accepted* *AE, MC, V* *No lunch.*

¢ ✕ **Fish Tales Market and Eatery.** This roadside eatery serves signature dishes such as oysters on a roll and fish of the day on grilled rye with coleslaw and melted cheese. You also can slurp lobster bisque or red conch chowder. Plan to dine early, as it's open only until 6:30. This is a no-frills kind of place with its own seafood market, a couple of picnic tables, and friendly service. ✉*MM 53, OS, 11711 Overseas Hwy.* ☎*305/743–9196 or 888/662–4822* *AE, MC, V* *Closed Sun.*

$ ✕ **Herbie's.** Since 1972, this has been the go-to spot for quick and affordable comfort food from cheeseburgers and fried oysters to shrimp scampi and filet mignon. You'll find all the local staples—conch, lobster tail, and fresh fish—to enjoy at picnic tables in the screened-in porch or inside where it's air-conditioned. ✉*MM 50.5, 6350 Overseas Hwy.* ☎*305/743–6373* *No credit cards* *Closed Sun. and Mon.*

$ ✕ **Key Colony Inn.** The inviting aroma of an Italian kitchen pervades this family-owned favorite. As you'd expect, the service is friendly and attentive. For lunch there are fish and steak entrées served with fries, salad, and bread. At dinner you can't miss with traditional dishes like veal Oscar and New York strip, or such specialties as seafood Italiano, a light dish of scallops and shrimp sautéed in garlic butter and served over a bed of linguine. The place is renowned for its Sunday brunch, served from November to April. ✉*MM 54, OS, 700 W. Ocean Dr., Key Colony Beach* ☎*305/743–0100* *AE, MC, V.*

$ ✕ **Keys Fisheries Market & Marina.** From the parking lot, this commercial warehouse flanked by fishing boats barely hints at the restaurant inside. Order at the window outside, pick up your food inside, then dine at one of the waterfront picnic tables under a plastic canopy. Fresh seafood (and a token hamburger) are the only things on the menu. A lobster Reuben ($13.95) served on thick slices of toasted bread is the signature dish. Other delights include the shrimpburger, whiskey-peppercorn scallops, and the Keys Kombo (broiled or grilled lobster, shrimp, scallops, and mahimahi for $25). There's also a 16-flavor ice-cream station and a bar serving beer and wine. ✉*MM 49, BS, end of 35th St.* ☎*305/743–4353 or 866/743–4353* 🌐*www.keysfisheries.com* ▭*MC, V.*

$ ✕ **7 Mile Grill.** With its whirling ceiling fans, this old-fashioned restaurant could serve as a location for a film set in the 1950s. The crowd is a mix of visitors charmed by its appearance and anglers from the nearby marina who just want some good grub. At the Marathon end of the Seven Mile Bridge, this restaurant's menu won't wow you, but you can count on friendly servers delivering comfort food for breakfast, lunch, and dinner. Standards on the mostly seafood menu include creamy shrimp bisque, crab cakes, beer-steamed shrimp, and mahimahi served grilled, blackened, or fried. Don't pass up the authentic key lime pie, which regularly wins the local paper's "Best in the Keys" award. Call ahead, as it's sometimes closed in August and September. ✉*MM 47, BS* ☎*305/743–4481* ▭*MC, V* ⊗*Closed Thurs. mid-Apr.–mid-Nov.*

¢ ✕ **The Stuffed Pig.** With only eight tables and a counter, this breakfast-and-lunch place is always hopping. The kitchen whips up daily lunch specials like meat loaf or pulled pork with hand-cut fries, but a quick glance around the room reveals that the all-day breakfast is the main draw. You can get the usual breakfast plates, but most newcomers opt for oddities like the lobster omelet, alligator tail and eggs, or "grits and grunts" (that's fish, to the rest of us). On a nice day, make your way to the shady backyard patio. If you can get past the unflattering name, you still might have a tough time swallowing the staff's sometimes surly attitude. ✉*MM 49, BS, 3520 Overseas Hwy.* ☎*305/743–4059* ▭*No credit cards* ⊗*No dinner.*

WHERE TO STAY

$ 🏨 **Crystal Bay Resort & Marina.** This resort is a blast from the past. The retro motel has a kitschy miniature golf course, shuffleboard courts, and a self-serve tiki bar. Of the selection of rooms and suites, Room 20 offers the best digs, with a bay view that goes on forever. We're told the Wright Brothers stayed in Unit 29—and who's to argue? The fish stories come fast and furious here. Many folks bring their boats and stay two or three weeks at a time; one guy came and never left. If all this sounds eccentrically charming to you, you'll have a grand old time here. If it sounds weird, stay away. **Pros:** Nice kitchens, friendly staff, casual atmosphere. **Cons:** Some rooms need updating, steep charge for extra guests. ✉MM 49, BS, 4900 Overseas Hwy. ☎305/289–8089 or 888/289–8089 ⊕www.crystalbayresort.com ⇨29 rooms ⌂In-room: kitchen (some), refrigerator. In-hotel: tennis courts, beachfront, water sports, no elevator, laundry facilities ▭D, MC, V.

★ $$$$ **Tranquility Bay.** Ralph Lauren might have designed the rooms at this luxurious beach resort. The 87 two- and three-bedroom town houses have gingerbread trim, white picket fences, and open-floor-plan interiors decorated in trendy cottage style. The picture-perfect theme continues with the palm-fringed pool and the sandy beach edged with a ribbon of blue bay (and echoed in the blue-and-white stripes of the poolside umbrellas). Guests look like models on a photo shoot: attractive young families enjoying themselves at the sunny decks, casual outdoor bar, or elegant restaurant. **Pros:** Secluded setting, gorgeous design, lovely crescent beach. **Cons:** A bit sterile, no real Keys atmosphere. ✉*MM 48.5, BS, 2600 Overseas Hwy.* ☎*305/289–0888 or 866/643–5397* ⊕*www.tranquilitybay.com* ⇨*87 rooms* ⌂*In-room: kitchen, refrigerator, DVD, Wi-Fi. In-hotel: 2 restaurants, bars, pool, gym, spa, beachfront, water sports, concierge, no-smoking rooms* ▭*AE, D, MC, V.*

SPORTS & THE OUTDOORS

BIKING

Tooling around on two wheels is a good way to see Marathon. There's easy cycling on a 1-mi off-road path that connects to the 2 mi of the Old Seven Mile Bridge leading to Pigeon Key.

"Have bikes, will deliver" could be the motto of **Bike Marathon Bike Rentals** (☎*305/743–3204*), which gets beach cruisers to your hotel door for $45 per week, including a helmet. It's open Monday through Saturday 9 to 4 and Sunday 9 to 2. **Overseas Outfitters** (✉*MM 48, BS* ☎*305/289–1670*) rents aluminum cruisers and hybrid bikes for $10 to $12 per day. The company also rents tandem bikes and children's bikes. It's open weekdays 9 to 6, Saturday 9 to 5, and Sunday 10 to 3.

BOATING

Sail, motor, or paddle: Whatever your choice of modes, boating is what the Keys is all about. Brave the Atlantic waves and reefs or explore the backcountry islands on the gulf side. If you don't have a lot of boating and chart-reading experience, it's a good idea to tap into local knowledge on a charter.

Captain Pip's (✉*MM 47.5, OS* ☎*305/743–4403 or 800/707–1692* ⊕*www.captainpips.com*) rents 19- to 24-foot outboards, $145 to $350 per day, as well as tackle and snorkeling gear. You also can charter a small boat with a guide, $620 to $685 for a half day and $875 to $925 for a full day. **Fish 'n' Fun** (✉*MM 53.5, OS* ☎*305/743–2275 or 800/471–3440* ⊕*www.fishnfunrentals.com*), next to the Boat House Marina, lets you get out on the water on 19- to 26-foot powerboats starting at $140 for a half day, $190 for a full day. The company offers free delivery in the Middle Keys. You also can rent Jet Skis and kayaks. For those who want a live-aboard vacation, **Florida Keys Bareboat Charters** (☎*305/743–0090* ⊕*www.floridakeysbareboatchartercompany.com*) rents 27-foot Catalina and Balboa sailboats for $200 a day, $950 a week. The fee includes home-port dockage.

FISHING

For recreational anglers, the deepwater fishing is superb in both bay and ocean. Marathon West Hump, one good spot, has depths ranging from 500 to more than 1,000 feet. Locals fish from a half-dozen bridges, including Long Key Bridge, the Old Seven Mile Bridge (once proclaimed the Eighth Wonder of the World), and both ends of Toms Harbor. Barracuda, bonefish, and tarpon all frequent local waters. Party boats and private charters are available.

Morning, afternoon, and night, fish for mahimahi, grouper, and other tasty catch aboard the 73-foot *Marathon Lady* (✉*MM 53, OS, at 117th St.* ☎*305/743–5580* ⊕*www.marathonlady.com*) that departs on half-day ($40) excursions from the Vaca Cut Bridge, north of Marathon. Join the crew for night fishing ($50) from 6:30 to midnight from Memorial Day to Labor Day; it's especially beautiful on a full-moon night. ★ Captain Jim Purcell, a deep-sea specialist for ESPN's *The American Outdoorsman*, provides one of the best values in fishing in the Keys. His **Sea Dog Charters** (✉*MM 47.5, BS* ☎*305/743–8255* ⊕*www.seadogcharters.net*), next to the 7 Mile Grill, has half- and full-day offshore, reef and wreck, and backcountry fishing trips, as well as fishing and snorkeling trips aboard 30- to 37-foot *boats*. The cost is $60 per person for a half day, regardless of whether your group fills the boat, and includes bait, light tackle, ice, and coolers. If you prefer an all-day private charter on a 37-foot boat, he offers those, too, for $850 for up to six people. A fuel surcharge may apply.

GOLF

Key Colony Golf & Tennis (✉*MM 53.5, OS, 8th St., Key Colony Beach* ☎*305/289–1533* 🌐*www.keycolonybeach.net/recreation.html*), a 9-hole course near Marathon, charges $9 for the course ($7 for each additional 9 holes), $3 per person for club rental, and $2 for a pull cart. There are no reserved tee times and there's no rush. Play from 7:30 to dusk. A little pro shop meets basic golf needs. Two lighted tennis courts are open from 7:30 to 10. Hourly rates are $4 for singles, $6 for doubles.

SCUBA DIVING & SNORKELING

Local dive operations take you Sombrero Reef and Lighthouse, the most popular down-under destination in these parts. For a shallow dive and some lobster-nabbing, Coffins Patch, off Key Colony Beach, is a good choice. A number of wrecks such as Thunderbolt serve as artificial reefs. Many operations out of this area will also take you to Looe Key Reef.

Hall's Diving Center and Career Institute (✉*MM 48.5, BS, 1994 Overseas Hwy.* ☎*305/743–5929 or 800/331–4255* 🌐*www.hallsdiving.com*) has been training divers for more than 40 years. Along with conventional twice-a-day snorkel and two-tank dive trips ($45 to $55) to the reefs at Sombrero Lighthouse and wrecks like the *Thunderbolt,* the company has more usual offerings like digital and video photography. Twice daily, **Spirit Snorkeling** (✉*MM 47.5 BS* ☎*305/289–0614* 🌐*www.spiritsnorkeling.net*) departs on snorkeling excursions to Sombrero Reef and Lighthouse Reef. For $30 a head, refreshments, snacks, and a freshwater shower are provided.

WATER SPORTS

For all your water sports rental needs, **Jerry's Charter Service** (✉*Banana Bay Resort & Marina, 4590 Overseas Hwy.* ☎*305/743–7298 or 800/775–2646*) is your one-stop place. It rents kayaks, Jet Skis, 12- to 25-foot day sailers, snorkel equipment, fishing rods, and power and pontoon boats.

SHOPPING

Bougainvillea House Gallery (✉*MM 53.5 BS, 12420 Overseas Hwy.33050* ☎*305/743–0808* 🌐*www.bougainvilleahouse-gallery.com*). Conveniently located next to the Marathon Chamber of Commerce, this artists co-op carries a surprising variety of art from pottery to fused glass jewelry to colorful fish and bird sculptures. It's closed Monday between June and September.

THE MIDDLE KEYS ESSENTIALS

For information on transportation, as well as contacts and resources to help you plan your trip to the Middle Keys, see ⇨ Florida Keys Essentials.

To research prices, get advice from other travelers, and book travel arrangements, visit www.fodors.com.

TOUR OPTIONS

AIR TOURS

Specializing in romantic sunset flights, Conch Air flies out of Marathon Airport in a 1935 Waco biplane for two passengers; scenic rides start at $74 per person.

Contacts **Conch Air** (*Marathon Airport, Marathon 33050 ☎ 305/395–1117* *www.conch-air.com*).

VISITOR INFORMATION

Contacts **Greater Marathon Chamber of Commerce & Visitor Center** (*✉ MM 53.5, BS, 12222 Overseas Hwy., Marathon ☎ 305/743–5417 or 800/262–7284 📠 305/289–0183* *www.floridakeysmarathon.com*).

The Lower Keys

4

WORD OF MOUTH

"The beach at Bahia Honda is the best in the Keys. In fact, it is one of the nicest beaches I have ever visited. The water is very shallow there and you can walk for a long way in knee-deep water that is so clean and clear that you would think it was a swimming pool."

–CarolSchwartz

"Drive on to Big Pine Key and out thru it to No Name Key. Find the Key deer and visit the No Name Pub for a late lunch."

–GBC

www.fodors.com/forums

Update by Chelle Koster Walton

BEGINNING AT BAHIA HONDA KEY, the islands of the Florida Keys become smaller, more clustered, and more numerous, a result of ancient tidal water flowing between the Florida Straits and the gulf. Here you're likely to see more birds and mangroves than other tourists, and more refuges, beaches, and campgrounds than museums, restaurants, and hotels. The islands are made up of two types of limestone, both denser than the highly permeable Key Largo limestone of the Upper Keys. As a result, fresh water forms in pools rather than percolating through the rock, creating watering holes that support alligators, snakes, deer, rabbits, raccoons, and migratory ducks. (Many of these animals can be seen in the National Key Deer Refuge on Big Pine Key.) Nature was generous with her beauty in the Lower Keys, which have both Looe Key Reef, arguably the Keys' most beautiful tract of coral, and Bahia Honda State Park, considered one of the best beaches in the world for its fine sand dunes, clear warm waters, and panoramic vista of bridges, hammocks, and azure sky and sea. Big Pine Key is fishing headquarters for a laid-back community that swells with retirees in the winter. South of it, the dribble of islands can flash by in a blink of an eye if you don't take the time to stop at a roadside eatery or check out tours and charters at the little marinas. They include Little Torch Key, Middle Torch Key, Ramrod Key, Summerland Key, Cudjoe Key, Sugarloaf Keys, and Saddlebunch Key. Lying offshore of Little Torch Key, Little Palm Island once welcomed U.S. presidents and other notables to its secluded fishing camp. It was also the location for the movie PT 109 about John F. Kennedy's celebrated World War II heroism. Today it still offers respite to the upper class in the form of an exclusive getaway resort accessible only by boat.

EXPLORING THE LOWER KEYS

In truth, the Lower Keys include Key West, but since it's covered in its own section and is as different from the rest of the Lower Keys as peanut butter is from jelly, this section covers just the keys between MM 37 and MM 9. The Seven Mile Bridge drops you into the lap of this homey, quiet part of the Keys.

Heed speed limits in these parts. They may seem incredibly strict given the traffic is lightest of anywhere in the Keys, but the purpose is to protect the resident Key deer population, and officers of the law pay strict attention.

LOWER KEYS TOP 5

- **Wildlife-viewing.** The Lower Keys are populated with all kinds of animals. Watch especially for Key deer but also other wildlife at the Blue Hole in National Key Deer Refuge.
- **Bahia Honda Key State Park.** Explore the beach and trails then camp for the night at Bahia Honda Key State Park.
- **Kayaking.** Get out in a kayak to spot birds in the Keys' backcountry wildlife refuges.
- **Snorkeling.** Grab a mask and fin and head to Looe Key Reef to see amazing coral formations and fish so bright and animated they look like cartoons.
- **Fishing.** All kinds of fishing is great in the Lower Keys. Cast from a bridge, boat, or shoreline flats for bonefish, tarpon, and other feisty catches.

ABOUT THE RESTAURANTS

Restaurants are fewer and farther between in these parts, and you won't find the variety of offerings in eateries closer to Miami. Mostly you'll find seafood joints where dinner is fresh off the hook and license plates or dollar bills stuck to the wall count for decor. For a special occasion, hop aboard the ferry at Little Torch Key to experience the global-trotting cuisine of the private resort of Little Palm Island. Restaurants may close for a two- to four-week vacation during the slow season—between mid-September and mid-November.

WHAT IT COSTS

¢	$	$$	$$$	$$$$
RESTAURANTS				
under $10	$10–$20	$20–$30	$30–$40	over $40
HOTELS				
under $100	$100–$150	$150–$200	$200–$250	over $250

Restaurant prices are per person for a main course at dinner. Hotel prices are for a standard double room, excluding 6% sales tax (more in some counties) and 1%–4% tourist tax.

ABOUT THE HOTELS

Fishing lodges, dive resorts, and campgrounds are the most prevalent type of lodging in this part of the Keys. Rates are generally much lower than other Keys, especially Key West, which makes this a good place to stay if you're on a budget.

BAHIA HONDA KEY

MM 38–36.

All of Bahia Honda Key is devoted to its eponymous state park, which keeps it in a pristine state. Besides the park's outdoor activities, it offers an up-close look of the original railroad bridge.

★ Fodor'sChoice Most first-time visitors to the region are dismayed by the lack of beaches. But then they discover sun-soaked Bahia Honda Key. The 524-acre **Bahia Honda State Park** sprawls across both sides of the highway, giving it 2½ mi of fabulous sandy coastline—three beaches in all—on both the Atlantic Ocean and the Gulf of Mexico. It's regularly declared the best beach in Florida, and you'll be hard pressed to argue. The sand is baby-powder soft, and the aqua water is warm, clear, and shallow. With their mild currents, the beaches are great for swimming, even with small fry. The snorkeling isn't bad, either; there's underwater life (soft coral, queen conchs, random little fish) just a few hundred feet offshore. Although swimming, kayaking, fishing, and boating are the main reasons to visit, you shouldn't miss biking along the 3½ mi of flat roads or hiking the Silver Palm Trail, with rare West Indian plants and several species found nowhere else in the Keys. Along the way you'll be treated to a variety of butterflies. Seasonal ranger-led nature programs might include illustrated talks on the history of the Overseas Railroad. There are rental cabins, a campground, snack bar, gift shop, 19-slip marina, and facilties for renting kayaks and arranging snorkeling tours. Get a panoramic view of the island from what's left of the railroad—the Bahia Honda Bridge. ⊠*MM 37, OS, 36850 Overseas Hwy.* ☎*305/872–2353* ⊕*www.floridastateparks.org/bahiahonda* *$3.50 for 1 person, $6 for 2 people, plus 50¢ per additional person* ⊙*Daily 8–sunset.*

4

WHERE TO STAY

★ $ **Bahia Honda State Park.** Elsewhere you'd pay big bucks for the wonderful water views available at these cabins on Florida Bay. Each two-bedroom unit has a full kitchen and bath and air-conditioning (but no television, radio, or phone). The park also has popular campsites suitable for either tents or motor homes. Some are directly on the beach—talk about a room with a view! Cabins and campsites book up early, so reserve up to 11 months before your planned visit. **Pros:** Great bayfront views, beachfront camping, affordable rates. **Cons:** Books up fast, area can be buggy. ⊠*MM 37, OS, 36850 Overseas Hwy.* ☎*305/872–2353 or 800/326–3521* ⊕*www.reserveamerica.com* *80 campsites, 48 RV sites, 32 tent sites; 3 duplex cabins* *In-room: no phone, kitchen, no TV. In-hotel: beachfront, water sports, bicycles, no elevator* *AE, D, MC, V.*

SPORTS & THE OUTDOORS

Bahia Honda Dive Shop (⊠*MM 37, OS* ☎*305/872–3210* ⊕*www.bahiahondapark.com*), the concessionaire at Bahia Honda State Park, manages a 19-slip marina; rents wet suits, snorkel equipment, and corrective masks; and operates twice-a-day offshore-reef snorkel trips ($29 plus $6 for equipment). Park visitors looking for other fun can rent kayaks ($10 per hour for a single, $18 for a double) and beach chairs.

BIG PINE KEY

MM 32–30.

Welcome to the Keys' most natural holdout, where wildlife refuges protect rare and endangered animals. Here you have left behind the commercialism of the Upper Keys for an authentic backcountry atmosphere. How could things get more casual than Key Largo, you might wonder? Find out by exiting U.S. 1 to explore the habitat of the charmingly diminutive Key deer or cast a line from No Name Bridge. Tours explore the expansive waters of National Key Deer Refuge and Great White Heron National Wildlife Refuge, one of the first such refuges in the country. Along with Key West National Wildlife Refuge, it encompasses more than 200,000 acres of water and more than 8,000 acres of land on 49 small islands. Besides its namesake bird, the Great White Heron National Wildlife Refuge provides habitat for uncounted species of birds and three species of sea turtles. It is the only U.S. breeding site for the endangered hawksbill turtle.

★ In the Florida Keys, more than 20 animals and plants are endangered or threatened. Among them is the diminutive Key deer, which stands about 30 inches at the shoulders and is a subspecies of the Virginia white-tailed deer. The 84,351-acre **National Key Deer Refuge** was established in 1957 to protect the dwindling population. These deer once roamed throughout the Lower and Middle Keys, but hunting, destruction of their habitat, and a growing human population caused their numbers to decline to 27 by 1957. The deer have made a comeback, increasing their numbers to between 600 and 750. The best place to see Key deer in the refuge is at the end of Key Deer Boulevard and on No Name Key, a sparsely populated island just east of Big Pine Key. Mornings and evenings are the best time to spot them. Deer may turn up along the road at any time of day, so drive slowly. Feeding them is against the law and puts them in danger. The refuge also has 22 listed endangered and threatened species of plants and animals, including five that are found nowhere else.

The **Blue Hole,** a quarry left over from railroad days, is the largest body of freshwater in the Keys. From the observation platform and nearby walking trail, you might see alligators, turtles, and other wildlife. There are two well-marked trails: the Jack Watson Nature Trail (2/3 mi), named after an environmentalist and the refuge's first warden; and the Fred Mannillo Nature Trail, one of the most wheelchair-accessible places to see an unspoiled pine rockland forest. The visitor center has exhibits on Keys biology and ecology. The refuge also provides information on the Key West National Wildlife Refuge and the Great White Heron National Wildlife Refuge. Accessible only by water, both are popular with kayak outfitters. ✉ *Visitor Center–Headquarters, Big Pine Shopping Center, 28950 Watson Blvd., MM 30.5, BS* ☎ *305/872–2239 or 305/872–0774* 🌐 *www.fws.gov/nationalkeydeer* 🎫 *Free* ⏲ *Daily sunrise–sunset; headquarters weekdays 8–5.*

WHERE TO EAT

¢ ✕ **Good Food Conspiracy.** Like good wine, this small natural-foods eatery and market surrenders its pleasures a little at a time. Step inside to the aroma of brewing coffee, and then pick up the scent of fresh strawberries or carrots blending into a smoothie, followed by the earthy odor of hummus. Order raw or cooked vegetarian and vegan dishes, organic soups and salads, and all-natural coffees and teas. Bountiful sandwiches include the popular organic turkey on a whole-wheat pita. If you can't sit down for a bite, stock up on healthful snacks like dried fruits, raw nuts, and carob-covered almonds. Dine early: the shop closes at 7 Monday to Saturday, and at 5 on Sunday. ✉ *MM 30.2, OS* ☎ *305/872–3945.*

$ ✕ **No Name Pub.** This no-frills honky-tonk has been around since 1936, delighting inveterate locals and intrepid vacationers who come for the excellent pizza, cold beer, and *interesting* companionship. The decor, such as it is, amounts to the autographed dollar bills that cover every inch of the place. The owners have conceded to the times by introducing a full menu, including a half-pound fried grouper sandwich, spaghetti and meatballs, and seafood baskets. The lighting is poor, the furnishings are rough, and the jukebox doesn't play the latest tunes. This former brothel–bait shop is just before the No Name Bridge. It's a bit hard to find, but worth the trouble if you want a singular Keys experience. ✉ *MM 30, BS, N. Watson Blvd.* ☎ *305/872–9115* 🌐 *www.nonamepub.com* 💳 *D, MC, V.*

WHERE TO STAY

★ ¢–$ **Big Pine Key Fishing Lodge.** There's a congenial atmosphere at this lively family-owned lodge-campground-marina. It's a happy mix of tent campers (who have the choicest waterfront real estate), RVers (who look pretty permanent), and motel-dwellers who like to mingle at the roof-top pool and challenge each other to a game of poker. Rooms have tile floors, wicker furniture, doors that allow sea breezes to waft through. A skywalk joins them with the pool and deck. Campsites range from rustic to full hookups. Everything is spotless—even the campground's bathhouse—and the service is good-natured and efficient. The staff will book you a room, sell you bait, or hook you up with a fishing charter. There are plenty of family-oriented activities, so the youngsters will never complain about being bored. Discounts are available for weeklong or longer stays. **Pros:** Local fishing crowd, nice pool, great price. **Cons:** RV park is too close to motel, deer will eat your food if you're camping. ✉*MM 33, OS, Box 430513* ☎*305/872–2351* *16 rooms; 158 campsites, 97 with full hookups, 61 without hookups* *In-room: kitchen (some), refrigerator (some). In-hotel: pool, no elevator, public Internet* *MC, V.*

$$$–$$$$ **Deer Run Bed & Breakfast.** Key deer wander the grounds of this beachfront B&B, set on a quiet street lined with buttonwoods and mangroves. The "natural beauty" angle is already covered here; innkeepers Jen DeMaria and Harry Appel are now working to elevate the level of lodgings. Two large oceanfront rooms are decorated in soothing earth tones and furnished with mahogany and pecan-wood furnishings. The beach-level unit is decorated in key lime and flamingo pink, with wicker furnishings, and the garden-view room is an eclectic mix that includes Victorian farmhouse doors serving as the headboard of the queen-size bed. Guests share a living room and a veranda. The animal-friendly atmosphere extends to the kitchen, with a mostly organic breakfast menu suitable for vegetarians. The breakfasts—perhaps flax pancakes with organic fruit or veggie scramble with soy sausage—come with Fair Trade coffee and tea. Guest rooms are stocked with organic cotton towels and cruelty-free toiletries. **Pros:** Quiet location, healthy breakfasts, enthusiastic owners. **Cons:** Exterior is cluttered, price is a bit high. ✉*MM 33, OS, 1997 Long Beach Dr.* ☎*305/872–2015* *www.deerrunfloridabb.com* *4 rooms* *In-room: refrigerator, Wi-Fi. In-hotel: beach-*

front, water sports, bicycles, no elevator, no kids under 18, no-smoking rooms ⊟*D, MC, V* ⊚*BP.*

SPORTS & THE OUTDOORS

BIKING

A good 10 mi of paved and unpaved roads run from MM 30.3, BS, along Wilder Road, across the bridge to No Name Key, and along Key Deer Boulevard into the National Key Deer Refuge. Along the way you might see some Key deer. Stay off the trails that lead into wetlands, where fat tires can do damage to the environment.

Marty Baird, owner of **Big Pine Bicycle Center** (☒*MM 30.9, BS* ☎*305/872–0130*), is an avid cyclist and enjoys sharing his knowledge of great places to ride. He's also skilled at selecting the right bike for the journey, and he knows his repairs, too. His old-fashioned single-speed, fat-tire cruisers rent for $8 per half day and $10 for a full day. Helmets, baskets, and locks are included. Although the shop is officially closed on Sunday, join Marty there most Sunday mornings at 8 in winter for a free off-road fun ride.

4

FISHING

Cast from No Name Key Bridge or hire a charter to take you into backcountry or deep waters for fishing year-round.

Fish with pros year-round in air-conditioned comfort with **Strike Zone Charters** (☒*MM 29.6, BS, 29675 Overseas Hwy.* ☎*305/872–9863 or 800/654–9560*). Deep-sea charter rates are $600 for a half day, $750 for a full day. It also offers flats fishing in the Gulf of Mexico.

KAYAKING

Captain Bill Keogh (naturalist, educator, photographer, and author of *The Florida Keys Paddling Guide*) operates Big Pine Kayak Adventures, which takes visitors into remote areas of two national wildlife refuges in the Lower Keys to explore mangrove hammocks, islands, creeks, and sponge and grass flats on kayak nature tours, shallow-water skiff ecotours, backcountry catamaran sailing cruises, and shallow-water fishing expeditions. Prices start at $50 per person for a three-hour tour.

Contacts **Big Pine Kayak Adventures** (*Box 431311, Big Pine Key 33043* ☎*305/872–7474* ⊕*www.keyskayaktours.com*).

SCUBA DIVING & SNORKELING

Close to Looe Key Reef, this is prime scuba and snorkeling territory. Some resorts cater to divers with dive boats that depart their own dock. Others can make arrangements for you.

Strike Zone Charters (✉*MM 29.6, BS, 29675 Overseas Hwy.* ☎*305/872–9863 or 800/654–9560*) leads dive excursions to the wreck of the 210-foot *Adolphus Busch* ($50), and scuba ($40) and snorkel ($30) trips to Looe Key Reef aboard glass-bottom boats. Strike Zone also offers a five-hour island excursion that combines snorkeling, fishing, and an island cookout for $49 per person. A large, dive shop is on-site.

WATER SPORTS

There's nothing like the vast expanse of pristine waters and mangrove islands preserved my national refuges from here to Key West. The mazelike terrain can be confusing, so it's wise to hire a guide at least the first time out.

★ **Big Pine Kayak Adventures** (✉*Old Wooden Bridge Fishing Camp, MM 30, BS,* ⊕ *Turn right at traffic light, continue on Wilder Rd. toward No Name Key* ☎*305/872–7474* 🌐*www.keyskayaktours.com*) makes it very convenient to rent kayaks by delivering them to your lodging or anywhere between Seven Mile Bridge and Stock Island. The company, headed by *The Florida Keys Paddling Guide* author Bill Keogh, will rent you a kayak and then ferry you—called taxi-yaking—to remote islands with clear instructions on how to paddle back on your own. Rentals are by the half day or full day. Group kayak tours ($50 for three hours) explore the mangrove forests of Great White Heron and Key Deer National Wildlife Refuges. Custom tours ($125 and up, four hours) transport you to exquisite backcountry areas teeming with wildlife. Kayak fishing charters are also popular.

LITTLE TORCH KEY

MM 29–10.

Little Torch Key and its neighbor islands, Ramrod Key and Summerland Key, are good jumping-off points for divers headed for Looe Key Reef. The islands also serve as a refuge for those who want to make forays into Key West but not stay in the thick of things.

NEED A BREAK? The aroma of rich, roasting coffee beans at Baby's Coffee (*✉MM 15, OS, Saddlebunch Keys ☎305/744-9866 or 800/523-2326*) arrests you at the door of "the Southernmost Coffee Roaster." Buy it by the pound or by the cup along with fresh-baked goods.

The undeveloped backcountry at your door makes Little Torch Key an ideal location for fishing and kayaking. Nearby **Ramrod Key,** which also caters to divers bound for Looe Key, derives its name from a ship that wrecked on nearby reefs in the early 1800s.

4

WHERE TO EAT

¢ ✕ **Geiger Key Marina Smokehouse.** There's a hint of the old Keys at this oceanfront marina restaurant where locals usually outnumber tourists. They come for the daily dinner specials: meat loaf on Monday, pasta on Tuesday, and so on. Weekends are the most popular; the place is packed on Saturday for steak-on-the-grill night and on Sunday for the chicken and ribs barbecue. Local fishermen head here for breakfast before heading out in search of the big ones. *✉MM 10, Geiger Key ☎305/296-3553 or 305/294-1230 🌐www.geigerkeymarina.com ▭MC, V.*

★ $$$$ ✕ **Little Palm Island Resort & Spa Restaurant.** The oceanfront setting calls to mind St. Barth's and the other high-end destinations of the Caribbean. Keep that in mind as you reach for the bill, which can also make you swoon. The restaurant at the exclusive Little Palm Island Resort—its dining room and adjacent outdoor terrace lit by candles and warmed by live music—is one of the most romantic spots in the Keys. The seasonal menu is a melding of French and Caribbean flavors, with exotic little touches. Think hearts of palm and mango salad with pink-pepper vinaigrette as a starter, followed by pan-seared divers scallops in a citrus beurre blanc with potato and lobster pancake. The weekend brunch buffet and the full-moon jazz dinners are very popular. The dining room is open to nonguests on a reservations-only basis. *✉MM 28.5, OS, 28500 Overseas Hwy. ☎305/872-2551 ⚠Reservations essential ▭AE, D, DC, MC, V.*

$$ ✕ **Mangrove Mama's Restaurant.** This could be the prototype for a Keys restaurant, given its shanty appearance, lattice trim, and roving sort of indoor-outdoor floor plan. Then there's the seafood, from the ubiquitous fish sandwich (fried, grilled, broiled, or blackened) to lobster tail, crab cakes,

and coconut shrimp. Burgers, steaks, and pasta round out the menu. Hidden in a grove of banana and palm trees, the place is opens for lunch and dinner. ✉*MM 20 BS, Sugarloaf Key* ☎*305/745–3030* ▭*AE, MC, V* ⊗*Closed Sept.*

$$ ✕ **Square Grouper.** Although this restaurant's food draws raves, its name earns snickers. (A "square grouper" is slang for bales of marijuana dropped into the ocean during the drug-running 1970s.) Owners Lynn and Doug Bell give the dishes whimsical touches, making them look as good as they taste. The seared sesame-encrusted tuna is lightly crunchy outside, like butter inside. The square grouper sandwich is a steaming pan-sautéed fillet served with key-lime tartar sauce on ciabatta. In an unassuming strip mall, the dining room is surprisingly suave, with linen-swathed tables and a wood-topped stainless-steel bar. ✉*MM 22.5, OS, Cudjoe Key* ☎*305/745–8880* ▭*AE, MC, V* ⊗*Closed Sun. and Mon. and several wks in summer.*

$$ ✕ **Sugar Loaf Lodge Restaurant.** If you're feeling peckish as you drive between Big Pine Key and Key West, there aren't a whole lot of choices. But here's a good place to stop for any meal, especially breakfast. A glass wall lets you admire the gulf from your table. Dinner, served outside, features Italian dishes like chicken piccata and osso buco. The chef gives a nod to what's local: snapper with key lime pepper glaze, for instance. ✉*MM 17 BS, Sugarloaf Key* ☎*305/745–3741* ▭*AE, D, MC, V.*

WHERE TO STAY

★ Fodor's Choice **Little Palm Island Resort & Spa.** *Haute tropicale*

$$$$ best describes this luxury retreat, and "second mortgage" might explain how some can afford the extravagant prices. But for those who can, it's worth the price. This property sits on a 5-acre palm-fringed island 3 mi offshore from Little Torch Key. The 28 oceanfront thatch-roof bungalow suites have slate-tile baths, mosquito netting–draped king-size beds, and British colonial–style furnishings. Other comforts include an indoor and outdoor shower, private veranda, separate living room, and comfy robes and slippers. Two Island Grand Suites are twice the size of the others and offer his-and-her bathrooms, an outdoor hot tub, and uncompromising ocean views. To preserve the quiet atmosphere, cell phones are verboten in public areas. **Pros:** Secluded setting, heavenly spa, easy wildlife viewing. **Cons:** Astronomic prices, can be too quiet for some. ✉*MM 28.5, OS,*

28500 Overseas Hwy. ☎305/872–2524 or 800/343–8567 ⊕www.littlepalmisland.com ⇨30 suites ♨In-room: no phone, safe, refrigerator, no TV, dial-up. In-hotel: restaurant, room service, bars, pool, gym, spa, beachfront, diving, water sports, no elevator, concierge, public Wi-Fi, airport shuttle, parking (no fee), no kids under 16, no-smoking rooms ▭AE, D, DC, MC, V ⊚MAP.

¢–$ **Looe Key Reef Resort.** If your Keys vacation is all about diving, you'll be well served at this scuba-obsessed operation. The closest place to stay to the stellar reef and affordable to boot, it's popular with the bottom-time crowd. Rooms are basic, but are perfect for sleeping between dives and hanging out at the tiki bar. The one suite is equipped with a fridge and microwave. Single rooms are available. **Pros:** Guests get discount on dive and snorkel trips, fun bar. **Cons:** Small rooms, unheated pool, close to road. *⊠MM 27.5 OS, Ramrod Key ☎305/872–2215 Ext. 2 or 800/942–5397 ⊕www.diveflakeys.com ⇨25 rooms, 1 suite ♨In room: Wi-Fi. In hotel: bar, pool, no elevator, public Wi-Fi ▭MC, V.*

$–$$ **Parmer's Resort.** Don't let the behind-the-Jehovah's-Witness-Hall-location put you off. Almost every room has a view of Pine Channel, with the lovely curl of Big Pine Key in the foreground. Waterfront cottages, with decks or balconies, are spread out on 5 landscaped acres, with a heated swimming pool and a five-hole putting green. There are water sports galore, and the staff will book you a kayak tour, a fishing trip, or a bike excursion, or tell you which local restaurants will deliver diner to your room. Value-minded couples (mostly European) flock here, sharing the landscape with 70-some tropical birds. So what if the decor feels a little grandma's-house and you have to pay extra if you want maid services? **Pros:** Bright rooms, pretty setting, good value. **Cons:** A bit out of the way, maid service costs extra, little shade around the pool. *⊠MM 28.7, BS, 565 Barry Ave. ☎305/872–2157 ⊕www.parmersresort.com ⇨18 rooms, 12 efficiencies, 15 apartments, 1 penthouse ♨In-room: no phone, kitchen (some). In-hotel: pool, no elevator, laundry facilities, public Internet, public Wi-Fi, no-smoking rooms ▭AE, D, MC, V ⊚CP.*

4

SPORTS & THE OUTDOORS

BOATING

Dolphin Marina (✉*28530 Overseas Hwy., Little Torch Key* ☎*305/872–2685* 🌐*www.dolphinmarina.net*) rents boats by the half day ($159 to $224) and full day ($214 to $279). The 20-foot boats have 115-horsepower engines and can carry up to six people. The 22-foot models have 150 horsepower for up to eight people.

SCUBA DIVING & SNORKELING

This is the closest you can get on land to Looe Key Reef, and that's where local dive operators love to head.

In 1744 the HMS *Looe,* a British warship, ran aground and sank on one of the most beautiful coral reefs in the Keys. Today, **Looe Key Reef** (✉*MM 27.5, OS, 216 Ann St., Key West* ☎*305/292–0311*) owes its name to the ill-fated ship. The 5.3-square-nautical-mi reef, part of the **Florida Keys National Marine Sanctuary,** has stands of elkhorn coral on its eastern margin, purple sea fans, and abundant sponges and sea urchins. On its seaward side, it drops almost vertically 50 to 90 feet. In its midst, **Shipwreck Trail** plots the location of nine historic wreck sites in 14 to 120 feet of water. Buoys mark the sites, and underwater signs tell the history of each site and what marine life to expect. Snorkelers and divers will find the sanctuary a quiet place to observe reef life—except in July, when the annual Underwater Music Festival pays homage to Looe Key's beauty and promotes reef awareness with six hours of music broadcast via underwater speakers. Dive shops and private charters transport hundreds of divers and snorkelers (more than 600 last year) to hear the spectacle, which includes classical, jazz, and New Age, Caribbean music, as well as a little Jimmy Buffett. There are even underwater Elvis imersonators. Rather than the customary morning and afternoon two-tank, two-location trips offered by most dive shops, **Looe Key Reef Resort & Dive Center** (✉*Looe Key Reef Resort, MM 27.5, OS, Box 509, Ramrod Key* ☎*305/872–2215 Ext. 2 or 800/942–5397* 🌐*www.diveflakeys.com*), the closest dive shop to Looe Key Reef, runs a single three-tank, three-location dive ($80 for divers, $40 for snorkelers). The maximum depth is 30 feet, so snorkelers and divers go on the same boat. On Wednesday, they run a similar dive that visits wrecks and reefs in the area ($80). The dive boat, a 45-foot Corinthian catamaran, is docked outside the full-service Looe Key Reef Resort.

WATER SPORTS

Rent a paddle-propelled vehicle for exploring local gulf waters at **Sugarloaf Marina** (✉*MM 17 GS, Sugarloaf Key* ☎*305/745–3135*). Rates for one- or two-person kayak and canoes start at $15 for one hour to $35 for a full day. Extra days are $25. The company also rents fishing rods ($5 per day) and snorkel sets ($8 per day). Delivery is free on multiple-day rentals.For a guided kayak tour, join Captain Andrea Paulson of **Reelax Charters** (✉*MM 17 GS, Sugarloaf Key* ☎*305/304–1392* 🌐*www.keyskayaking.com*). Customized charters start at four hours for $60 per person, and can include snorkeling and beaching on a secluded island in the Keys backcountry.

THE LOWER KEYS ESSENTIALS

For information on transportation, as well as contacts and resources to help you plan your trip to the Lower Keys, see ☞ *Florida Keys Essentials.*

To research prices, get advice from other travelers, and book travel arrangements, visit www.fodors.com.

TOUR OPTIONS

AIR TOURS

Fantasy Dan's Airplane Rides depart from Sugarloaf Key Airport; passengers can spot sharks, sting rays, and other reef life on sightseeing rides that price at $20 to $50 per person (sunset and champagne flights are available by special arrangement).

Contacts **Fantasy Day's Airplane Rides** (✉*Sugarloaf Key Airport, MM 17, Sugarloaf Key* ☎*305/745–2217.*

BOAT TOURS

Strike Zone Charters has glass-bottom-boat excursions into the backcountry and Atlantic Ocean. The five-hour Island Excursion ($49 plus fuel surcharge) emphasizes nature and Keys history; besides close encounters with birds, sea life, and vegetation, there's a fish cookout on an island. Snorkel and fishing equipment, food, and drinks are included. This is one of the few nature outings in the Keys with wheelchair access.

Contacts **Strike Zone Charters** (✉*MM 29.6, BS, 29675 Overseas Hwy., Big Pine Key* ☎*305/872–9863 or 800/654–9560*).

VISITOR INFORMATION

Contacts **Big Pine and the Lower Keys Chamber of Commerce** (✉ *MM 31, OS, 31020 Overseas Hwy.* 📫 *Box 430511, Big Pine Key 33043* ☎ *305/872–2411 or 800/872–3722* 📠 *305/872–0752* 🌐 *www.lowerkeyschamber.com*).

EN ROUTE. **The huge object that looks like a white whale floating over Cudjoe Key (MM 23–21) is not a figment of your imagination. It's Fat Albert, a radar balloon that monitors local air and water traffic.**

Key West

5

WORD OF MOUTH

"We had lunch at Blue Heaven in Bahama Village. The food was forgettable but the setting, complete with live music on stage and live chickens underfoot, was worth traveling a long way for."

–Ackislander

"There are many water activities to do from the harbors at Key West, like snorkeling, fishing, or visiting Dry Tortugas Island, which is a full-day trip."

–CollegeMom

www.fodors.com/forums

Revised & Updated by Chelle Koster Walton

SITUATED 150 MI FROM MIAMI, 90 mi from Havana, and an immeasurable distance from sanity, this end-of-the-line community has never been like anywhere else. Even after it was connected to the rest of the country—by the railroad in 1912 and by the highway in 1938—it maintained a strong sense of detachment. The U.S. acquired Key West from Spain in 1821, along with the rest of Florida. The Spanish had named the island Cayo Hueso, or Bone Key, after the Native American skeletons they found on its shores. In 1823 President James Monroe sent Commodore David S. Porter to chase pirates away. For three decades, the primary industry in Key West was wrecking—rescuing people and salvaging cargo from ships that foundered on the nearby reefs. According to some reports, when pickings were lean the wreckers hung out lights to lure ships aground. Their business declined after 1849, when the federal government began building lighthouses.

In 1845 the army began construction on Fort Taylor, which kept Key West on the Union side during the Civil War. After the fighting ended, an influx of Cubans unhappy with Spain's rule brought the cigar industry here. Fishing, shrimping, and sponge-gathering became important industries, as did pineapple canning. Through much of the 19th century and into the 20th, Key West was Florida's wealthiest city in per-capita terms. But in 1929 the local economy began to unravel. Cigar making moved to Tampa, Hawaii dominated the pineapple industry, and the sponges succumbed to blight. Then the Depression hit, and within a few years half the population was on relief.

Tourism began to revive Key West, but that came to a halt when a hurricane knocked out the railroad bridge in 1935. To help the tourism industry recover from that crushing blow, the government offered incentives for islanders to turn their charming homes—many of them built by shipwrights—into guesthouses and inns. The wise foresight has left the town with more than 100 such lodgings, a hallmark of Key West vacationing today. In the 1950s, the discovery of "pink gold" in the Dry Tortugas boosted the economy of the entire region. Catching Key West shrimp required a fleet of up to 500 boats and flooded local restaurants with some of the sweetest shrimp alive. The town's artistic community found inspiration in the colorful fishing boats.

Key West reflects a diverse population: Conchs (natives, many of whom trace their ancestry to the Bahamas), freshwater Conchs (longtime residents who migrated from somewhere else years ago), Hispanics (primarily Cuban immigrants), recent refugees from the urban sprawl of mainland Florida, military personnel, and an assortment of vagabonds, drifters, and dropouts in search of refuge. The island was once a gay vacation hot spot, and it remains a decidedly gay-friendly destination. Some of the most renowned gay guesthouses, however, no longer cater to an exclusively gay clientele. Key Westers pride themselves on their tolerance of all peoples, all sexual orientations, and even all animals. Most restaurants allow pets, and it's not surprising to see stray cats, dogs, and even chickens roaming freely through the dining rooms. The chicken issue is one that government officials periodically try to bring to an end, but the colorful fowl continue to strut and crow, particularly in the vicinity of Old Town's Bahamian Village.

Although the rest of the Keys are known for outdoor activities, Key West has something of a city feel. Few open spaces remain, as promoters continue to churn out restaurants, galleries, shops, and museums to interpret the city's intriguing past. As a tourist destination, Key West has a lot to sell—an average temperature of 79°F, 19th-century architecture, and a laid-back lifestyle. Yet much has been lost to those eager for a buck. Duval Street looks like a miniature Las Vegas lined with garish signs for T-shirt shops and tour company offices. Cruise ships dwarf the town's skyline and fill the streets with day-trippers gawking at the hippies with dogs in their bike baskets, gay couples walking down the street holding hands, and the oddball lot of locals, some of whom bark louder than the dogs.

EXPLORING KEY WEST

Key West is the one place in the Keys where you could conceivably do without a car, especially if you plan on staying around Old Town. Even if you've driven the 106 mi down the chain, you're probably ready to abandon your car in the hotel parking lot. Trolleys, buses, bikes, scooters, and feet are more suitable alternatives. To explore on your own, pick up a copy of Sharon Wells' "Walking & Biking Guide to Historic Key West." It is organized into 16 different tours according to your areas of interest. To explore the beaches, New Town, and Stock Island, you'll probably need a car.

KEY WEST TOP 5

- **The Dry Tortugas.** Do a day trip to Dry Tortugas National Park for snorkeling and hiking away from the throngs; you can choose either a ferry or a flight.
- **Watching the Sunset.** Revel in both the beautiful sunset and the gutsy performers at Mallory Square's nightly celebration.
- **The Conch Train.** Hop aboard the Conch Train for a narrated tour of the town's tawdry past and rare architectural treasures.
- **Bar-Hopping.** Nightlife rules in Key West. Do the "Duval Crawl," the local version of club hopping. But first fortify yourself at one of the town's exceptional restaurants.
- **The Hemingway Connection.** Visit Ernest Hemingway's historic home for a taste of Key West's literary past.

PELICAN PATH. **Pelican Path is a free walking guide to Key West published by the Old Island Restoration Foundation. The guide discusses the history and architecture of 43 structures along 25 blocks of 12 Old Town streets. Pick up a copy at the Chamber of Commerce.**

ABOUT THE RESTAURANTS

Keys restaurants get their most exotic once you reach Key West, and you can pretty much find anything you want (except a bargain). Pricier restaurants serve tantalizing fusion cuisine that reflects the influence of Cuba and other Caribbean islands. Tropical fruits and citrus figure prominently on the menus, and the mango, papaya, and passion fruit show up on the lists of beverages. Of course, there are plenty of places that serve local seafood. Key West stays true to island character with a selection of "hole-in-the-wall" places where it doesn't get any more colorful.

ABOUT THE HOTELS

Key West's lodgings include historic cottages, restored Conch houses, and large resorts. Quaint guesthouses, the town's trademark, offer a true island experience in residential neighborhoods near Old Town's restaurants, shops, and clubs. A few rooms cost as little as $65 a night in the off-season, but most range from $100 to $300. Some guesthouses and inns do not welcome children under 16, and many do not permit smoking.

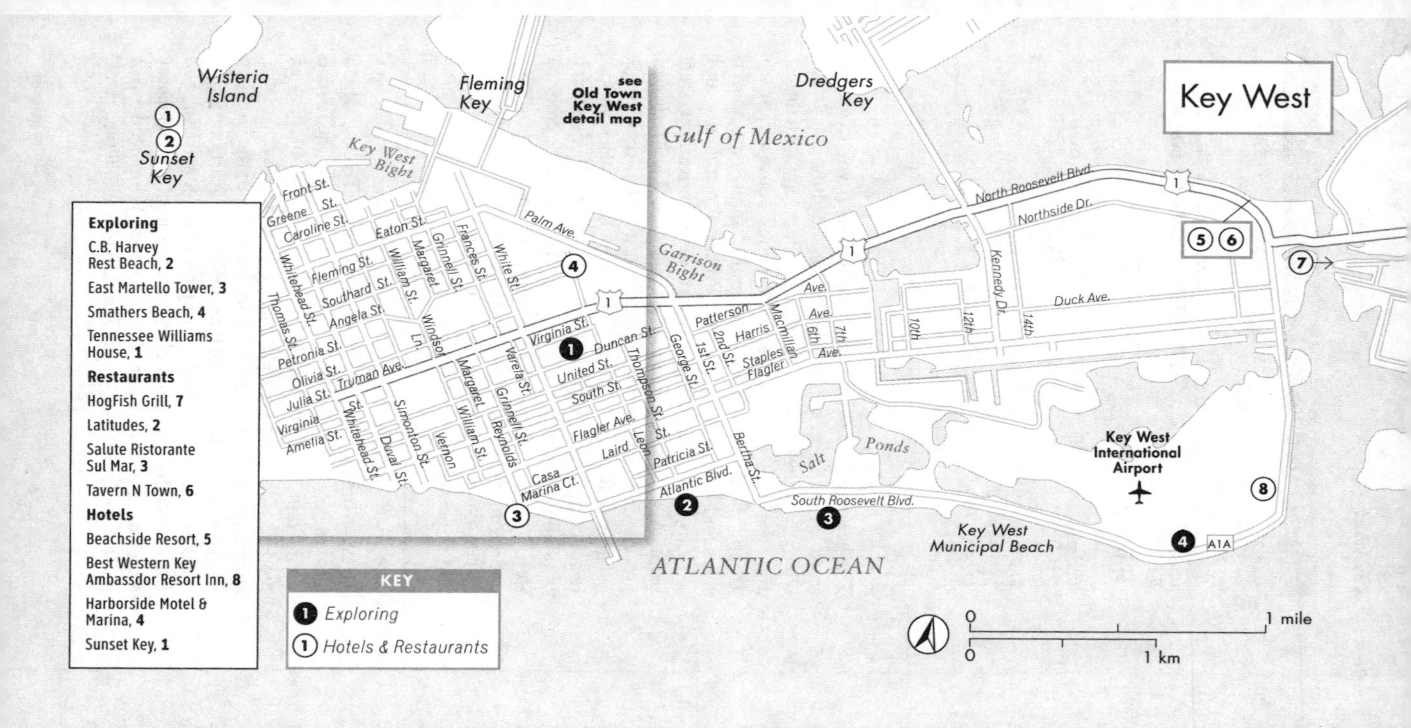
Key West
Exploring
C.B. Harvey Rest Beach, 2
East Martello Tower, 3
Smathers Beach, 4
Tennessee Williams House, 1
Restaurants
HogFish Grill, 7
Latitudes, 2
Salute Ristorante Sul Mar, 3
Tavern N Town, 6
Hotels
Beachside Resort, 5
Best Western Key Ambassdor Resort Inn, 8
Harborside Motel & Marina, 4
Sunset Key, 1
KEY
Exploring
Hotels & Restaurants
see Old Town Key West detail map
Wisteria Island
Sunset Key
Fleming Key
Dredgers Key
Gulf of Mexico
Key West Bight
Garrison Bight
Key West International Airport
Key West Municipal Beach
Salt Ponds
ATLANTIC OCEAN
North Roosevelt Blvd.
Northside Dr.
South Roosevelt Blvd.
Duck Ave.
Kennedy Dr.
Palm Ave.
Truman Ave.
Atlantic Blvd.
Bertha St.
A1A
0
1 mile
0
1 km

WHAT IT COSTS				
¢	$	$$	$$$	$$$$
RESTAURANTS				
under $10	$10–$20	$20–$30	$30–$40	over $40
HOTELS				
under $100	$100–$150	$150–$200	$200–$250	over $250

Restaurant prices are per person for a main course at dinner. Hotel prices are for a standard double room, excluding 6% sales tax (more in some counties) and 1%–4% tourist tax.

OLD TOWN

The heart of Key West, this historic Old Town area runs from White Street to the waterfront. Beginning in 1822, wharves, warehouses, chandleries, ship-repair facilities, and eventually in 1891 the U.S. Custom House sprang up around the deep harbor to accommodate the navy's large ships and other sailing vessels. Wreckers, merchants, and sea captains built lavish houses near the bustling waterfront. A remarkable number of these fine Victorian and pre-Victorian structures have been restored to their original grandeur and now serve as homes, guesthouses, shops, restaurants, and museums. These, along with the dwellings of famous writers, artists, and politicians who've come to Key West over the past 175 years, are among the area's approximately 3,000 historic structures. Old Town also has the city's finest restaurants and hotels, lively street life, and popular nightspots.

A GOOD TOUR

To cover many sights, take the Old Town Trolley, which lets you get off and reboard a later trolley, or the Conch Tour Train. Old Town is also manageable on foot, bicycle, moped, or golf cart–like electric cars. The area is expansive, so you'll want either to pick and choose from the stops on this tour or break it into two or more days. Start on Whitehead Street at the **Ernest Hemingway Home & Museum**, and then cross the street and climb to the top of the **Lighthouse Museum** for a spectacular view. Return to Whitehead Street and follow it north to Angela Street, where you'll turn right.

At Margaret Street, the **City Cemetery** is worth a look for its above-ground vaults and unusual headstone inscriptions. Head north on Margaret Street, turn left onto Southard Street, then right onto Simonton Street. Halfway up the block, **Nancy Forrester's Secret Garden** occupies Free School Lane. After wandering among the blossoms, head west on Southard Street to Duval Street, turn right, and look at the lovely tiles and woodwork in the **San Carlos Institute**. Return again to Southard Street, turn right, and follow it through Truman Annex to **Fort Zachary Taylor State Park**.

Walk west into Truman Annex to see the **Harry S Truman Little White House Museum**, President Truman's vacation residence. Return east on Caroline and turn left on Whitehead to visit the **Audubon House and Gardens**, honoring the famed artist and naturalist. Follow Whitehead north to Greene Street and turn left to see the salvaged sea treasures of the **Mel Fisher Maritime Heritage Society Museum**. At Whitehead's northern end are the **Key West Aquarium** and the **Key West Museum of Art and History**, the former historic U.S. Custom House. By late afternoon you should be ready to cool off with a dip or catch a few rays at the beach. From the aquarium, head east two blocks to the end of Simonton Street, where you'll find the appropriately named **Simonton Street Beach**. On the Atlantic side of Old Town is **South Beach**, named for its location at the southern end of Duval Street. If you've brought your pet, stroll a few blocks east to **Dog Beach**, at the corner of Vernon and Waddell streets. A little farther east is **Higgs Beach–Astro Park**, on Atlantic Boulevard between White and Reynolds streets. As the sun starts to sink, return to the north end of Old Town and follow the crowds to Mallory Square, behind the aquarium, to watch Key West's nightly sunset spectacle. (Those lucky enough may see a green flash—the brilliant splash of green or blue that sometimes appears as the sun sinks into the ocean on a clear night.) For dinner, head east on Caroline Street to **Historic Seaport at Key West Bight**, a renovated area where there are numerous restaurants and bars.

If you're not entirely a do-it-yourselfer, **Key West Promotions** (✉ *422 Fleming St.* ☎ *305/744–9804* 🌐 *www.keywestwalkingtours.com*) offers a variety of guided walking tours, including a pub crawl and restaurant tour.

5

GAY & PROUD

With its official motto being "One Human Family," Key West has long been a favorite of the gay and lesbian community. In fact, Key West wouldn't be the same without the gay people who renovated many of the ramshackle homes and guesthouses. Following are a couple of the gay-specific activities Key West offers.

Home of the Key West Business Guild, the **Gay & Lesbian Community Center** (✉*513 Truman Ave.* ☎*305/292–3223* or *800/535–7797* 🌐*www.gaykeywestfl.com*) hosts events, movie nights, and support groups. Stop at the visitor center for information on gay accommodations and attractions. It's open daily 9 to 5.

Decorated with a rainbow, the **Gay & Lesbian Trolley Tour** (✉*513 Truman Ave.* ☎*305/294–4603* 🌐*www.gaykeywestfl.com*rumbles around the town beginning at 10:50 every Saturday. The 70-minute tour highlighting Key West's gay history costs is $25.

The name says it all. **Skinny Dipper Cruises** (✉*Garrison Bight Marina* ☎*305/240–0527* 🌐*www.skinnydippercruises.com*) offers clothing-optional excursions. Sunset sails are $75 per person, while longer charter cruises are $125 per person.

TIMING

Allow two full days to see all the Old Town museums and homes, especially with a little shopping thrown in. For a narrated trip on the tour train or trolley, budget 1 hour to ride the loop without getting off, an entire day if you plan to get off and on at some of the sights and restaurants.

WHAT TO SEE

❻ **Audubon House and Gardens.** If you've ever seen an engraving by ornithologist John James Audubon, you'll understand why his name is synonymous with birds. See his works in this three-story house, which was built in the 1840s for Captain John Geiger and filled with period furniture. It now commemorates Audubon's 1832 stop in Key West while he was traveling through Florida to study birds. A children's room makes his work accessible to youngsters. Docents lead a guided tour that identify the rare indigenous plants and trees. ✉*205 Whitehead St.* ☎*305/294–2116* or

877/294–2470 ⊕www.audubonhouse.com ✉$11 ⊙Daily 9:30–5, last tour starts at 4.

★ ⑯ **City Cemetery.** You can learn almost as much about a town's history through its cemetery as through its historic houses. Key West's celebrated 20-acre burial place may leave you wanting more, with headstone epitaphs such as "I told you I was sick" and, for a wayward husband, "Now I know where he's sleeping at night." Among the interesting plots are a memorial to the sailors killed in the sinking of the battleship USS *Maine,* carved angels and lambs marking graves of children, and grand aboveground crypts that put to shame many of the town's dwellings for the living. There are separate plots for Catholics, Jews, and refugees from Cuba. You're free to walk around the cemetery on your own, but the best way to see it is on a 60-minute tour given by the staff and volunteers of the Historic Florida Keys Foundation. Tours leave from the main gate, and reservations are required. ✉*Margaret and Angela Sts.* ☎*305/292–6718* ✉*$15* ⊙*Daily sunrise–6* PM*, tours Tues. and Thurs. at 9:30; call for additional times.*

⑳ **Dog Beach.** Next to Louie's Backyard, this small beach—the only one in Key West where dogs are allowed—has a shore that's a mix of sand and rocks. ✉*Vernon and Waddell Sts.* ☎*No phone* ✉*Free* ⊙*Daily sunrise–sunset.*

㉔ ★ **Eco-Discovery Center.** Walk through a model of Key Largo's Aquarius, the world's only underwater ocean laboratory, to discover what lurks beneath the sea. Opened in 2007, this 6,400-square-foot underwater attraction encourages visitors to venture through a variety of Florida Key habitats, from pinelands, beach dunes, and mangroves to the deep sea. Touch-screen computer displays and live underwater cameras show off North America's only contiguous barrier coral reef. ✉*35 East Quay Rd., at end of Southard St. in Truman Annex* ☎*305/809–4750* ⊕*floridakeys.noaa.gov* ✉*Free* ⊙*Tues.–Sat. 9–4.*

❶ ★ **Ernest Hemingway Home & Museum.** Amusing anecdotes pepper the guided tours of Ernest Hemingway's home. While living here between 1931 and 1942, Hemingway wrote about 70% of his life's work, including classics like *For Whom the Bell Tolls.* Few of his belongings remain, and there's little about his actual work, but photographs help you visualize his day-to-day life. The supposed descendants of Hemingway's cats—many named for actors, artists, and authors—have free rein of the property. Tours begin every

5

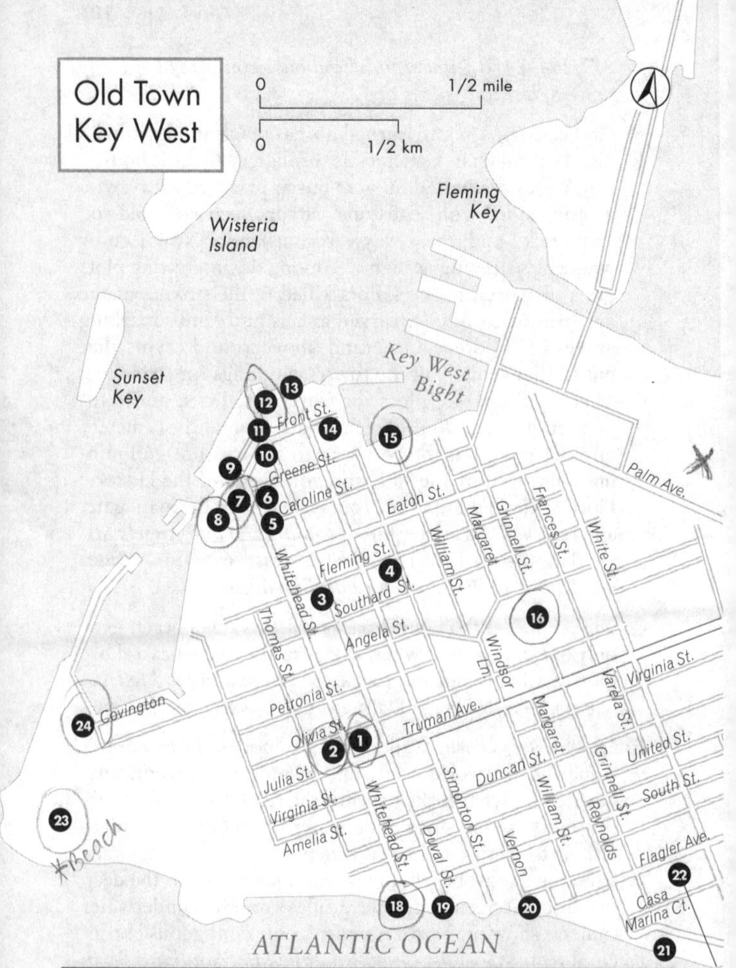

Audubon House and Gardens, **6**

City Cemetery, **16**

Dog Beach, **20**

Eco-Discovery Center, **24**

Ernest Hemingway Home & Museum, **1**

Fort Zachary Taylor Historic State Park, **23**

Harry S Truman Little White House Museum, **8**

Heritage House Museum & Robert Frost Cottage, **5**

Higgs Beach-Astro City Playground, **21**

Historic Seaport at Key West Bight, **15**

Key West Aquarium, **11**

Key West Butterfly & Nature Conservatory, **17**

Key West Museum of Art and History, **9**

Key West Shipwreck Historeum, **10**

Lighthouse Museum, **2**

Mallory Square & Pier, **12**

Mel Fisher Maritime Museum, **7**

Nancy Forrester's Secret Garden, **4**

Pirate Soul Museum, **14**

San Carlos Institue, **3**

Simonton Street Beach, **13**

South Beach, **19**

The Southernmost Point, **18**

West Martello Tower, **22**

10 minutes and take 25 to 30 minutes; then you're free to explore on your own. ✉*907 Whitehead St.* ☎*305/294–1136* 🌐*www.hemingwayhome.com* 🎟*$12* ⏲*Daily 9–5.*

NEED A BREAK? **Check out the pretty palm garden next to the Key West Library at 700 Fleming Street, just off Duval. This leafy, outdoor reading area, with shaded benches, is the perfect place to escape the frenzy and crowds of downtown Key West. There's free Internet access in the library, too.**

㉓ ★ **Fort Zachary Taylor Historic State Park.** Construction of the fort began in 1845, but construction was halted during the Civil War. Even though Florida seceded from the Union, Yankee forces used the fort as a base to block Confederate shipping. More than 1,500 Confederate vessels were detained in Key West's harbor. The fort, finally completed in 1866, was also used in the Spanish-American War. Take a 30-minute guided tour of this National Historic Landmark at noon and 2. In February, a celebration called Civil War Heritage Days includes costumed reenactments and demonstrations. From mid-January to mid-April, the park serves as an open-air gallery for pieces created for Sculpture Key West. The park's beach is the best in Key West. There's an adjoining picnic area with barbecue grills and shade trees, a snack bar, and rental equipment, including snorkeling gear and kayaks. ✉*End of Southard St., through Truman Annex* ☎*305/292–6713* 🌐*www.floridastateparks.org/forttaylor* 🎟*$3.50 for 1 person, $6 for 2 people, 50¢ per additional person* ⏲*Daily 8–sunset, tours noon and 2.*

❽ **Harry S Truman Little White House Museum.** In a letter to his wife during one of his visits, President Harry S. Truman wrote, "Dear Bess, you should see the house. The place is all redecorated, new furniture and everything." If he visited today, he'd be similarly impressed. There's a photographic review of visiting dignitaries and permanent audiovisual and artifact exhibits on the Florida Keys as a presidential retreat; Ulysses S. Grant, John F. Kennedy, and Jimmy Carter are among the chief executives who passed through here. Tours lasting 45 minutes begin every 15 minutes until 4:15. On the grounds of **Truman Annex,** a 103-acre former military parade grounds and barracks, the home served as a winter White House for presidents Truman, Eisenhower, and Kennedy. ✉*111 Front St.* ☎*305/294–9911* 🌐*www.trumanlittlewhitehouse.com* 🎟*$12* ⏲*Daily 9–5, grounds sunrise–6; last tour at 4:30.*

❺ **Heritage House Museum & Robert Frost Cottage.** A seven-generation Key West family has collected and assembled local artifacts in their lovely Caribbean Colonial home built in the late 1830s. In addition to original furnishings, visitors can tour the exhibited artifacts and the garden out back. Poet Robert Frost spent many winters in the garden's cottage, where he often entertained luminaries like Tennessee Williams and Gloria Swanson. Today you can hear readings as you enjoy the orchids and other blossoming foliage. In April it hosts the Key West Robert Frost Poetry Festival. ✉*410 Caroline St.* ☎*305/296–3573* 🌐*www.heritagehouse-museum.org* 🎫*$7 for guided tour, $5 for self-guided tour* ⏲*Mon.–Sat. 10–4.*

㉑ **Higgs Beach–Astro City Playground.** This Monroe County park is a popular sunbathing spot. But bather beware: the Natural Resources Defense Council lists this as one of the Florida beaches that often exceeds acceptable levels of bacteria. A nearby grove of Australian pines provides shade, and the West Martello Tower provides shelter should a storm suddenly sweep in. Kayak and beach chair rentals are available, as is a volleyball net. The beach also has a marker commemorating the gravesite of 295 enslaved Africans who died after being rescued from three South America–bound slave ships in 1860. Across the street, **Astro City Playground** is popular with young children. ✉*Atlantic Blvd. between White and Reynolds Sts.* ☎*No phone* 🎫*Free* ⏲*Daily 6 AM–11 PM.*

⓯ **Historic Seaport at Key West Bight.** What used to be a funky—in some places even seedy—part of town is now an 8½-acre historic restoration project of 100 businesses, including waterfront restaurants, open-air bars, museums, clothing stores, bait shops, dive shops, docks, a marina, the Waterfront Market, and the Key West Rowing Club. It's all linked by the 2-mi waterfront **Harborwalk,** which runs between Front and Grinnell streets, passing big ships, schooners, sunset cruises, fishing charters, and glass-bottom boats. Additional construction continues on outlying projects. ✉*100 Grinnell St.* ☎*305/293–8309* 🌐*www.keywestseaport.com.*

NEED A BREAK? **Get your morning (or afternoon) buzz at Coffee Plantation (✉*713 Caroline St.* ☎*305/295–9808* 🌐*www.coffeeplantationkeywest.com*), where you can also hook up to the Internet in the comfort of a homelike setting in a circa-1890**

CLOSE UP

Hemingway Was Here

In a town where Pulitzer Prize–winning writers are almost as common as coconuts, Ernest Hemingway stands out. Bars and restaurants around the island claim that he ate or drank there (except Bagatelle, where the sign reads "Hemingway Never Liked This Place"), and though he may not have quenched his formidable thirst at all of them, his larger-than-life image continues to grow.

Hemingway came to Key West in 1928 at the urging of writer John dos Passos and rented a house with his second wife, Pauline Pfeiffer. They spent winters in the Keys, and in 1931 Pauline's wealthy uncle Gus gave the couple the house at 907 Whitehead Street. Now known as the Ernest Hemingway Home & Museum, it's Key West's number one tourist attraction. In 1935, when the visitor bureau first included the house in a tourist brochure, Hemingway promptly built the high brick wall that surrounds it today.

During his time in Key West, Hemingway penned some of his most important works, including *A Farewell to Arms, To Have and Have Not, Green Hills of Africa,* and *Death in the Afternoon.* His rigorous schedule consisted of writing almost every morning in his second-story studio above the pool, then promptly descending the stairs at midday. By afternoon and evening he was ready for drinking, fishing, swimming, boxing, and hanging around with the boys.

One close friend was Joe Russell, a craggy fisherman and owner of the bar Sloppy Joe's, now at 201 Duval Street. Russell and Charles Thompson introduced Hemingway to deep-sea fishing, which became fodder for his writing. Another of Hemingway's loves was boxing. He set up a ring in his yard and paid local fighters to box with him, and he refereed matches at Blue Heaven, then a saloon at 729 Thomas Street.

Hemingway honed his macho image dressed in cutoffs and old shirts and took on the name Papa. In turn, he gave his friends new names and used them as characters in his stories. Joe Russell became Freddy, captain of the *Queen Conch* charter boat in *To Have and Have Not.*

Hemingway stayed in Key West for 11 years before leaving Pauline for his third wife. Pauline and their two sons stayed on in the house until 1951.

–Jim & Cynthia Tunstall

conch house. Poets, writers, and minstrels sometimes show up to perform while you munch pastries or luncheon sandwiches and wraps and sip your hot or cold espresso beverage.

11 **Key West Aquarium.** Feed a nurse shark and explore the fascinating underwater realm of the Keys without getting wet at this kid-friendly aquarium. Hundreds of tropical fish and sea creatures live here. A touch tank enables you to handle starfish, sea cucumbers, horseshoe and hermit crabs, even horse and queen conchs—living totems of the Conch Republic. Built in 1934 by the Works Progress Administration as the world's first open-air aquarium, most of the building has been enclosed for all-weather viewing. Guided tours, included in the admission price, include shark petting and feedings. *1 Whitehead St. 305/296–2051 www.keywestaquarium.com $11 Daily 10–6; tours at 11, 1, 3, and 4:30.*

The Key West Butterfly & Nature Conservatory. This air-conditioned refuge for butterflies, birds, and the human spirit gladdens the soul with hundreds of colorful wings—more than 50 species of butterflies alone—in a lovely glass-encased bubble. Waterfalls, artistic benches, paved pathways, birds, and lush, flowering vegetation elevate this above most butterfly attractions. The gift shop is worth a visit on its own. *1316 Duval St. 305/296–2988 or 800/939–4647 www.keywestbutterfly.com $10 Daily 9–5.*

17

★ Fodor's Choice **Key West Museum of Art and History.** When Key West was designated a U.S. port of entry in the early 1820s, a customhouse was established. Salvaged cargoes from ships wrecked on the reefs were brought here, setting the stage for Key West to become for a time the richest city in Florida. After a $9 million restoration, the imposing red-brick-and-terra-cotta Richardsonian Romanesque–style building has reopened as a museum and art gallery. Smaller galleries have long-term and changing exhibits about the history of Key West, including a Hemingway room and a fine collection of folk artist Mario Sanchez's wood paintings. *281 Front St. 305/295–6616 www.kwahs.com $10 Daily 9–5.*

9

10 **Key West Shipwreck Historeum Museum.** Much of Key West's history, early prosperity, and interesting architecture come from ships that ran aground on its coral reef. Artifacts from the circa-1856 Isaac Allerton, which yielded $150,000

worth of wreckage, comprises the museum portion of this multi-faceted attraction. Actors, films, and lasers add a bit of Disneyesque drama. The final highlight is climbing to the top the lookout tower, a reproduction of the 20 or so towers used by Key West wreckers during the town's salvaging heydays. ✉*1 Whitehead St.* ☎*305/292–8990* 🌐*www.shipwreckhistoreum.com* 💵*$11* ⏱*Daily 9:40–5.*

❷ **Lighthouse Museum.** For the best view in town, climb the 88 steps to the top of this 1847 lighthouse. The 92-foot structure has a Fresnel lens, which was installed in the 1860s at a cost of $1 million. The keeper lived in the adjacent 1887 clapboard house, which now exhibits vintage photographs, ship models, nautical charts, and lighthouse artifacts from all along the Key reefs. ✉*938 Whitehead St.* ☎*305/295–6616* 🌐*www.kwahs.com* 💵*$10* ⏱*Daily 9:30–5; last admission at 4:30.*

5

⓬ **Mallory Square and Pier.** For cruise ship passengers, this is the disembarkation point for an attack on Key West. For practically every visitor, it's the requisite venue for a nightly sunset celebration that includes street performers—human statues, sword swallowers, tightrope walkers, musicians, and more—plus craft vendors, conch fritter fryers, and other regulars who defy classification. (Wanna picture with my pet iguana?) With all the activity, don't forget to watch the main show: a dazzling tropical sunset. ✉*Mallory Sq.* ☎*No phone.*

❼ **Mel Fisher Maritime Museum.** In 1622 two Spanish galleons laden with riches from South America foundered in a hurricane 40 mi west of the Keys. In 1985 diver Mel Fisher recovered the treasures from the lost ships, the *Nuestra Senora de Atocha* and the *Santa Margarita.* Fisher's incredible adventure tracking these fabled hoards and battling the state of Florida for rights is as amazing as the loot you'll see, touch, and learn about in this museum. Artifacts include a gold bar worth $15,000 and a 77.76-carat natural emerald crystal worth almost $250,000. Exhibits on the second floor rotate and might cover slave ships, including the excavated 17th-century *Henrietta Marie,* or the evolution of Florida maritime history. ✉*200 Greene St.* ☎*305/294–2633* 🌐*www.melfisher.org* 💵*$12* ⏱*Weekdays 8:30–5, weekends 9:30–5.*

❹ **Nancy Forrester's Secret Garden.** It's hard to believe that this green escape still exists in the middle of Old Town Key West. Despite damage by hurricanes and pressures from developers, Nancy Forrester has maintained her naturalized garden for more than 35 years. Growing in harmony are rare palms and cycads, ferns, bromeliads, bright gingers and heliconias, gumbo-limbo trees strewn with orchids and vines, and a colorful crew of birds, reptiles, cats, and a few surprises. An art gallery has botanical prints and environmental art. One-hour private tours cost $15 per person, four-person minimum. *1 Free School La.* *305/294–0015* *www.nancyforrester.com* *$10* *Daily 10–5.*

Pirate Soul Museum. Enter if you dare! This $10 million (14) attraction combines an animatronic Blackbeard, hands-on exhibits about buccaneers, and a collection of nearly 500 artifacts, including the only authentic surviving pirate chest in America, dating back to the 1600s. Don't miss the Disney-produced, three-dimensional sound program that takes you below decks into a completely dark mock prison cell. *524 Front St.* *305/292–1113* *www.piratesoul.com* *$15* *Daily 9–7.*

(3) **San Carlos Institute.** South Florida's Cuban connection began long before Fidel Castro was born. The institute was founded in 1871 by Cuban immigrants. Now it contains a research library and museum rich with the history of Key West and 19th- and 20th-century Cuban exiles. Cuban patriot Jose Mart delivered speeches from the balcony of the auditorium, and opera star Enrico Caruso sang in the opera house, which reportedly has exceptional acoustics. It's frequently used for concerts, lectures, films, and exhibits. *516 Duval St.* *305/294–3887* *Free* *Tues.–Fri. 1:30–7, weekends 11–5.*

(13) **Simonton Street Beach.** This small beach facing the gulf is a great place to watch boat traffic in the harbor. Parking, however, is difficult. There are restrooms and a boat ramp. *North end of Simonton St.* *No phone* *Free* *Daily 7 AM–11 PM.*

(17) **South Beach.** On the Atlantic, this stretch of sand, also known as City Beach, is popular with travelers staying at nearby motels. The Natural Resources Defense Council lists it as one of Florida's beaches that often exceeds accepted levels of bacteria. Enjoy the water, but from afar perhaps. It has limited parking. *Foot of Duval St.* *No phone* *Free* *Daily 7 AM–11 PM.*

(18) **The Southernmost Point.** Possibly the most-photographed site in Key West, this is a must-see for many visitors. Who

wouldn't want their picture taken next to the big striped buoy that marks the southernmost spot in the continental United States? A plaque next to it honors Cubans who lost their lives trying to escape to America. ✉ *Whitehead and South Sts.* ☎ *No phone*

㉒ **West Martello Tower.** Within the ruins of this Civil War–era fort is the Key West Garden Club, which maintains lovely gardens of native and tropical plants. It also holds art, orchid, and flower shows in March and November and leads private garden tours in March. ✉ *Atlantic Blvd. and White St.* ☎ *305/294–3210* 🌐 *www.keywestgardenclub.com* *Donation welcome* ⏲ *Tues.–Sat. 9:30–5.*

ALWAYS CELEBRATING. **Key West has a growing calendar of festivals and artistic and cultural events—including the Conch Republic Celebration in April and the Halloween Fantasy Fest in October. December brings festivity in the form of a lighted boat parade at the Historic Seaport and New Year's Eve revelry that rivals any in the nation. Few cities of its size—a mere 2 mi by 4 mi—celebrate with the joie de vivre of this one.**

5

NEW TOWN

The Overseas Highway splits as it enters Key West, the two forks rejoining to encircle New Town, the area east of White Street to Cow Key Channel. The southern fork runs along the shore as South Roosevelt Boulevard (Route A1A) skirts Key West International Airport. Along the north shore, North Roosevelt Boulevard (U.S. 1) passes the Key West Welcome Center. Part of New Town was created with dredged fill. The island would have continued growing this way had the Army Corps of Engineers not determined in the early 1970s that it was detrimental to the nearby reef.

A GOOD TOUR

Attractions are few in New Town. The best way to take in the sights is by car or moped. Take South Roosevelt Boulevard from the island's entrance to the historical museum exhibits at **East Martello Tower**, near the airport. Continue past the Riggs Wildlife Refuge salt ponds and stop at **Smathers Beach** for a dip, or continue west onto Atlantic Boulevard to **C.B. Harvey Rest Beach**.

CLOSE UP

The Conch Republic

Beginning in the 1970s, pot smuggling became a source of income for islanders who knew how to dodge detection in the maze of waterways in the Keys. In 1982, the U.S. Border Patrol threw a roadblock across the Overseas Highway just south of Florida City to catch drug runners and undocumented aliens. Traffic backed up for miles as Border Patrol agents searched vehicles and demanded that the occupants prove U.S. citizenship. Officials in Key West, outraged at being treated like foreigners by the federal government, staged a protest and formed their own "nation," the so-called Conch Republic. They hoisted a flag and distributed mock border passes, visas, and Conch currency. The embarrassed Border Patrol dismantled its roadblock, and now an annual festival recalls the city's victory.

TIMING

Allow one to two hours to include brief stops at each attraction. If your interests lie in art, gardens, or Civil War history, you'll need three or four hours. Throw in time at the beach and make it a half-day affair.

WHAT TO SEE

❷ **C. B. Harvey Rest Beach.** This beach and park were named after Cornelius Bradford Harvey, former Key West mayor and commissioner. It has half a dozen picnic areas, dunes, and a wheelchair and bike path. ✉*Atlantic Blvd., east side of White St. Pier* ☎*No phone* 💵*Free* ⏲*Daily 7 AM–11 PM.*

❸ ★ **East Martello Tower.** This Civil War citadel was *semper paratus,* or "always ready" as the U.S. Coast Guard motto says, but like most of Florida during the war it never saw a lick of action. Today it serves as a museum, with historical exhibits about the 19th and 20th centuries. Among the latter are relics of the USS *Maine,* a Cuban refugee raft, and books by famous writers—including seven Pulitzer Prize winners—who have lived in Key West. The tower, operated by the Key West Art and Historical Society, also has a collection of Stanley Papio's "junk art" sculptures and Cuban folk artist Mario Sanchez's chiseled and painted wooden carvings of historic Key West street scenes.

3501 S. Roosevelt Blvd. *305/296–3913* *www.kwahs.com* *$6* *Weekdays 10-4, weekends 9:30-4:30.*

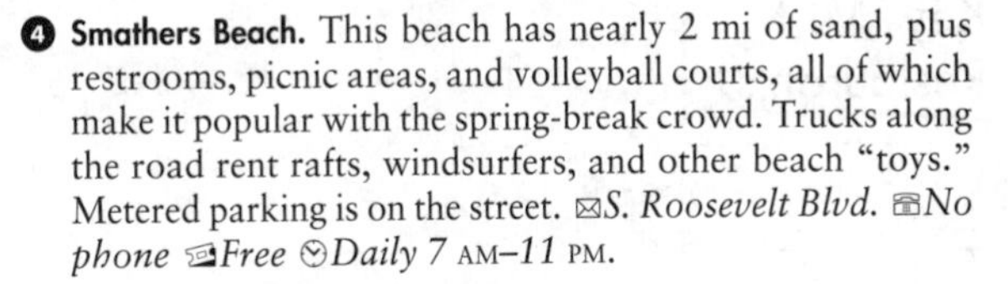

4 **Smathers Beach.** This beach has nearly 2 mi of sand, plus restrooms, picnic areas, and volleyball courts, all of which make it popular with the spring-break crowd. Trucks along the road rent rafts, windsurfers, and other beach "toys." Metered parking is on the street. *S. Roosevelt Blvd.* *No phone* *Free* *Daily 7 AM–11 PM.*

1 **Tennessee Williams House.** You cannot tour the inside of this cottage, but you can pay homage with a visit to the site where one of America's greatest playwrights—and one of the Keys' earliest gay residents of note—lived for nearly 40 years and penned a great many classics. *1431 Duncan St.*

5

WHERE TO EAT

Bring your appetite, a sense of daring, and a lack of preconceived notions about propriety. A meal in Key West can mean overlooking the crazies along Duval Street, watching roosters and pigeons battle for a scrap of food that may have escaped your fork, relishing the finest in what used to be the dining room of some 19th-century Victorian home, or gazing out at boats jockeying for position in the marina. And that's just the diversity of the setting. Seafood dominates local menus, but the treatment afforded that fish or crustacean can range from Cuban and New World to Asian and Continental.

AMERICAN

¢ × **Lobo's Mixed Grill.** If White Castle has attained national cult status with its burgers, then the equivalent among Key West denizens might very well be Lobo's belly buster. The 7-ounce, charcoal-grilled chunk of ground chuck is thick and juicy and served with lettuce, tomato, and pickle on a toasted bun. The choice of 30 wraps (rib eye, oyster, grouper, and others) is equally popular. The menu includes salads and quesadillas, as well as a fried-shrimp-and-oyster combo. Beer and wine are also served. This outdoor eatery closes at 6, so eat early. Lobo's offers free delivery within Old Town. *5 Key Lime Sq., east of intersection of Southard and Duval Sts.* *305/296–5303* *www.loboskeywest.com* *No credit cards* *Closed Sun. Apr.–early Dec.*

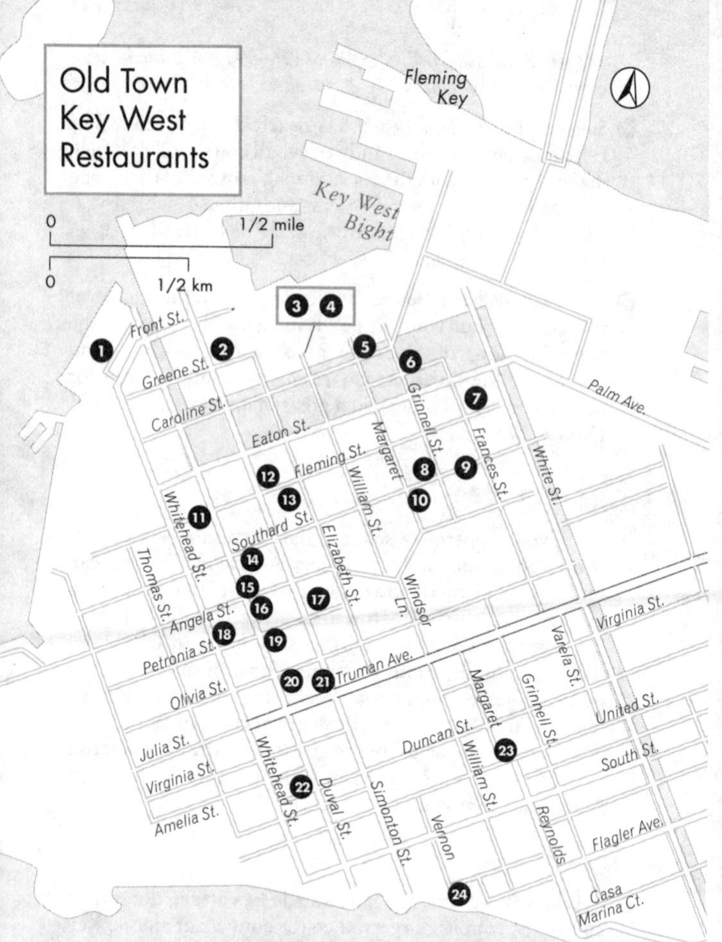

Ambrosia, **12**

Alice's Key West Restaurant, **22**

Blue Heaven, **18**

B. O.'s Fish Wagon, **5**

The Cafe, A Mostly Vegetarian Place, **14**

Café Marquesa, **13**

Café Solé, **9**

Conch Republic Seafood Company, **2**

Croissants de France, **19**

El Meson de Pepe's, **1**

El Siboney, **23**

Finnegan's Wake Irish Pub and Eatery, **6**

Half Shell Raw Bar, **4**

The Island House Café, **7**

Jimmy Buffett's Margaritaville Cafe, **11**

Lobo's Mixed Grill, **15**

Louie's Backyard, **24**

Mangia Mangia, **8**

Mangoes, **16**

Michael's Restaurant, **10**

915 Duval, **20**

Pisces, **21**

Seven Fish, **17**

Turtle Kraals, **3**

$$ ✕ **Mangoes.** The outdoor dining patio with potted plants, twinkling lights, and oversize umbrellas is the place to see and be seen on lively Duval Street. The chef struts his stuff with dishes like mustard-rubbed rack of lamb, grilled filet mignon, pan-seared veal chop, potato-crusted salmon, and Grand Marnier–glazed duck breast. All are well prepared and rarely disappoint. Adventurous diners may find more satisfaction in the salads and starters, which are often more imaginative. Try the lightly crisped tempura-fried ahi tuna or the conch spring rolls with Asian spiced vegetables. Then sit back and watch the weird world go by. ✉*700 Duval St.* ☎*305/292–4606* 🌐*www.mangoeskeywest.com* ▭ *D, MC, V.*

$$ ✕ **Michael's Restaurant.** White tablecloths, subdued lighting, and romantic music give Michael's the feel of an urban getaway. Garden seating reminds that you are in the Keys. Chef-owner Michael Wilson flies in prime rib, cowboy steaks, and rib eyes from Allen Brothers in Chicago, which has supplied top-ranked steakhouses for more than a century. Also on the menu is a melt-in-your-mouth grouper stuffed with jumbo lump crab, veal chop stuffed with mozzarella and prosciutto and topped with a mushroom demi-glace, and a variety of fondue dishes (try the pesto pot, spiked with hot pepper and basil). The Hemingway (mojito-style) and the Third Degree (raspberry vodka and white crčme de cacao) top the martini menu. ✉*532 Margaret St.* ☎*305/295–1300* 🌐*www.michaelskeywest.com* ▭*AE, MC, V* ⊙*No lunch.*

5

CAJUN

$ ✕ **Jimmy Buffett's Margaritaville Cafe.** If you must have your cheeseburger in paradise, it may as well be here, where you can chew along with the song playing endlessly on the sound system. The first of Buffet's line of chain eateries, it belongs here more than anywhere else, but quite frankly it's more about the name, music, and attitude (and margaritas) than the food. The menu has a Cajun-Caribbean flair with such offerings as blackened hot dog, grilled andouille sausage with red beans and rice, broiled yellowtail snapper, and barbecued ribs. Live bands pack the place come dinner and into the wee hours. ✉*500 Duval St.* ☎*305/292–1435* 🌐*www.margaritaville.com* ▭*AE, D, MC, V.*

CARIBBEAN

$ ✕ **El Meson de Pepe's.** If you want to get a taste of the island's Cuban heritage, this is the place. Perfect for after Mallory Square sunset, you can dine al fresco or in the dining room on refined versions of Cuban classics. Begin with a mega-sized mojito while you enjoy the basket of bread and savory sauces. The expansive menu offers *tostones rellenos* (green plantains with different traditional fillings), *ceviche* (raw fish "cooked" in lemon juice), and more. Choose from Cuban specialties such as roasted pork in a cumin sauce and ropa vieja (shredded beef stew). At lunch, Cuban sandwiches and smaller versions of dinner's most popular entrées are served to an enthusiastic crowd. A salsa band performs outside at the bar during sunset celebration. ✉*Mallory Sq., 410 Wall St.* ☎*305/295–2620* 🌐*www.elmesondepepe.com* ▭*AE, D, MC, V.*

$ ✕ **El Siboney.** Dining at this family-style restaurant is like going to Mom's for Sunday dinner—if your mother is Cuban. The dining room is noisy, and the food is traditional cubanano. There's a well-seasoned black-bean soup, a memorable paella, and local fish served grilled, stuffed, and breaded. Dishes come with plantains, bread, and two sides. To make a good thing even better, the prices are very reasonable. ✉*900 Catherine St.* ☎*305/296–4184* ▭*D, MC, V.*

ECLECTIC

★ Fodor'sChoice ✕ **Alice's Key West Restaurant.** A rather plain
$$ storefront gives way to a warm and cozy dining room, where chef-owner Alice Weingarten serves her trademark "fusion confusion" fare. Color, zing, and spice are her main ingredients. The spring rolls, for example, are filled with blackened shrimp, fire-roasted corn, and goat cheese. The Brazilian-style pan-seared skirt steak is served with garlicky chimichurri sauce and green chili and Manchego cheese mashed potatoes, and the Greek-style shrimp is accompanied by kalamata olive-studded mashed potatoes. Save room for her extra special key lime pie made with lime curd and a chocolate lined crust. The place is open for breakfast, too. Eggs, home fries, and toast go for as little as $4. ✉*1114 Duval St.* ☎*305/292–5733* 🌐*www.aliceskeywest.com* ▭*AE, D, MC, V.*

★ ✕ **Blue Heaven.** The outdoor dining area here is often referred
$$ to as "the quintessential Keys experience," and it's hard to argue. There's much to like about this historic restaurant

where Hemingway refereed boxing matches and customers cheered for cockfights. Although these events are no more, the free-roaming chickens and cats add that "what-a-hoot" factor. Nightly specials include black bean soup, seared sea scallops, and sautéed yellowtail snapper in citrus beurre-blanc sauce. Desserts and breads are baked on the premises; the banana bread is a hit during "breakfast with the roosters," and the lobster benedict with key-lime hollandaise is divine. ■TIP→**Dinner can be crowded and service spotty; your best bet is to come for breakfast or lunch.** ✉ *729 Thomas St.* ☎ *305/296–8666* 🌐 *www.blueheavenkw.com* *Reservations not accepted* ▭ *AE, D, MC, V* ⊗ *Closed Labor Day–mid-Oct.*

★ $ ✕ **The Cafe, A Mostly Vegetarian Place.** You don't have to be a vegetarian to love this New Age café. Local favorites include homemade soup, veggie burgers (order them with a side of sweet potato fries), portobello mushroom salad, and grilled Gorgonzola pizza. For bigger appetites there are offerings like the Szechuan-style vegetable stir-fry. On Sunday, there's a new brunch menu. ✉ *509 Southard St.* ☎ *305/296–5515* ▭ *MC, V.*

★ Fodor'sChoice $$$ ✕ **Café Marquesa.** It's showtime in the display kitchen as Chef Susan Ferry, who trained with Norman Van Aken at his Coral Gables restaurant, works her magic. Ferry presents eight or more entrées each night, and although every dish is a sure bet, frequent guests call attention to the peppercorn-dusted seared yellowfin tuna, the ginger coconut almond–crusted hogfish, and the pan-roasted duck breast. End your meal on a sweet note with Key Lime Napoleon with tropical fruits and berries. There's also a fine selection of wines and a choice of microbrewery beers. Adjoining the intimate Marquesa Hotel, the dining room is relaxed and elegant. ✉ *600 Fleming St.* ☎ *305/292–1244* 🌐 *www.marquesa.com* ▭ *AE, DC, MC, V* ⊗ *No lunch.*

$$ ✕ **The Island House Café.** For men only, this café has an excellent wine list and a menu with global flair. Dinner entrées range from standards like meat loaf to more unusual offerings like yellowtail snapper with curry sauce. The nearby gardens and pool area are a clothing-optional space, so this place has one of the island's most unusual views. ✉ *Island House, 1129 Fleming St.* ☎ *305/294–6284* 🌐 *www.islandhousekeywest.com* ▭ *AE, D, DC, MC, V.*

$$$ ✕ **Latitudes.** For a special treat, take the short boat ride to lovely Sunset Key for lunch or dinner on the beach. Creativity and quality ingredients combine for dishes that are bound to impress as much as the setting. For lunch, the

seafood quesadilla with chipotle dressing and avocado salsa is a fine example of the chef's use of local foods. At dinner, start with the crispy lobster cakes or seared yellowfin tuna stacked with mango, then move on to something with a slight Italian accent, such as yellowtail snapper with citrus risotto or bacon-crusted "prime rib" of wild salmon with crispy polenta. The short menu also has something to please meat-eaters and vegetarians. ✉*Sunset Village, 245 Front St.* ☎*305/292–5300 or 888/477–7786* 🌐*www.sunsetkeyisland.com* *Reservations essential* 💳*AE, D, DC, MC, V.*

$$$ ✕ **Louie's Backyard.** Feast your eyes on a steal-your-breath-away view and beautifully presented dishes prepared by executive chef Doug Shook. Once you get over sticker shock on the seasonally changing menu (appetizers cost around $14 to $16; entrées hover around the $35 mark), settle in and enjoy dishes like oven-roasted salmon on a crisp potato cake, grilled tuna with Japanese noodles, or grilled chili-rubbed pork chop with smoked applesauce. Louie's key lime pie has a gingersnap crust and is served with a raspberry coulis. Come for lunch if you're on a budget; the menu is less expensive (but still expect to pay about $17 for your entrée) and the view is just as fantastic. For night owls, the Afterdeck Bar serves cocktails on the water until the wee hours. ✉*700 Waddell Ave.* ☎*305/294–1061* 🌐*www.louiesbackyard.com* *Reservations essential* 💳 *MC, V.*

$$ ✕ **915 Duval.** Twinkling lights draped along the upper and lower porches of this century-old Victorian mansion add an touch. If you like to sample and sip, you'll appreciate the variety of smaller plate selections and wines by the glass. Amply portioned tapas include adventurous combos like the bacon-wrapped dates stuffed with sweet garlic and soy citrus, clams and chorizo, Thai-style beef salad rolls, and the signature "tuna dome," with fresh crab, lemon-miso dressing, and an ahi tuna sashimi wrapping. There are also larger plates if you're craving something like grilled double pork chops or steak frite. Dine outdoors and people-watch along upper Duval, or sit at a table inside while listening to light jazz. ✉*915 Duval St.* ☎*305/296–0669* 🌐*www.915duval.com* 💳*AE, MC, V* ⏲*No lunch.*

★ $$$ ✕ **Pisces.** Don't be dismayed when you see the sign for Pisces on the Café des Artistes building: Chef Andrew Berman and staff are still there. They've changed the name, updated the menu, and gone contemporary with a stylish granite bar and sparkling mirrors. Some old favorites remain on the menu, such as "lobster tango mango," flambéed in cognac and served with a saffron-basil butter sauce and sliced mangoes. Other dishes include veal chops with wild mushrooms and champagne-braised black grouper. Menu names sounded better when they were in French, but the taste lost nothing in the translation. ✉ *1007 Simonton St.* ☎ *305/294–7100* 🌐 *www.pisceskeywest.com* 💳 *AE, MC, V* ⊗ *No lunch.*

$$ ✕ **Tavern N Town.** Chef Norman Van Aken returned to Key West after making his name synonymous with Miami-style cuisine. Once head chef at Louie's Backyard, he has brought his highly acclaimed brand of new world cuisine to the Beachside Resort. This handsome dual restaurant will ultimately serve an intimate space for a set menu that he designs nightly in back. For now, the only part that is open is the Tavern, a warm room where a friendly bar provides ambience and open kitchen adds lovely aromas from the wood-fired oven. The menu focuses on simply prepared fish and meat dishes, such as pork with smoky plantain cream. Nightly scheduled specials offer affordable favorites such as pasta carbonara. The key lime pie gets extra tang from a pomegranate sauce. The restaurant is also open for breakfast and lunch. ✉ *Beachside Resort, 3841 N. Roosevelt Blvd.* ☎ *305/296–8100 or 800/546–0885* 🌐 *www.beachsidekeywest.com* ✍ *Reservations essential* 💳 *AE, D, DC, MC, V.*

5

FRENCH

★ $$$ ✕ **Café Solé.** Welcome to the self-described "home of the hog snapper." The confusing slogan refers to an award-winning dish of deliciously roasted local fish seasoned with shrimp and red peppers. This little piece of France is concealed behind a high wall and a gate in a residential neighborhood. Inside, Chef John Correa shows culinary wizardry that extends well beyond the hog. Marrying his French training with local ingredients, he creates delicious takes on classics, including Portobello mushroom soup, mangrove snapper with champagne-pesto sauce, and some of the best bouillabaisse that you'll find outside of Marseilles. From the land, there is filet mignon with a wild-mushroom demi-glace. If you can't decide, a three-course tasting dinner costs $27. ✉ *1029 Southard St.* ☎ *305/294–0230* 🌐 *www.cafesole.com* 💳 *D, DC, MC, V.*

$ ✕ **Croissants de France.** Pop into the bakery for something sinfully French to take with you, or spend some people-watching time at the sidewalk café next door. There's a delightful selection of American and French breakfasts (the poached eggs on brioche with creamy mustard sauce is worth every gram of cholesterol). Quiches, galettes, and crepes put the mais oui in lunch. The selection of salads appeals to American palates. Finish off lunch with a dessert crepe—the coconut with banana, chocolate and ice cream perhaps—or a chocolate éclair or key lime tart from the bakery. ✉*816 Duval St.* ☎*305/294–2624* 🌐*www.croissantsdefrance.com* 💳*AE, D, MC, V* ⊙*Closed Wed. No dinner.*

IRISH

$ ✕ **Finnegan's Wake Irish Pub and Eatery.** "Come for the beer. Stay for the food. Leave with the staff," is the slogan of this popular pub. The pictures of Beckett, Shaw, Yeats, and Wilde on the walls and the creaky wood floors underfoot exude Irish country warmth. The certified Angus beef is a bit pricey ($30 for an 18-ounce rib eye), but most of the other dishes are bargains. Traditional fare includes bangers and mash, chicken potpie, and colcannon—rich mashed potatoes with scallions, sauerkraut, and melted white cheddar cheese. Bread pudding soaked topped with a honey-whiskey sauce is a true treat. There's live music on weekends and daily happy hours from 4 to 7 and midnight to 2 featuring nearly 30 beers on tap. ✉*320 Grinnell St.* ☎*305/293–0222* 💳*AE, D, MC, V.*

ITALIAN

★ $ ✕ **Mangia Mangia.** This longtime favorite serves large portions of homemade pastas that can be matched with any of the homemade sauces. Tables are arranged in a brick garden hung with twinkling lights and in a nicely dressed-up dining room in an old house. Everything that comes out of the open kitchen is outstanding, including the *bollito misto di mare* (fresh seafood sautéed with garlic, shallots, and white wine) or the memorable spaghettini "schmappellini," thin pasta with asparagus, tomatoes, pine nuts, and Parmesan. The wine list—with more than 350 offerings—includes old and rare vintages, but also has a good under-$20 selection. ✉*900 Southard St.* ☎*305/294–2469* 🌐*www.mangia-mangia.com* 💳*AE, D, MC, V* ⊙*No lunch.*

★ $ ✕ **Salute Ristorante Sul Mare.** This colorful restaurant sits on Higgs Beach, giving it one of the island's best lunch views (and a bit of sand and salt spray on a windy day). The dinner menu includes inventive homemade pasta dishes like cappellini with calamari, capers, olives, and tomatoes, or linguine with shrimp, tomatoes, garlic, and basil. Start with a salad of mixed greens, feta, artichoke hearts, olives, and roasted red pepper or the bean soup with grilled bread. At lunch there are bruschetta, panini, and clams marinara, as well as a fresh-fish sandwich. ✉*1000 Atlantic Blvd., Higgs Beach* ☎*305/292–1117* ▭*AE, MC, V* ⊙*No lunch Sun.*

JAPANESE

$$ ✕ **Ambrosia.** Ask any savvy local where to get the best sushi on the island and you'll undoubtedly be pointed to this tiny wood-and-tatami paneled dining room tucked away in a quiet neighborhood. Grab a seat at the sushi bar and watch owner and head sushi chef Masa prepare an impressive array of super-fresh sashimi delicacies. You can't go wrong with the ambrosia special, a sampler of five kinds of sashimi. There's an assortment of lightly fried tempura and teriyaki dishes and a killer bento box at lunch. Enjoy it all with a cup of sake or a cold glass of Sapporo beer. ✉*Santa Maria Resort,1401 Simonton St.* ☎*305/293–0304* ▭*AE, MC, V.*

SEAFOOD

¢ ✕ **B. O.'s Fish Wagon.** What started out as a fish house on wheels appears to have broken down on the corner of Caroline and William Streets and is today the cornerstone for one of Key West's junkyard-chic dining institutions. From the outside, it looks as though a hurricane deposited a pile of debris; the only sign that it's a restaurant is the wood-plank counter looking out at Caroline Street. Step up to the window and order the specialty: a grouper sandwich fried or grilled and topped with key-lime sauce. Other choices include fish nuts (don't be scared, they're just fried nuggets), hot dogs, and shrimp or soft-shell crab sandwich. Talk sass with your host and find a picnic table or take a seat at the plank. Grab some paper towels off one of the rolls hanging around and busy yourself reading graffiti, license plates, and irreverent signs. It's a must-do Key West experience. ✉*801 Caroline St.* ☎*305/294–9272* ▭*No credit cards.*

$ ✕ **Conch Republic Seafood Company.** Because of its location where the fast ferry docks, Conch Republic does a brisk business. It's huge, open-air, and on the water, so the place is hard to miss. The menu is ambitious, offering more than just standard seafood fare. The baked oysters callaloo (a spinachlike green), for instance, are a Caribbean-style twist on oysters Rockefeller. The grilled or fried shrimp basket comes with a trio of sauces, including the house mixture. Paella, grilled fish, seafood stir-fry, and steaks are some other options. Live music adds to the decibel level. ✉*631 Greene St. at Elizabeth St.* ☎*305/294–4403* 🌐*www.conchrepublicseafood.com* ▭*AE, D, MCV.*

$ ✕ **Half Shell Raw Bar.** Smack-dab on the docks, this legendary institution gets its name from the oysters, clams, and peel 'n' eat shrimp that are departure point for its seafood-based diet. It's not clever recipes or fine dining (or even air-conditioning) that packs 'em in; it's fried fish, po'boy sandwiches, and seafood combos. For a break from the deep fryer, try the fresh and light conch ceviche, "cooked" with lime juice. The potato salad is flavored with dill and the "Pama Rita" is a new twist in Margaritaville. ✉*Lands End Village at Historic Seaport, 231 Margaret St.* ☎*305/294–7496* 🌐*www.halfshellrawbar.com* ▭*AE, MC, V.*

$ ✕ **Hogfish Grill.** It's worth a drive to Stock Island, the next island up from Key West, to sit along one of Florida's last surviving working waterfronts, watch the shrimpers and fishermen unloading their catch, and indulge in the freshness you're witnessing at this down-to-earth spot. Hogfish is of course the specialty. The "Killer Hogfish Sandwich comes on Cuban Bread. Sprinkle it with one of the house hot sauces. Other favorites include lobster rolls or pulled pork sandwiches at lunch and fish tacos, shrimp quesadillas, or smoked ribs at dinner. ✉*6810 Front St., Stock Island* ☎*305/293–4041* ▭*D, MC, V.*

★ $ ✕ **Seven Fish.** A local hot spot, this off-the-beaten-track eatery is good for an eclectic mix of dishes like tropical shrimp salsa, wild-mushroom quesadilla, seafood marinara, and sometimes even an old-fashioned meat loaf with real mashed potatoes. Those in the know arrive early to snag one of the 12 or so tables clustered in the bare-bones dining room. ✉*632 Olivia St.* ☎*305/296–2777* 🌐*www.7fish.com* ▭*AE, MC, V* ⊗*Closed Tues. No lunch.*

$ ✕ **Turtle Kraals.** Named for the kraals, or corrals, where sea turtles were once kept until they went to the cannery, this place calls to mind the island's history. Today, much smaller box turtles provide live entertainment at 6 on Monday and Friday, when folks cheer on contestants in a turtle race. The menu offers an assortment of marine cuisine that includes seared jerk tuna, seafood enchiladas, and mango crab cakes. The open-walled restaurant overlooks the marina at the Historic Seaport. ✉*231 Margaret St.* ☎*305/294–2640* 🌐*www.turtlekraals.com* ▭ *MC, V.*

WHERE TO STAY

Historic cottages, restored century-old Conch houses, and large resorts are among the offerings in Key West, with the majority charging between $100 and $300 a night. In high season, December through March, you'll be hard pressed to find a decent room for less than $200, and most places raise prices considerably during holidays. Many guesthouses and inns do not welcome children under 16, and most do not permit smoking indoors. Most tariffs include an expanded continental breakfast and, often, afternoon wine or snack.

GUESTHOUSES

★ $$$$ **Ambrosia Key West.** If you desire personal attention, a casual atmosphere, and a dollop of style, stay at these twin inns spread out on nearly 2 acres. Ambrosia is more intimate, with themed rooms such as the Treetop, Sailfish Suites, and Havana Cabana. Ambrosia Too is a delightful art-filled hideaway. Rooms and suites have original work by local artists, wicker or wood furniture, and spacious bathrooms. Each has a private entrance and deck, patio, or porch. Poolside continental breakfast is included, and children are welcome. **Pros:** Spacious rooms, poolside breakfast, friendly staff. **Cons:** On-street parking can be tough to come by. ✉ *615, 618, 622 Fleming St.* ☎ *305/296–9838 or 800/535–9838* 🌐 *www.ambrosiakeywest.com* *22 rooms, 3 town houses, 1 cottage, 6 suites* *In-room: kitchen (some), refrigerator. In-hotel: 3 pools, bicycles, no elevator, concierge, public Wi-Fi, parking (no fee), some pets allowed (fee), no-smoking rooms* *AE, D, MC, V* *CP.*

$–$$ **Angelina Guest House.** The high rollers and ladies of the night were chased away long ago, but this charming guesthouse revels in its past as a gambling hall and bordello. In the heart of Old Town Key West, it's a home away from home that offers simple, clean, attractively priced accommodations. Accommodations range from small rooms sharing a bath to spacious rooms with king beds and sleeper sofas. Built in the 1920s, this yellow-and-white clapboard building has second-floor porches, gabled roofs, and a white picket fence. The current owners prettied the rooms with flower-print curtains and linens and added homemade cinnamon rolls, which receive rave reviews in the guest book, to the breakfast bar. A lagoon-style pool, fountain, and old-brick walkways accent a lovely garden. **Pros:** Good

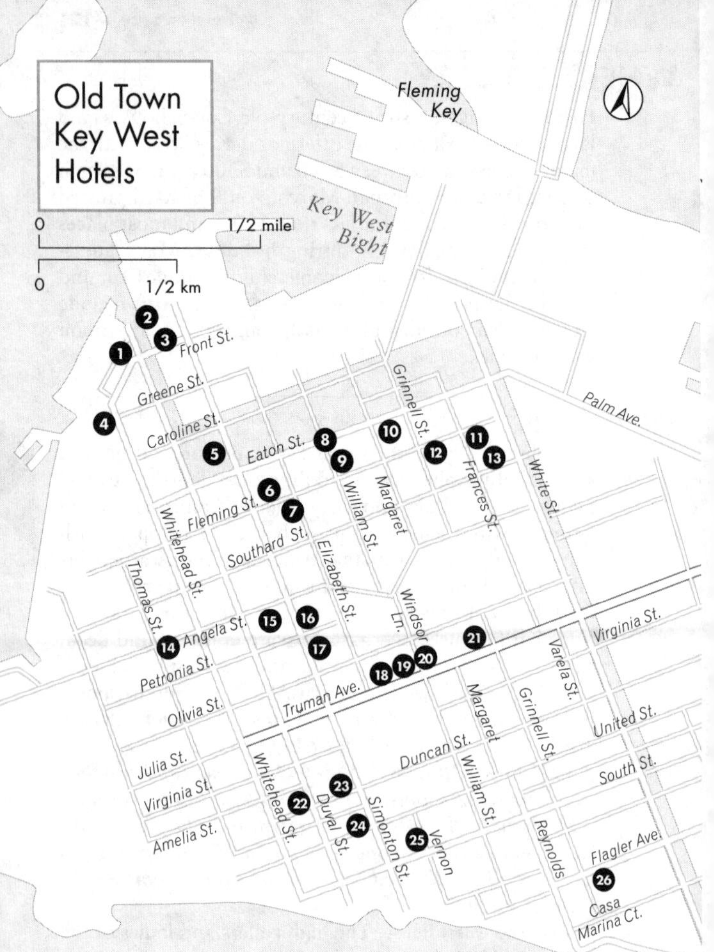

Ambrosia Key West, **6**
Angelina Guest House, **14**
Azul Key West, **21**
Casa Marina Resort, **26**
Courtney's Place, **16**
Eden House, **12**
The Gardens Hotel, **15**
Heron House Court, **11**
Hyatt Key West Resort & Spa, **3**
Island City House Hotel, **9**
Island House, **13**
Key Lime Inn, **18**
La Pensione, **20**
Marquesa Hotel, **7**
Merlin Guesthouse, **17**
Mermaid & the Alligator, **19**
Ocean Breeze Inn, **25**
Ocean Key Resort, **1**
Pearl's Rainbow, **23**
Pier House Resort & Caribbean Spa, **2**
Popular House/ Key West B&B, **8**
Simonton Court, **5**
Southernmost Hotel & Resorts, **24**
Speakeasy Inn, **22**
Westin Key West Resort & Marina, **4**
Westwinds Inn, **10**

value, nice garden, friendly staff. **Cons:** Thin walls, basic rooms, shared balcony. ✉*302 Angela St.* ☎*305/294–4480 or 888/303–4480* 🌐*www.angelinaguesthouse.com* *13 rooms* *In-room: no phone, refrigerator (some), no TV. In-hotel: pool, bicycles, no elevator, no kids under 18, no-smoking rooms* *D, MC, V* *CP.*

$$$–$$$$ **Azul Key West.** The ultramodern—nearly minimalistic—redo of this classic Queen Anne mansion is a break from the sensory overload of Key West's other abundant Victorian guesthouses. The adults-only boutique hotel, 3˝ blocks from Duval Street, combines original trim and shiny wood floors with sleek furnishings, including a curved frosted glass and chrome check-in desk, leather loungers, and a state-of-the-art sound system. Spacious, serene rooms, some with private verandas, have leather headboards, flat-screen TVs, and remote-controlled fans and lights. **Pros:** Lovely building, marble-floored baths, luxurious linens. **Cons:** On a busy street, weekend surcharge. ✉*907 Truman Ave.* ☎*305/296–5152 or 888/253–2985* 🌐*www.azulhotels.us* *10 rooms, 1 suite* *In-room: Wi-Fi. In-hotel: pool, bicycles, no elevator, public Wi-Fi, no kids under 21, no-smoking rooms* *AE, D, MC, V* *CP.*

$$$–$$$$ **Courtney's Place.** If you like kids, cats, and dogs, you'll feel right at home in this collection of accommodations ranging from cigar-maker cottages to shotgun houses. The interiors are equally varied in coloring and furnishings, but all the rooms have at least a refrigerator, microwave, and coffeepot, if not a full kitchen. The family-owned property is tucked into a residential neighborhood, though within easy walking distance of Duval Street. All rooms are not created equal here; the tiny Room 5 is tucked into an attic space. **Pros:** Near Duval Street, fairly priced. **Cons:** Small parking lot, dated bed linens. ✉*720 Whitemarsh La.* ☎*305/294–3480 or 800/869–4639* *305/294–7019* 🌐*www.courtneysplacekeywest.com* *6 rooms, 2 suites, 2 efficiencies, 8 cottages* *In-room: kitchen (some), refrigerator, Wi-Fi. In-hotel: pool, bicycles, no elevator, concierge, laundry facilities, parking (no fee), some pets allowed (fee), no-smoking rooms* *AE, MC, V* *CP.*

★ $$ **Eden House.** From the vintage metal rockers on the street-side porch to the old neon hotel sign in the lobby, this 1920s rambling Key West mainstay hotel is high on character, low on gloss. You'll get a taste of authentic old Key West, without sacrificing convenience, comfort, or budget. Rooms come in all shapes and sizes, from shared-bath basic to large apartments with full kitchens and private decks or porches. The spacious outdoor area is shaded by towering palms. Grab a book and plop in a hammock in the outdoor library, tucked into a sun-dappled corner with a gurgling waterfall and potted bonsai. **Pros:** Sunny garden, hot tub is actually hot, daily happy hour around the pool. **Cons:** Cutesy signage is overdone. ✉ *1015 Fleming St.* ☎ *305/296–6868 or 800/533–5397* 🌐 *www.edenhouse.com* *36 rooms, 8 suites.* *In-room: kitchen (some), refrigerator (some). In-hotel: restaurant, pool, bicycles, no elevator, public Internet, public Wi-Fi, parking (no fee), no-smoking rooms* ▭ *MC, V.*

★ Fodor's Choice **The Gardens Hotel.** Built in 1875, this gloriously shaded property covers a third of a city block in Old Town. Peggy Mills, who bought it as a private estate in 1931, coiffed it with orchids, ponytail palms, and black bamboo. She added walks, fountains, and *tinajones* (earthen pots) imported from Cuba. After her death in 1971, the property was turned into a romantic inn that offers several types of accommodations, from standard rooms with garden and courtyard views to a two-bedroom carriage house suite. Decorated with Bahamian plantation-style furnishings, the quiet and elegant rooms are a luxurious tropical retreat. Most have private verandas. Rates include Continental breakfast. **Pros:** Luxurious bathrooms, secluded garden seating, free phone calls. **Cons:** Hard to get reservations. ✉ *526 Angela St.* ☎ *305/294–2661 or 800/526–2664* 🌐 *www.gardenshotel.com* *17 rooms* *In-room: refrigerator, Wi-Fi. In-hotel: bar, pool, spa, no elevator, concierge, public Wi-Fi, parking (no fee), no kids under 16, no-smoking rooms* ▭ *AE, D, MC, V* *CP.*
$$$$

$$$ **Heron House Court.** Formerly called Fleur de Key Guesthouse, this circa 1900 inn provides everyone with a warm welcome. Its Conch-style architecture harks back to the property's origins as a boardinghouse and cigar makers' cottages. Standard rooms in the main house are small, so opt for a superior room, slightly more expensive but a great deal larger. Airy, bright rooms have tiled floors and a complementary mix of antiques and reproductions, and are tastefully decorated in tropical colors. The guest rooms are nicer than the public areas, which include a pool and weathered deck. **Pros:** Complimentary weekend wine hours, fluffy bathrobes. **Cons:** Faces noisy Eaton Street, owner's suite smells musty. ✉ *412 Frances St.* ☎ *305/296–4719 or 888/265–2395* 🌐 *www.heronhousecourt.com* *2 suites, 14 rooms* *In-room: refrigerator. In-hotel: pool, no eleva-*

tor, concierge, public Wi-Fi, no kids under 21, no-smoking rooms ▭*AE, D, MC, V* 🍽*CP.*

$$$$ **Island City House Hotel.** An oasis with brick walkways, tropical plants, a a canopy of palms sets this convivial guesthouse apart from the pack. The vintage-1880s Island City House has wraparound verandas, pine floors, and charm to spare. Arch House, a former carriage house, has a dramatic entry that opens into a lush courtyard. Although all suites front on busy Eaton Street, only Nos. 5 and 6 face it. A reconstructed cigar factory has become the poolside Cigar House, with spacious rooms, porches, decks, and plantation-style teak and wicker furnishings. The private tropical garden wraps around a spacious pool area. Children are welcome—a rarity in Old Town guesthouses. **Pros:** Private gardens, knowledgeable staff. **Cons:** Spotty Wi-Fi service, no front desk staff at night, some rooms are small. ✉*411 William St.* ☎*305/294–5702 or 800/634–8230* 🌐*www.islandcityhouse.com* *24 suites* *In-room: kitchen (some), Wi-Fi (some). In-hotel: pool, bicycles, no elevator, laundry facilities, concierge, public Wi-Fi, no-smoking rooms* ▭*AE, DC, MC, V* 🍽*CP.*

$$$ **Island House.** Geared specifically toward gay men, this hotel features a health club, a video lounge, a café and bar, and rooms in historic digs. Clothing is optional everywhere but in the gym. **Pros:** Lots of privacy, just the place to get that all-over tan. **Cons:** No women allowed. ✉*1129 Fleming St.* ☎*305/294–6284 or 800/890–6284* 🌐www.islandhousekeywest.com *34 rooms* *In-room: safe, refrigerator, VCR, dial-up, Wi-Fi. In-hotel: restaurant, bar, pool, public Internet, public Wi-Fi* ▭*AE, D, DC, MC, V.*

$$$$ **Key Lime Inn.** This 1854 Grand Bahama–style house on the National Register of Historic Places succeeds by offering amiable service, a great location, and simple rooms with natural-wood furnishings. The cluster of pastel-painted cottages, surrounded by white picket fences, has a residential feel, a bit like a beach colony without the beach, or the backlot of a movie set. The least-expensive Cabana rooms, some with patios, surround the pool. The Garden Cottages have one room; some include a porch or balcony. Some rooms in the historic Maloney House have a porch or patio. **Pros:** Free parking, some rooms have private patios. **Cons:** Standard rooms are pricey, pool faces a busy street, mulch-covered paths. ✉*725 Truman Ave.* ☎*305/294–5229 or 800/549–4430* 🌐*www.keylimeinn.com* *37 rooms* *In-room: safe, refrigerator (some), dial-up. In-hotel: pool,* *no elevator, public Wi-Fi, parking (no fee), no-smoking rooms* ⊟*AE, D, MC, V* 🍽*CP.*

★ $$$–$$$$ **Mermaid & the Alligator.** An enchanting combination of flora and fauna makes this 1904 Victorian house a welcoming retreat. The property is bathed in palms, banyans, birds of paradise, and poincianas, with cages of colorful, live parrots and swarms of butterflies adding tropical punch. Rooms are Caribbean colonial–inspired, with wood-slat floors, elegant trim, and French doors. The color scheme—key lime, cantaloupe, and other rich colors—couldn't be more evocative of the Keys. Some downstairs rooms open onto the deck, pool, and gardens designed by one of the resident owners, a landscape designer. Upstairs rooms overlook the gardens. An extensive breakfast is served poolside. **Pros:** Inviting hot tub, massage pavilion, island getaway feel. Cons: Minimum stay requires, dark public areas, cheesy plastic lawn chairs. ✉*729 Truman Ave.* ☎*305/294–1894 or 800/773–1894* 🌐*www.kwmermaid.com* ⇨*9 rooms* ♿*In-room: no phone, no TV, Wi-Fi. In-hotel: pool, no elevator, public Internet, public Wi-Fi, no kids under 16, no-smoking rooms* ⊟*AE, MC, V* 🍽*CP.*

$$ **La Pensione.** Hospitality and period furnishings make this 1891 home, once owned by a cigar executive, a wonderful glimpse into Key West life in the late 19th century. All rooms have private baths and king-size or double beds. All but one have sitting areas—the exception being a handicapped-accessible room. None have televisions, but not to worry, there's plenty of entertainment on nearby Duval Street. Rates include daily Continental breakfast in the dining room or on the veranda. **Pros:** Pine-paneled walls, off-street parking, some rooms have wraparound porches. **Cons:** Street-facing rooms are noisy, baths need updating. ✉*809 Truman Ave.* ☎*305/292–9923 or 800/893–1193* 🌐*www.lapensione.com* ⇨*9 rooms* ♿*In-room: no TV, Wi-Fi. In-hotel: pool, no elevator, public Wi-Fi, parking (no fee), no kids under 18* ⊟*AE, D, MC, V* 🍽*CP.*

★ $$ **Merlin Guesthouse.** Key West guesthouses don't usually welcome families, but this laid-back jumble of rooms and suites is an exception. If you can live with a few flaws, you'll grab a bargain. Accommodations in the 1930s Simonton House, with four-poster beds, are most suitable for couples. The one- and two-bedroom suites are popular with families. Bright, roomy cottages are perfect if you want a bit more privacy. Get a room in the back, if you are bothered by noise. The leafy courtyard and pool area are where guests hang out day and night. **Pros:** Good location near

THE HOLIDAYS KEY WEST STYLE

On New Year's Eve, Key West celebrates the turning of the calendar page with three separate ceremonies that parody New York's dropping-of-the-ball drama. Here they let fall a 6-foot conch shell from Sloppy Joe's Bar, a pirate wench from the towering mast of the Liberty Clipper at the Historic Seaport, and a drag queen (elegantly decked out in a ball gown and riding an oversized red high-heel shoe) at Bourbon Street Pub. You wouldn't expect any less from America's most outrageous city.

Key West is one of the nation's biggest party towns, so the celebrations here take on a colorful hue. In keeping with Key West's rich maritime heritage, its two-night Bight Before Christmas takes place one mid-December weekend at Key West Bight. The Lighted Boat Parade creates a quintessential Florida spectacle with fanciful fireworks, live music, and decorated vessels of all shapes and sizes.

Tennessee Williams Theatre stages a Key West version of Nutcracker Suite. In this unorthodox retelling, the heroine sails the *Lemonade Sea* to a coral reef and is submerged in a diving bell. (What? No sugarplum fairies?) Between Christmas and New Year's Day, the Holiday House and Garden Tour is another yuletide tradition.

Duval Street, good rates. **Cons:** Neighbor noise, common areas are dated. ✉*811 Simonton St.* ☎*305/296–3336 or 800/642–4753* 🌐*www.merlinguesthouse.com* *10 rooms, 6 suites, 4 cottages* *In-room: no phone, safe, kitchen (some), refrigerator (some), Wi-Fi. In-hotel: pool, no elevator, public Internet, public Wi-Fi, no-smoking rooms* *AE, D, MC, V* *CP.*

$$$ **Pearl's Rainbow.** This guesthouse, which caters to lesbians and gay-friendly women, occupies an 1886 cigar factory. It's home to Pearl's Patio, a women-only bar. The Strand restaurant serves breakfast, lunch, and evening snacks. Rooms range from basic to deluxe, and are comfortable, clean, and well-appointed. **Pros:** Full breakfast, plenty of privacy. **Cons:** No men allowed, bar attracts late-night partiers. ✉*525 United St.* ☎*305/292–1450 or 800/749–6696* 🌐*www.pearlsrainbow.com* *32 rooms, 6 suites* *In-room: refrigerator, kitchen (some), Wi-Fi. In-hotel: restaurant, bar, pools, Internet, public Wi-Fi* *AE, D, MC, V* *BP.*

★ **Popular House/Key West Bed & Breakfast.** Local art—large, $-$$$ splashy canvases, a mural in the style of Gauguin—decorate the walls at this lodging. Handmade textiles (owner Jody Carlson is a talented weaver) drape chairs, couches, and beds. You'll find both inexpensive rooms with shared bath and luxury rooms with all the amenities, as the owners reason that budget travelers deserve the same good style (and lavish tropical continental breakfast) as their well-heeled counterparts. Less-expensive rooms burst with bright colors; the hand-painted dressers add a whimsical flourish. Balconies on the second-floor rooms overlook the gardens. Spacious (and more expensive) third-floor rooms are decorated with a paler palette and original furniture. **Pros:** Feels like an art gallery, tiled outdoor shower, hot tub and sauna area is a welcome hangout. **Cons:** Some rooms are small. *415 William St. 305/296–7274 or 800/438–6155 www.keywestbandb.com 10 rooms, 6 with bath In-room: no phone, no TV, Wi-Fi (some). In-hotel: pool, bicycles, no elevator, public Internet, public Wi-Fi, no kids under 18, no-smoking rooms AE, D, DC, MC, V CP.*

$$-$$$ **Speakeasy Inn.** During Prohibition, Raul Vasquez made this place popular by smuggling in liquor from Cuba. Today, the booze is legal, and there's even a daily happy hour. The Speakeasy Inn is still well known, only now its reputation is for having reasonably priced rooms within walking distance of the beach. Accommodations have bright white walls offset by bursts of color in rugs, pillows, and seat cushions. Queen-size beds and tables are fashioned from salvaged pine. The rooms are basic, but some have nice touches like claw-foot tubs. Room 1 has a deck that's good for people-watching. **Pros:** Good location, reasonable rates, high-quality cigars at the attached cigar store. **Cons:** No pool, basic decor. *1117 Duval St. 305/296–2680 or 800/217–4884 www.speakeasyinn.com 4 suites, 4 studios In-room: refrigerator, Wi-Fi. In-hotel: bicycles, no elevator, public Internet, public Wi-Fi, no-smoking rooms AE, D, MC, V CP.*

$$-$$$ **Westwinds Inn.** This cluster of historic gingerbread-trimmed houses has individually decorated rooms that make you feel right at home. The buildings spread throughout luxuriant gardens with two swimming pools (one heated) just a couple of blocks from the Historic Key West Seaport. The library provides a spot to read, grab snacks from the communal refrigerator and microwave, and hook up to wireless Internet. Breakfast poolside is generous. **Pros:**

Away from Old Town's bustle, lots of character, affordable rates. **Cons:** Small lobby, confusing layout, a long walk from Duval Street. ✉*914 Eaton St.* ☎*305/296–4440 or 800/788–4150* 🌐*www.westwindskeywest.com* *25 rooms and suites* *In room: Wi-Fi (some). In hotel: pools, laundry facilities, public Wi-Fi, no elevators, no kids under age 12, no-smoking rooms* *D, MC, V* *CP.*

HOTELS

$$$$ **Beachside Resort.** The new kid on the block, this hotel vies for convention business with the biggest ballroom in Key West. It also appeals to families with its spacious condo units decorated with impeccable good taste. Designer furnishings reflect the resort's waterfront location. Frette linens on the beds, real china in the kitchens, and marble hot tubs add touches of luxury. Rooms have spiral staircases down to the gardens and up to the rooftop sundecks. Families enjoy the beach and pool area, while the resort's Norman Van Aken restaurant is a serious perk for the connoisseur crowd. **Pros:** Private beach, shuttle to downtown and the airport, poolside cabanas. **Cons:** Packed with conventions, can't walk to Old Town, cookie-cutter facade. ✉*3841 N. Roosevelt Blvd., New Town* ☎*305/296–8100 or 800/546–0885* 🌐*www.beachsidekeywest.com* *93 rooms, 129 1- to 3-bedroom suites* *In room: kitchen, Ethernet, Wi-Fi. In hotel: 3 restaurants, room service, bars, pool, gym, concierge, public Wi-Fi, airport shuttle, parking (fee), no-smoking rooms* *AE, D, DC, MC, V.*

$$$ **Best Western Key Ambassador Resort Inn.** You know what to expect from this chain hotel: well-maintained rooms, predictable service, and competitive prices. This one also happens to be on a 7-acre piece of property with ocean views next to the airport. Accommodations are cheerful, if uninspired, with Caribbean-style furniture and linens in coordinated tropical colors. All have screened-in balconies. The palm-shaded pool looks over the Atlantic, and a covered picnic area with a large barbecue grill encourages socializing. **Pros:** Big pool area, popular tiki bar. **Cons:** Airport noise, lacks personality. ✉*3755 S. Roosevelt Blvd., New Town* ☎*305/296–3500 or 800/432–4315* 🌐*www.keyambassador.com* *100 rooms* *In-room: refrigerator, dial-up, Wi-Fi. In-hotel: 2 restaurants, bar, pool, laundry facilities, concierge, public Wi-Fi, airport shuttle, parking (no fee), no-smoking rooms* *AE, D, DC, MC, V* *CP.*

5

★ **Casa Marina Resort.** At any moment, you expect the landed gentry to walk across the oceanfront lawn, just as they did when this 13-acre resort was built back in the 1920s. Set on a private beach, it has the same richly appointed lobby with beamed ceilings, polished pine floor, and original art. Guest rooms are stylishly decorated with armoires and wicker chairs that add a lot of warmth. Fluffy bathrobes and luxurious designer toiletries make it feel like boutique hotel. Two-bedroom loft suites with balconies face the ocean. The main building's ground-floor lanai rooms open onto the lawn, and the pools have a nice view of the Atlantic. **Pros:** The area's nicest resort beach, historic setting, away from the crowds. **Cons:** Long walk to Old Town, showing signs of age. *1500 Reynolds St. 305/296–3535 or 866/397–6342 www.casamarinaresort.com 239 rooms, 72 suites In-room: safe, dial-up, Wi-Fi. In-hotel: restaurant, room service, bars, tennis courts, pools, gym, spa, beachfront, diving, water sports, bicycles, children's programs (ages 4–12), laundry service, concierge, public Internet, public Wi-Fi, airport shuttle, no-smoking rooms AE, D, DC, MC, V.*

$$$$

$$$$ **Hyatt Key West Resort & Spa.** Boasting its own beach, the Hyatt Key West is one of few resorts where you can walk in the sand, then along the streets of Old Town. A top-to-bottom renovation in 2007 transformed this hotel into a tropical escape with plenty of panache. It offers a wide range of water sports, fine dining in two restaurants, and fitness amenities—all with an eye toward keeping green. Rooms are bright and airy, with walk-in showers with rain showerheads, and balconies that overlook the gulf. They pamper you with little extras such as down comforters and fluffy robes. **Pros:** Away from the bustle of Old Town, on the beach, plenty of activities. **Cons:** Beach is small, charge for wireless connections, chain-hotel feel. *601 Front St. 305/809–1234 www.keywest.hyatt.com 7 rooms In-room: safe, dial-up, Wi-Fi. In-hotel: 2 restaurants, room service, bars, pool, gym, spa, beachfront, diving, water sports, laundry service, concierge, public Wi-Fi, parking (fee), no-smoking rooms AE, D, DC, MC, V.*

★ Fodor'sChoice **Marquesa Hotel.** In a town that prides itself on its laid-back luxury, this complex of four restored 1884 houses stands out. Guests—typically shoeless in Marquesa robes—relax among richly landscaped pools, rock waterfalls, and peaceful gardens. Elegant rooms surround a courtyard and have antique and reproduction furnishings, creamy-white and aqua fabrics, and marble baths. The

$$$$

lobby resembles a Victorian parlor, with Audubon prints, vases overflowing with flowers, and photos of early Key West. The clientele is well traveled and affluent 40- to 70-year-olds, mostly straight, but the hotel is very gay-friendly. **Pros:** Elegant setting, romantic atmosphere, deluxe baths. **Cons:** Street-facing rooms can be noisy, expensive rates. ✉*600 Fleming St.* ☎*305/292–1919 or 800/869–4631* 🌐*www.marquesa.com* *27 rooms* *In-room: safe, refrigerators, dial-up, Wi-Fi. In-hotel: restaurant, room service, pools, no elevator, laundry service, concierge, public Wi-Fi, no kids under 14, no-smoking rooms* ▭*AE, DC, MC, V.*

★ $$$$ **Ocean Key Resort.** A pool and lively open-air bar and restaurant sit on Sunset Pier, a perfect place perfect to watch the sun sink into the horizon. Toast the day's end from private balconies that extend from spacious rooms that are both stylish and homey. High ceilings, hand-painted furnishings, sleigh beds, wooden chest, and lavish whirlpool tubs create a personally designed look. This is a full-service resort, with excellent amenities like a great on-site spa. **Pros:** Well-trained staff, lively pool scene, best spa on the island. **Cons:** Confusing layout, too bustling for some. ✉*Zero Duval St.* ☎*305/296–7701 or 800/328–9815* 🌐*www.oceankey.com* *75 rooms, 25 suites* *In-room: kitchen (some), refrigerator, dial-up, Wi-Fi. In-hotel: 2 restaurants, room service, bars, pool, spa, diving, water sports, bicycles, laundry service, concierge, public Wi-Fi, parking (fee), some pets allowed, no-smoking rooms* ▭*AE, D, DC, MC, V.*

★ $$$$ **Pier House Resort & Caribbean Spa.** The staff here goes out of its way to pamper you, and the location—on a quiet stretch of beach at the foot of Duval—is ideal as a buffer from, and gateway to, the action. It's a sprawling complex of weathered gray buildings, including an original Conch house. The courtyard is dotted with tall coconut palms and hibiscus blossoms, and rooms are cozy and colorful, with a water, pool, or garden view. In 2008, the resort opened six top-of-the-line suites extending over the water with sunset views. The rest of the rooms were completely redecorated. Rooms nearest the public areas can be noisy. **Pros:** Beautiful beach, good location, nice spa. **Cons:** Lots of conventions, cookie-cutter feel, poolside rooms are small. ✉*1 Duval St.* ☎*305/296–4600 or 800/723–2791* 🌐*www.pierhouse.com* *113 rooms, 29 suites* *In-room: refrigerator, VCR (some), dial-up, Wi-Fi. In-hotel: 2 restaurants, room service, bars, pool, gym, spa, beachfront, bicycles,* *laundry service, concierge, public Wi-Fi, no-smoking rooms* ⊟*AE, D, DC, MC, V.*

★ **Simonton Court.** A small world all its own, this lodging makes you feel deliciously sequestered from Key West's crasser side, but close enough to get there on foot. The "basic" rooms are in an old cigar factory, each with its own unique decor. There's also a restored shotgun house and cottages. But top of the line are the units occupying a Victorian home and the townhouse facing the property's pool and breakfast brick-paved courtyard. **Pros:** Lots of privacy, well-appointed accommodations, friendly staff. **Cons:** Minimum stays required in high season. ✉*320 Simonton St.* ☎*305/294–6386 or 800/944–2687* 🌐*www.simontoncourt.com* *14 rooms, 12 suites* *In room: safe, kitchen (some), refrigerator. In-hotel: pools, no kids under age 18, no-smoking rooms* ⊟ *D, DC, MC, V* *CP.*
$$$$

★ **Southernmost Hotel & Resorts.** This hotel offers resort-style accommodations at motel prices. Its location on the quiet end of Duval means you don't have to deal with the hustle and bustle of downtown unless you want to (it's within a 20-minute walk). Cookie-cutter rooms are spacious, bright, and airy, and have cottage-style furnishings and the required tropical color schemes. Grab a cold drink from the Tiki Hut bar and join the crowd around the pool, or venture across the street to the beach. Looking for something more upscale and intimate? **Pros:** Pool attracts a lively crowd, access to nearby properties, free parking. **Cons:** Public beach is small. ✉*1319 Duval St.* ☎*305/296–6577 or 800/354–4455* *305/294–8272* 🌐*www.southernmostresorts.com* *127 rooms* *In-room: safe, refrigerator, dial-up, Wi-Fi (some). In-hotel: bar, pool, beachfront, laundry facilities, public Wi-Fi, parking (no fee), no-smoking rooms* ⊟*AE, D, DC, MC, V* *CP.*
$$–$$$

★ **Sunset Key.** This private island retreat feels complete cut off from the world, yet you're just minutes away from the action. Board a 10-minute launch to 27-acre Sunset Key, where you'll find sandy beaches, swaying palms, flowering gardens, and a delicious sense of privacy. A favorite of yacht owners, the hotel has a 40-slip marina. The comforts are first-class at the cluster of one-, two- and three-bedroom cottages at the water's edge. Baked goods, freshly squeezed juice, and a newspaper are delivered each morning. Each of the accommodations has a kitchen, but you can use the grocery shopping service or hire a private chef (both for a fee, of course). You can use all the facilities at the Westin Key West Resort in Old Town. But be
$$$$

warned that you may never want to leave Sunset Key and its great restaurants, pretty pool, and very civilized beach complete with attendants and cabanas. **Pros:** Peace and quiet, roomy verandas, free 24-hour shuttle. **Cons:** Luxury doesn't come cheap. *✉245 Front St. ☎305/292–5300 or 888/477–7786 ⊕www.sunsetkeyisland.com ⇨37 cottages ♁In-room: safe, kitchen, DVD, VCR, dial-up. In-hotel: restaurant, bars, room service, tennis courts, pool, gym, beachfront, laundry facilities, laundry service, concierge, public Internet, parking (fee), no-smoking rooms ▭AE, D, DC, MC, V ⊚CP.*

$$$$ **Westin Key West Resort & Marina.** This charming waterfront resort huddles around its 40-slip marina in the middle of Old Town. It has all the elegant touches associated with the Westin name, including the Heavenly Bed and Starbucks coffee in the rooms. As sister resort to Sunset Key, guests have limited access to the private island resort via a short shuttle boat ride. Most of the rooms, which are large by Key West standards, look out on the Gulf of Mexico. All have sunny yellow color schemes, and some have steam baths and jetted tubs. **Pros:** Good location, good amenities, access to Sunset Key. **Cons:** Feels too big for Key West, always crowded, conference clientele. *✉245 Front St. ☎305/294–4000 ⊕www.westin.com/keywest ⇨146 rooms, 32 suites ♁In-room: safe, refrigerator, dial-up, Wi-Fi. In-hotel: 4 restaurants, room service, bars, pool, gym, water sports, concierge, public Wi-Fi, parking (fee), some pets allowed, no-smoking rooms ▭AE, D, DC, MC, V.*

MOTELS

$–$$ **Harborside Motel & Marina.** This little motel neatly packages three appealing characteristics—affordability, safety, and a pleasant location between Old Town and New Town. Units are boxy and basic, with little patios, ceramic-tile floors, and lots of peace and quiet. For on-the-water living, book one of the four stationary houseboats; each sleeps four. Sportfishing charters leave from here, and there's a fish-cleaning table on the dock. Pros: Waterfront bars, grills for cookouts, friendly fishing atmosphere. Cons: Rooms need sprucing up. *✉903 Eisenhower Dr. ☎305/294–2780 or 800/501–7823 ⊕www.keywestharborside.com ⇨14 efficiencies, 4 houseboats ♁In-room: kitchen. In-hotel: pool, no elevator, laundry facilities ▭AE, D, DC, MC, V.*

$$ **Ocean Breeze Inn.** What this simple South Beach area motel lacks in style it makes up for in value. Less than $200 a night during high season? Practically unheard of

in Key West. Rooms, with peachy floral colors and wicker furniture, are clustered around a tiny pool. Some are quite spacious with high ceilings, kitchenettes, and dining-sitting areas. Pros: Free parking, clean and spacious rooms, the staff remembers your name. Cons: Bland decor, small pool, no staff after 6 PM. ✉ *625 South St.* ☎ *305/296–2829 or 877/879–2362* 🌐 *www.oceanbreezeinn.com* ➪ *15* ♨ *In-room: kitchen (some). In-hotel: pool, no elevator, no-smoking rooms* ▭ *D, DC, MC, V.*

VACATION RENTALS

The Key West Innkeepers Association is an umbrella organization for dozens of local properties. Vacation Rentals Key West lists historic cottages, homes, and condominiums for rent. Key West Welcome Center gets a lot of walk-in business because of its location on U.S. 1 at the entrance to Key West. Rent Key West Vacations specializes in renting vacation homes and condos for a week or longer. Vacation Key West lists all kinds of properties throughout Key West.

Key West Innkeepers Association (✉ *Key West* ☎ *800/492–1911* 🌐 *www.keywestinns.com*). **Vacation Rentals Key West** (✉ *1511 Truman Ave., Key West* ☎ *305/292–7997 or 800/621–9405* 📠 *305/294–7501* 🌐 *www.keywestvacations.com*). **Key West Welcome Center** (✉ *24746 Overseas Hwy., Summerland Key* ☎ *305/296–4444 or 800/284–4482* 🌐 *www.keywestwelcomecenter.com*). **Rent Key West Vacations** (✉ *1107 Truman Ave., Key West* ☎ *305/294–0990 or 800/833–7368* 🌐 *www.rentkeywest.com*). **Vacation Key West** (✉ *100 Grinnell St., Key West* ☎ *305/295–9500 or 800/595–5397* 🌐 *www.vacationkw.com*).

NIGHTLIFE & THE ARTS

NIGHTLIFE

Rest up: Much of what happens in Key West does so after dark. Open your mind and have a stroll. Scruffy street performers strum next to dogs in sunglasses. Characters wearing parrots or iguanas try to sell you your photo with their pet. Brawls tumble out the doors of Sloppy Joe's. Drag queens strut across stages in Joan Rivers garb. Tattooed men lick whipped cream off of women's body parts. And margaritas flow like a Jimmy Buffett tune.

BEST OF THE BARS. Southernmost Scavenger Hunt's "Best of the Bars" challenge has teams of two to five touring the bars of Key West for clues, libations, and prizes. It hosts the event at 7 PM most Fridays, Saturdays, and Sundays, starting at Sloppy Joe's. The cost is $20 to $35 per person. For information, call ☎305/292–9994 or visit 🌐www.keywesthunt.com.

BARS & LOUNGES

No matter your mood, **Durty Harry's** (✉*208 Duval St.* ☎*305/296–4890*) can fill the bill. The mega-size entertainment complex has live music in a variety of indoor-outdoor bars including Rick's Dance Club Wine & Martini Bar and the tiny Red Garter strip club.

Belly up to the bar for a cold mug of the signature Hog's Breath Lager at the infamous **Hog's Breath Saloon** (✉*400 Front St.* ☎*305/296–4222* 🌐*www.hogsbreath.com*), a must-stop on the Key West bar crawl. Live bands play daily 1 PM–2 AM.

Capt. Tony's Saloon (✉*428 Greene St.* ☎*305/294–1838*) was the original Sloppy Joe's in the mid-1930s, when Hemingway was a regular. Later, a young Jimmy Buffett sang here and made this watering hole famous in his song "Last Mango in Paris." Bands play nightly.

Ride the mechanical bucking bull, listen to live bands croon cry-in-your-beer tunes, and grab some pretty decent chow at the indoor-outdoor spread known as **Cowboy Bill's Honky Tonk Saloon** (✉*610-1/2 Duval St.* ☎*305/295–8219* 🌐*www.cowboybillskw.com*) Wednesday brings—we kid you not—Sexy Bikini Bull Riding.

Pause for a libation at the open-air **Green Parrot Bar** (✉*601 Whitehead St., at Southard St.* ☎*305/294–6133*). Built in 1890, the bar is said to be Key West's oldest. The sometimes-rowdy saloon has locals outnumbering out-of-towners, especially on weekends when bands play.

A youngish, touristy crowd, sprinkled with aging Parrot Heads, frequents **Margaritaville Café** (✉*500 Duval St.* ☎*305/292–1435*), owned by former Key West resident and recording star Jimmy Buffett, who has been known to perform here. The drink of choice is, of course, a margarita. There's live music nightly, as well as lunch and dinner.

Nightlife at the **Pier House** (✉*1 Duval St.* ☎*305/296–4600 or 800/723–2791*) begins with a steel-drum band to celebrate the sunset on the beach, then moves indoors to the piano bar for live jazz.

The **Schooner Wharf Bar** (✉ *202 William St.* ☎ *305/292–3302*), an open-air waterfront bar and grill in the historic seaport district, retains its funky Key West charm. Its margarita ranks among Key West's best.

There's more history and good times at **Sloppy Joe's** (✉ *201 Duval St.* ☎ *305/294–5717*), the successor to a famous 1937 speakeasy named for its founder, Captain Joe Russell. Decorated with Hemingway memorabilia and marine flags, the bar is popular with travelers and is full and noisy all the time. A Sloppy Joe's T-shirt is a de rigueur Key West souvenir, and the gift shop sells them like crazy.

The **Top Lounge** (✉ *430 Duval St.* ☎ *305/296–2991*) is on the 7th floor of the La Concha Crowne Plaza and is one of the best places in town to view the sunset and enjoy live entertainment.

Love karaoke? Get it out of your system at **Two Friends Patio Lounge**(✉ *512 Front St.* ☎ *305/296–3124* 🌐 *www.twofriendskeywest.com*), the self-proclaimed "Key West King of Karoake." The singing starts nightly at 8 PM.

In the best traditions of a 1950s cocktail lounge, **Virgilio's** (✉ *524 Duval St.* ☎ *305/296–8118*) serves chilled martinis to the soothing tempo of live jazz and blues nightly.

GAY & LESBIAN BARS

Key West's largest gay bar, **Aqua** (✉ *711 Duval St.* ☎ *305/294–0555)* hosts drag shows, karaoke contests, and live entertainment at three bars, including one outside on the patio.

Pick your entertainment at the **Bourbon Street Complex** (✉ *722–801 Duval St.* ☎ *305/296–1992*), a club within an all-male guesthouse. There are two nightly drag shows in the 801 Bourbon Bar and 10 video screens along with dancers grooving to the latest music spun by DJs at the Bourbon Street Pub.

Part of a men's resort, **Island House Café + Bar** (✉ *Island House, 1129 Fleming St.* ☎ *305/294–6284 or 800/890–6284)* serves frozen and other cocktails along with creative cuisine in tropical gardens with a pool where clothing is optional.

CLOSE UP

Margarita Madness

Mojitos, martinis, and caipirinhas may be the popular drinks in Miami's South Beach, but in Key West the margarita Jimmy Buffett crooned about is still alive and well.

Every bar and club serves them, either the version classic or in dozens of variations. Every bartender claims to make the best. Here are some that rank tops in their category.

At the **Half Shell Raw Bar,** the Raw Bar Rita, made with 1800 Reposado Tequila, has a funky green glow. The Pama Rita, which the menu claims is "for the health nut," is much prettier, dyed and flavored with a splash of red Pama liqueur and fueled with Herradura Silver. It scores best in the novelty category.

Although **El Meson de Pepe** brags about its mojitos, its Gold Margarita, made with El Jimador Reposado, is no slouch. It goes especially well with a basket of Cuban bread served with addictive red and green dipping sauces. It rates tops for its ability to play well with food.

At Bagatelle's **Toucan Bar,** the Patron's Margarita, named for its brand of top-shelf tequila, gets points for being smooth, almost creamy. It's the perfect balance of tart and sweet. The view of Duval Street adds to the enjoyment.

At **Mangoes,** the Mangorita is naturally the signature drink. Very tropical, but made with Cuervo and Marie Brizard, it ranks in the "tourist drink" category.

The Cabo Rita at **Conch Republic Seafood Company** is named for a type of tequila called Cabo Wabo Reposado (say that three times after sampling a few). It gets bolstered with triple sec, but isn't too sweet. This is a strong contender in the classic category.

At Jimmy Buffett's **Margaritaville** one would expect high competition. Buffett on the stereo makes a margarita go down just right, with or without a shaker of salt. The Herradura Silver tequila is a good start, but the dash of Cointreau makes the Uptown Margarita heavy on the sweet.

Schooner Wharf's Schoonerita takes top rating in the classic class. The bartender shakes the cocktail and squeezes in a healthy dose of real lime juice at the end. Made with Sauza tequila, it comes served in a proper glass birdbath-shape vessel, although this one has a stem in the shape of a cactus. (South-of-the-border kitsch and margaritas go well together.)

LaTeDa Hotel and Bar (✉*1125 Duval St.* ☎*305/296–6706 or 877/528–3520*) hosts female impersonators (catch Christopher Peterson when he's on stage) and riotously funny cabaret shows nightly in the Crystal Room Cabaret Lounge. Gays and non-gays both enjoy the shows. There's also live entertainment nightly, including the popular local singer Lenore Troia, in the Terrace Garden Bar and smooth piano jazz and pricey martinis in the ultracool lounge bar.

Pearl's Patio (✉*Pearl's Rainbow, 525 United St. between Duval and Simonton Sts.* ☎*305/293–9805 ext. 156 or 800/749–6696*) is Key West's only all-female bar. It features a full range of drinks, a menu of light dishes, and weekly women's movies.

THE ARTS

Catch the classics and the latest art, independent, and foreign films shown daily by the **Key West Film Society** (✉*416 Eaton St.* ☎*305/295–9493*) in the two-screen Tropic Cinema theater.

Sebrina Alfonso directs the **Key West Symphony** (✉*Tennessee Williams Fine Arts Center, 5901 College Rd.* ☎*305/292–1774*) during the winter season.

With more than 20 years' experience, the **Red Barn Theatre** (✉*319 Duval St.* ☎*305/296–9911 or 866/870–9911*), a small professional theater, performs dramas, comedies, and musicals, including works by new playwrights.

On Stock Island, the **Tennessee Williams Fine Arts Center** (✉*Florida Keys Community College, 5901 College Rd.* ☎*305/296–1520*) presents chamber music, dance, jazz concerts, and dramatic and musical plays with major stars, as well as other performing arts events.

Home to the Key West Players, the community-run **Waterfront Playhouse** (✉*Mallory Sq.* ☎*305/294–5015*) is a mid-1850s wrecker's warehouse that was converted into a 180-seat regional theater presenting comedy and drama from December to June. It claims to be Florida's longest continuously running theater company.

SCULPTURE KEY WEST. **Key West bursts with art, especially every year between January and April when artists unveil their latest works at two exhibitions in Fort Zachary Taylor State Park and West Martello Tower. More than 30 artists from around the**

country are selected to bring their contemporary sculpture for outdoor exhibitions. In years past, sculptures have ranged from a dinosaur surfacing in a pond and a giant Key West chicken to heads floating in the water and abstract formations suggesting sea and seaside vegetation.

SPORTS & THE OUTDOORS

Unlike the rest of the region, Key West isn't known for outdoor pursuits. But everyone should devote at least half a day to relaxing on a boat tour, heading out on a fishing expedition, or pursuing some other adventure at sea. The ultimate excursion is a boat or seaplane trip to Dry Tortugas National Park for snorkeling and exploring Fort Jefferson. Other excursions cater to nature-lovers, scuba divers and snorkelers, and folks who would just like to get out in the water and enjoy the scenery and sunset. For those who prefer their recreation land-based, biking is the way to go. Hiking is limited, but walking the streets of Old Town provides plenty of exercise.

5

BIKING

Key West was practically made for bicycles, but don't let that lull you into a false sense of security. Narrow and one-way streets along with car traffic result in several bike accidents a year. Some hotels rent or lend bikes to guests; others will refer you to a nearby shop and reserve a bike for you. Rentals usually start at about $12 a day, but some places also rent by the half-day. ■TIP→ **Lock up; bikes—and porch chairs!—are favorite targets for local thieves.**

Eaton Bikes (✉*830 Eaton St.* ☎*305/294–8188*) ⊕*www.eatonbikes.com* has tandem, three-wheel, and children's bikes in addition to the standard beach cruisers ($18 for first day) and seven-speed cruisers ($20). It delivers free to all Key West rentals. **Keys Moped & Scooter** (✉*523 Truman Ave.* ☎*305/294–0399*) rents beach cruisers with large baskets for $10 a day. Rates for scooters start at $30. Look for the huge American flag on the roof. **Moped Hospital** (✉*601 Truman Ave.* ☎*305/296–3344 or 866/296–1625* ⊕*www.mopedhospital.com*) supplies balloon-tire bikes with yellow safety baskets for adults and kids ($12 per day), as well as mopeds ($40) and double-seater scooters ($65).**Paradise Scooter Rentals** (✉*112 Fitzpatrick St.* ☎*305/923–6063* *www.paradisescooterrentals.com*) rents bikes $12 a day and scooters for $60 to $85 a day.

BOATING

Key West is surrounded by marinas, so it's easy to find what you're looking for, whether it's sailing with dolphins or paddling in the mangroves.

At **Key West Eco-Tours** (*Historic Seaport* *305/294–7245* *www.ecokeywest.com*), the sail-kayak-snorkel excursions take you into backcountry flats and mangrove forests. The 4½-hour trip costs $90 per person and includes lunch. Three-hour kayak-only tours costs $75 per single kayak, $120 per double and includes snacks. Sunset sails and private charters are also available. **The Schooner Liberty** (*Schooner Wharf at the Historic Seaport* *305/292–0332* *www.libertyfleet.com*) makes a dramatic statement as it passes Mallory Square. In addition to the very popular sunset cruises ($57), the 80-foot tall ship also does two-hour morning and afternoon sails ($35). Even more eye-catching, the 125-foot multi-masted **Liberty Clipper** hosts dinner and music excursions on Tuesday, Thursday, and Sunday. Cost is $79 for 2½ hours; two-hour sunset voyages with drinks and appetizers only are offered Wednesday, Friday, and Saturday for $65. **Sunset Culinaire Tours** (*5555* College Rd. *305/296–0982* *www.sunsetculinaire.com*) serves a full menu of gourmet meals with fine wine and beer aboard a sleek cruising yacht every evening at sunset. The cost is $75 per person.

FISHING

Any number of local fishing guides can take you to where the big ones are biting, either in the backcountry for snapper and snook or to the deep water for the marlins and shark that brought Hemingway here in the first place.

FISH GUIDE. Chambers of commerce, marinas, and dive shops offer free Teall's Guides (*Box 522409, Marathon Shores* *305/872–3123*) with land and nautical charts pinpointing popular fishing and diving areas throughout the Keys.

Key West Fishing Pro Guides (*866/259–4205* *www.keywestproguides.com*) has several different trips, including flats and backcountry fishing ($400 for a half day) and reef and offshore fishing ($600 for half day). **Key West Bait and**

Tackle (✉241 *Margaret St.* ☎305/292–1961 🌐*www.keywestbaitandtackle.com*) carries live bait, frozen bait, and fishing equipment. It also has the Live Bait Lounge, where you can sip ice-cold beer while telling fish tales.

GOLF

Not in the least a golfing destination, Key West does have one course on Stock Island. Make your tee times early in season.

Key West Resort Golf Course (✉*6450 E. College Rd.* ☎*305/294–5232*) is an 18-hole, par 70 course on the bay side of Stock Island. Greens fees are $165.

KAYAKING

Lazy Dog Kayak Guides (✉*5114 Overseas Hwy., Key West* ☎*305/295–9898* 🌐*www.lazydog.com*)runs four-hour guided sea-kayak-snorkel tours around the mangrove islands just east of Key West. The $60 charge covers transportation, bottled water, a snack, and supplies, including snorkeling gear. A $35 two-hour guided kayak tours is also available.

SCUBA DIVING & SNORKELING

The Florida Keys National Marine Sanctuary extends along Key West and beyond to the Dry Tortugas. Key West National Wildlife Refuge further protects the pristine waters. Most divers don't make it this far out in the Keys, but if you're looking for a day of diving as a break from the nonstop party in Old Town, expect to pay about $45 and upward for a two-tank dive. Serious divers can book dive trips to the Dry Tortugas.

Captain's Corner (✉*Corner of Greene and Elizabeth* ☎*305/296–8865* 🌐*www.captainscorner.com*), a PADI-certified dive shop, has classes in several languages and twice-daily snorkel and dive trips ($40–$45) to reefs and wrecks aboard the 60-foot dive boat *Sea Eagle*. Equipment rental is extra.Safely dive the coral reefs without getting a scuba certification with **Snuba of Key West** (✉*Garrison Bight Marina, Palm Ave. between Eaton St. and N. Roosevelt Blvd.* ☎*305/292–4616* 🌐*www.snubakeywest.com*). Ride out to the reef on a catamaran, then follow your guide underwater for a one-hour tour of the coral reefs. You wear a regulator with a breathing hose that is attached to a floating air tank on the surface. No prior diving or snorkeling experience is necessary, but you must know how to swim. The $99 price includes beverages.

SHOPPING

On these streets you'll find colorful local art of widely varying quality, key limes made into everything imaginable, and the raunchiest T-shirts in the civilized world. Browsing the boutiques—with frequent pub stops along the way—makes for an entertaining stroll down Duval Street. Cocktails certainly help the appreciation of some goods, such as the figurine of a naked man blowing bubbles out his backside or the swashbuckling pirate costumes that are not just for Halloween anymore.

Where to start? **Bahama Village** is an enclave of spruced-up shops, restaurants, and vendors leading the way in the restoration of the historic district where black Bahamians settled in the 19th century. The village lies roughly between Whitehead and Fort streets and Angela and Catherine streets. Hemingway frequented the bars, restaurants, and boxing rings in this part of town.

ARTS & CRAFTS

Key West is filled with art galleries, and the variety is truly amazing. Much is locally produced by the town's large artist community, but many galleries carry international artists from as close as Haiti and as far away as France. Local artists do a great job of preserving the island's architecture and spirit.

At **Alan S. Maltz Gallery**(✉ *1210 Duval St.* ☎ *305/294–0005)*, the owner captures the state's nature and character in stunning portraits.

Art@830 (✉ *830 Caroline St., Historic Seaport* ☎ *305/295–9595* 🌐 *www.art830.com)* carries a little bit of everything, from pottery to paintings. Most outstanding is its selection of glass art, particularly the jellyfish lamps.

Cuba, Cuba! (✉ *814 Duval St.* ☎ *305/295–9442*) stocks paintings, sculptures, and photos by Cuban artists.

The **Gallery on Greene** (✉ *606 Greene St.* ☎ *305/294–1669*) showcases politically incorrect art by Jeff MacNelly and three-dimensional paintings by Mario Sanchez. This is the largest gallery exhibition space in Key West.

The oldest private art gallery in Key West, **Gingerbread Square Gallery** (✉*1207 Duval St.* ☎*305/296–8900*), represents local and internationally acclaimed artists, including Sal Salinero and John Kiraly, in media ranging from graphics to art glass.

Haitian art connoisseurs will love the bright colors in the paintings, the bead-and-sequin work in the handicrafts, and fine metal sculptures at the **Haitian Art Company** (✉*600 Frances St.* ☎*305/296–8932*).

Historian, photographer, and painter Sharon Wells opened **KW Light Gallery** (✉*1203 Duval St.* ☎*305/294–0566*) to showcase her own fine art photography and paintings, as well as the works of other national artists. You can find historic photos here as well.

Lucky Street Gallery (✉*1130 Duval St.* ☎*305/294–3973*) sells high-end contemporary paintings. There are also a few pieces of jewelry by internationally recognized Key West–based artists. Changing exhibits, artist receptions, and special events make this a lively venue.

Pelican Poop (✉*314 Simonton St.* ☎*305/296–3887*) sells Caribbean art in a tropical courtyard garden. The owners buy directly from Caribbean artisans every year, so the prices are very attractive.

Potters Charles Pearson and Timothy Roeder can be found at **Whitehead St. Pottery** (✉*322 Julia St.* ☎*305/294–5067*), where they display their porcelain stoneware and raku-fired vessels. The setting, around two koi ponds with a burbling fountain, is as sublime as the art.

Glass Reunion (✉*825 Duval St.* ☎*305/294–1720*) showcases a collection of wild and impressive fine art glass. It's worth a stop in just to see the imaginative and over-the-top glass chandeliers, jewelry, dishes, and platters.

BOOKS

The **Key West Island Bookstore** (✉*513 Fleming St.* ☎*305/294–2904*) is a home-away-from-home for the large Key West writers' community. It carries new, used, and rare titles. It specializes in Hemingway, Tennessee Williams, and South Florida mystery writers.

CIGARS

Cigars, once Key West's major industry, survives in small shops throughout Old Town. In many places such as **Conch Republic Cigar Factory** (✉*512 Greene St.* ☎*305/295–9036 or 800/317–2167* 🌐*www.conch-cigars.com*) a cigar-roller is at work to demonstrate hand-rolling techniques. The shop sells a variety of flavored and unflavored varieties.

CLOTHING & FABRICS

Take home a shopping bag full of scarlet hibiscus, fuchsia heliconias, blue parrot fish, and even pink flamingos from the **Seam Shoppe** (✉*1114 Truman Ave.* ☎*305/296–9830*), which has in the city's widest selection of tropical fabrics.

Since 1964, **Key West Hand Print Fabrics** (✉*201 Simonton St.* ☎*305/294–9535 or 800/866–0333*) has vibrant tropical fabrics and resort wear for men and women. It's in Curry Warehouse, a brick building erected in 1878 to store tobacco.

A pair of **Kino Sandals** (✉*107 Fitzpatrick St.* ☎*305/294–5044* 🌐*www.kinosandalfactory.com* ⊙*Closed Sun. in off-season*) was once a public declaration that you'd been to Key West. The attraction? You can watch these inexpensive items being made. The factory has been churning out several styles since 1966. Walk up to the counter, grab a pair, try them on, and lay down some cash. It's that simple.

The surf is definitely not up in Key West, but the surfer attitude is. **Shirley Can't Surf** (✉*624 Duval St.* ☎*305/292–1009*) is crammed with surf wear, including its own brand T-shirts proclaiming this the southernmost surf shop since 1965. It also stocks skateboarding equipment.

Get beach ready with colorful towels from **Towels of Key West** (✉*806 Duval St.* ☎*305/292–1120 or 800/927–0316*). There are more than 45 towel unique designs, some you'd expect, others more whimsical. All are hand-sewn on the island.

Don't leave town without a browse through the legendary **Fairvilla Megastore** (✉*520 Front St.* ☎*305/292–0448*), where you'll find an astonishing array of fantasy wear, outlandish costumes (check out the pirate section), and other "interesting" souvenirs.

FOOD & DRINK

The **Blond Giraffe** (*✉802 Duval St. ☎305/293–7874 ✉614 Front St. ☎305/296–2020 ✉1209 Truman Ave. ☎305/295–6776 ✉107 Simonton St. ☎305/296–9174*) turned an old family recipe for key lime pie into one of the island's success stories. You'll often encounter a line out the door waiting for a pie with delicate pastry, sweet-tart custard filling, and thick meringue topping. The key lime rum cake is the best-selling product for shipping home. For a snack on the run, try the pie on a stick.

You'll be pleasantly surprised with the fruit wines sold at the **Key West Winery** (*✉103 Simonton St. ☎305/292–1717 or 866/880–1717*). Display crates hold bottles of wines made from blueberries, blackberries, pineapples, cherries, mangoes, watermelons, tomatoes, and, of course, key limes. Stop in for a free tasting.

Fausto's Food Palace (*✉522 Fleming St. ☎305/296–5663 ✉1105 White St. ☎305/294–5221*) is a market in the traditional town-square sense. Since 1926, Fausto's has been the spot to catch up on the week's gossip and to chill out in summer—it has groceries, organic foods, marvelous wines, a sushi chef on duty from 8 to 6, and box lunches to go.

If you like it hot, you'll love **Peppers of Key West** (*✉602 Greene St. ☎305/295–9333 or 800/597–2823 ⊕www.peppersofkeywest.com*). The shop has hundreds of sauces, salsas, and sweets guaranteed to light your fire.

You'll spend your first five minutes at the family-owned **Waterfront Market** (*✉201 William St. ☎305/296–0778*) wondering how to open a franchise in your hometown. The upscale market sells items from around the world, including health food, organic produce, fresh salads, gourmet coffees, imported cheeses, baked goods, and more. Don't miss the fish market, arguably the best in town; there's also a juice bar, sushi, and vegan dishes.

GIFTS & SOUVENIRS

Like a parody of Duval Street T-shirt shops, the hole-in-the-wall **Art Attack** (*✉606 Duval St. ☎305/294–7131*) throws in every icon and trinket anyone nostalgic for the days of peace and love might fancy: beads, necklaces, harmony bells, and psychedelic T-shirts. Best sellers are photographic postcards of Key West by Tony Gregory. It's open until 11 nightly.

Part museum, part shopping center, **Cayo Hueso y Habana** (✉*410 Wall St., Mallory Sq.* ☎*305/293–7260* 🌐*www.historictours.com/keywest/cayoh.htm*) occupies a circa-1879 warehouse with a hand-rolled cigar shop, one-of-a-kind souvenirs, a Cuban restaurant, and exhibits that tell of the island's Cuban heritage. Outside a memorial garden pays homage to the island's Cuban ancestors.

Fast Buck Freddie's (✉*500 Duval St.* ☎*305/294–2007*) sells a classy, hip selection of gifts, including every flamingo item imaginable. It also carries such imaginative items as a noise-activated rat in a trap and a raccoon tail in a bag.

Half Buck Freddie's (✉*920 Caroline St.* ☎*305/294–2007*) is the discount-outlet store for Fast Buck's.

★ For that unique (but slightly overpriced) souvenir of your trip to Key West head to **Montage** (✉*512 Duval St.* ☎*305/395–9101 or 877/396–4278*), where you'll discover hundreds of handcrafted signs of popular Key West guesthouses, inns, hotels, restaurants, bars, and streets. If you can't find what you're looking for, they'll make it for you.

HEALTH & BEAUTY

Key West Aloe (✉*540 Greene St., at Simonton St.* ☎*305/293–1885 or 800/445–2563*) was founded in a garage in 1971. Today it produces some 300 perfume, sunscreen, and skin-care products for men and women.

EXCURSION TO DRY TORTUGAS NATIONAL PARK

70 mi southwest of Key West.

Dry Tortugas National Park covers 64,657 acres, of which only 40 acres (on seven small islands) are dry. And they're *very* dry. Lack of freshwater earned the island group part of its name back in the days of the Spanish conquistadores. The other part of the name referred to the abundance of sea turtles that then—and still today to a lesser degree—populate its waters. Diving and snorkeling these waters rate high in the logbooks of bottom-timers from around the planet.

The typical visitor from Key West, however, makes it no farther than the waters of Garden Key. Home to 19th-century Fort Jefferson, it is the destination for seaplane and fast ferry tours out of Key West. With 2½ to 4½ hours to spend on the island, visitors have time to tour the mammoth fort-come-prison and then cool off with mask and snorkel along the fort's moat wall.

History buffs might remember long-deactivated Fort Jefferson, the largest brick building in the western hemisphere, as the prison that held Dr. Samuel Mudd, who unwittingly set John Wilkes Booth's leg after the assassination of Abraham Lincoln. Three other men were also held there for complicity in the assassination. Original construction on the fort began in 1846 and continued for 30 years, but was never completed because the invention of the rifled cannon made it obsolete. That's when it became a Civil War prison and later a wildlife refuge. In 1935, President Franklin Roosevelt declared it a national monument due to its historic and natural value.

The brick fort acts as a gigantic almost 16-acre reef. Around its moat walls, coral grows and schools of snapper, grouper, and wrasses hang out. To reach the offshore coral heads requires about 15 minutes of swimming over sea grass beds. The reef formations blaze with the color and majesty of brain coral, swaying sea fans, and flitting tropical fish. It takes a bit of energy to swim the distance, but the water depth pretty much measures under 7 feet all the way, allowing for sandy spots to stop and rest. (Standing in sea grass meadows and on coral is detrimental to marine life.)

Serious snorkelers and divers head out farther offshore to epic formations, including Palmata Patch, one of the few surviving concentrations of elkhorn coral in the Keys. Day-trippers congregate on the sandy beach to relax in the sun and enjoy picnics. Overnight tent campers have use of restroom facilities and achieve a total getaway from noise, lights, and civilization in general. Remember that no matter how you get here, the park's $5 admission fee must be paid in cash.

The park has set up with signage a self-guided tour that takes about 45 minutes. Budget more time if you're into photography, because the scenic shots are hard to pass up. Ranger-guided tours are also available at certain times. Check in at the visitor center for a schedule. The small office also shows an orientation video, sells books and other educational materials, and, most importantly, provides a blast of air-conditioning on hot days.

Birders in the know bring binoculars to watch some 100,000 nesting sooty terns at their only U.S. nesting site, Bush Key, adjacent to Garden Key. Noddy terns also nest in the spring. During winter migrations, birds fill the airspace so thickly it appears they're falling from the sky, birders say. More than 300 species have been spotted in the park's seven islands, including frigatebirds, boobies, cormorants, and white-tailed tropic birds. Bush Key is closed to foot traffic during nesting season, January through September. *Box 6208, Key West 305/242–7700 www.nps.gov/drto.*

The underwater sightseeing commences long before you get wet on **Seaplanes of Key West.** The 45-minute trip to the Dry Tortugas skims above the trademark windowpane-clear waters of the Florida Keys. The seaplane perspective provides an awesome experience that could result in a stiff neck from craning to look out the window and down from 500 feet above. In the Flats that edge Key West, you can spot stingrays, sea turtles, and sharks in the shallow water. In the area dubbed The Quicksands, water plunges to 30-foot depths and sand undulates in dune-like formations. Shipwrecks also festoon these waters; here's where Mel Fisher harvested treasure from the Atocha and Margarita. His 70-foot work ship, the Arbutus, deteriorated and eventually sank at the northern edge of the treasure sites. With its mast poking out above water, it's easy to spot and fun to photograph. From there, the water deepens from emerald hues to shades of deep blue as depths reach 70 feet. Seaplanes of Key West's most popular trip is the half-day option, where you spend about 2½ on Garden Key. The seaplanes leave during your stay, so be prepared to carry all of your possessions with you. The half-day tour costs $229 per person. The morning trip beats the ferries to the island, so you'll have it to yourself until the others arrive. Snorkeling equipment, soft drinks, and birding lists are supplied. *Key West International Airport, 3471 S. Roosevelt Blvd., Key West 305/294–0709 or 800/950–2359 www.seaplanesofkeywest.com.*

DID YOU KNOW? **The Dry Tortugas lies in the Central Time Zone. Seaplanes of Key West pilots like to tell their passengers that they land 15 minutes before they take off.**

If you want to save some money or have a fear of small planes, consider the fast catamaran **Yankee Freedom II**. The ferry to Dry Tortugas National Park takes 2¼ hours each way. The time passes quickly on the uncramped vessel (it holds 250 passengers, but limits its trip to 100). It's equipped with three restrooms, two freshwater showers, and two bars (open on return trip only). Stretch out on two decks: one an air-conditioned salon with cushioned seating, the other an open sundeck with sunny and shaded seating. You can also spot the same creatures and wrecks visible from the seaplane tour, albeit with a less impressive view. Continental breakfast and lunch are included. On arrival to Garden Key, a naturalist leads a 40-minute guided tour, followed by lunch and a free afternoon for swimming, snorkeling, and exploring. The tour allows you approximately 4½ on Garden Key and generally gets you back to Key West by 5:30, in time for Sunset Celebration. The vessel is ADA-certified for visitors using wheelchairs. ✉*Lands End Marina, 240 Margaret St., Key West* ☎*305/294–7009 or 800/634–0939* 🌐*www.yankeefreedom.com* 🎟*$149* ⏲*Trips daily at 8 AM.*

Smaller and more economical, **Sunny Days Fast Cat** follows pretty much the same schedule as the ferry and includes the same perks, but promises a more stable and slightly speedier ride aboard its sleek, lighter catamaran. Guests can roam the air-conditioned cabin and rear sundeck and can use a freshwater shower once back on board. Camping transportation rates are about $30 higher per person. ✉*Historic Key West Seaport, Greene and Elizabeth Streets, Key West* ☎*305/292–6100 or 800/236–7937* 🌐*www.drytortugasferry.com* 🎟*$120* ⏲*Trips daily at 8 AM.*

WHERE TO STAY

⛺ **Dry Tortugas National Park.** A cluster of trees and a foundation of sand define the park's small camping area. The grounds aren't very private during the day, but after the seaplanes and ferries leave, it doesn't get more peaceful anywhere on this earth. Its eight sites each accommodate six people and three tents. Costing $3 per person per night, they are available on a first-come, first-served basis. There's also a group site available to for up to 40 people (15 tents) with advance reservations. Note that there's no water available and campers must carry off whatever they bring onto the island. No open fires are allowed, only camp stoves and charcoal briquettes used in the grills. Pack your food carefully to keep it safe from the island's controlled rat population. Restrooms are locked from 10 to 3, but campers are allowed to use facilities aboard the ferries. *Picnic tables, grills, swimming (ocean)* *8 tent sites* *Dry*

Tortugas National Park, Garden Key, Box 6208, Key West ☎305/664–4815 or 305/242–7700 (group site reservations) 🌐www.nps.gov/drto 💰$3.

KEY WEST ESSENTIALS

For information on transportation, as well as contacts and resources to help you plan your trip to Key West, see ⇨ Florida Keys Essentials.

To Whom It May Concern: research prices, get advice from other travelers, and book travel arrangements, visit www.fodors.com

TOUR OPTIONS

AIR TOURS

Island Aeroplane Tours flies up to two passengers in a 1941 Waco, an open-cockpit biplane; tours range from an eight-minute overview of Key West ($90 for two) to a 45-minute reef and wreck excursion ($295 for two).

Seaplanes of Key West has half- and full-day trips to the Dry Tortugas, where you can explore Fort Jefferson, built in 1846, and snorkel on the beautiful protected reef. Soft drinks and snorkel equipment are included in the $229 half-day, $405 full-day per-person fee, plus a $5 park fee.

Contacts **Island Aeroplane Tours** (✉*Key West Airport, 3469 S. Roosevelt Blvd.* ☎*305/294–8687* 🌐*www.keywestairtours.com*). **Seaplanes of Key West** (✉*Key West Airport, 3471 S. Roosevelt Blvd.* ☎*305/294–0709 or 800/950–2359* 🌐*www.seaplanesofkeywest.com*).

BICYCLE TOURS

Lloyd's Original Tropical Bike Tour, led by a 30-year Key West veteran, explores the natural, noncommercial side of Key West at a leisurely pace, stopping on backstreets and in backyards of private homes to sample native fruits and view indigenous plants and trees; at City Cemetery; and at the Medicine Garden, a private meditation garden. The behind-the-scenes tours run two hours and cost $35, including bike rental.

Contacts **Lloyd's Original Tropical Bike Tour** (✉*Truman Ave. and Simonton St., Key West* ☎*305/304–4700* 🌐*www.lloydstropicalbiketour.com*).

BOAT TOURS

Victoria Impallomeni, a 34-year wilderness guide and marine scientist, invites nature lovers—and especially children—aboard the *Imp II*, a 25-foot Aquasport, for four-hour ($500) and seven-hour ($700) Dancing Dolphin Spirit Charters ecotours that frequently include encounters with wild dolphins. While island-hopping, you visit underwater gardens, natural shoreline, and mangrove habitats. For her Dolphin Day for Humans tour, she pulls you through the water, equipped with mask and snorkel, on a specially designed "dolphin water massage board." Sometimes dolphins follow the boat and swim among participants. Tours also include Sacred Sound Healing Retreats, a self-transformational retreat useing vibrations, and sounds. All equipment is supplied. Tours leave from Murray's Marina.

M/V *Discovery*'s glass-bottom boats have submerged viewing rooms for 360-degree marine watching ($40).

For something with more of an adrenaline boost, book with White Knuckle Thrill Boat Ride. The speed boat holds up to 12 people for doing 360s, fishtails, and other on the water stunts in the gulf. Cost is $59 each.

Contacts **Dancing Dolphin Spirit Charters** (✉ *MM 5 OS at Murray's Marina, 5710 U.S. 1, Key West* ☎ *305/304–7562 or 888/822–7366* 🌐 *www.captainvictoria.com*). **Murray's Marina** (✉ *5710 U.S. Hwy. 1, MM 5, Key West* ☎ *305/296–0364* 🌐 *www.murraymarine.com*). **M/V** *Discovery* (✉ *Land's End Marina, 251 Margaret St., Key West* ☎ *305/293–0099 or 800/262–0099* 🌐 *www.discoveryunderseatours.com*).**White Knuckle Thrill Boat Ride** (✉ *Hurricane Hole Marina 5130 Overseas Hwy., Key West* ☎ *305/797–0459* 🌐 *www.whiteknucklethrillboatride.com*).

BUS TOURS

The Conch Tour Train is a 90-minute narrated tour of Key West, traveling 14 mi through Old Town and around the island. Board at Mallory Square or Angela Street and Duval Street depot every half-hour (9–4:35 from Mallory Square). The cost is $27 (go online for discounted tickets).

Old Town Trolley operates trolley-style buses, departing from the Mallory Square and Roosevelt Boulevard depots every 30 minutes (9–4:30 from Mallory Square, later at other stops), for 90-minute narrated tours of Key West. The smaller trolleys go places the larger Conch Tour Train won't fit. You may disembark at any of 10 stops and reboard a later trolley. The cost is $27, but you can save a little by booking online.

Key West Business Guild's 75-minute Gay & Lesbian Historic Trolley Tours highlight the contributions gay and lesbian writers, artists, politicians, designers, and celebrities have made to Key West's past. Tours, which cost $27, depart Saturday at 11 AM from 512 South Street. Look for the rainbow flags on the trolley.

Contacts **Conch Tour Train** (*Key West 305/294–5161 or 800/868–7482 www.conchtrain.com*).**Old Town Trolley** (*201 Front St.Key West 305/296–6688 or 800/868–7482 www.oldtowntrolley.com*). **Key West Business Guild** (*513 Truman Ave. Box 1208, Key West 305/294–4603 or 800/535–7797 www.gaykeywestfl.com*).

WALKING TOURS

In addition to publishing several good guides on Key West, the Historic Florida Keys Foundation conducts tours of the City Cemetery Tuesday and Thursday at 9:30.

As the former state historian in Key West and the current owner of a historic-preservation consulting firm, Sharon Wells of Island City Strolls knows plenty about Key West. She's authored many works, including the annually revised "Walking and Biking Guide to Historic Key West," which has 14 self-guided tours of the historic district. It's available at guesthouses, hotels, and Key West bookstores. If that whets your appetite, sign on for one of her walking or biking tours, including the Famous Writers and Artists of Key West and the Off-the-Beaten-Track Old Town tour, which cost $25, with a four-person minimum.

Key West's Ghosts & Legends offers nightly tours at 7 and 9 ($18), including a visit to the Old City Morgue, haunted Victorian mansions, and the Key West Cemetery to hear fascinating and sometimes bone-chilling stories of real-life events and people. *Tours meet at Duval and Caroline streets.* Reservations are required.

For a more spectacular spiritual experience, tag along with The Original Ghost Tours' 90-minute, lantern-led stroll around Old Town. It departs nightly from the Crowne Plaza La Concha Hotel at 430 Duval Street and costs $15.

For graden lovers, the Orchid Lady takes visitors to three hidden historic and exotic gardens daily in the morning and afternoon. The 90-minute tour costs $25.

Contacts **Historic Florida Keys Foundation** (✉ *510 Greene St., Old City Hall, Key West* ☎ *305/292-6718*). **Island City Strolls** (✉ *Box 56, Key West* ☎ *305/294-8380* 🌐 *www.seekeywest.com*). **Key West's Ghosts & Legends Haunted Tour** (✉ *Tours meet at Duval and Caroline streets* 📫 *Box 1807, Charleston, SC* ☎ *305/294-1713 or 866/622-4467* 🌐 *www.keywestghosts.com*). **The Orchid Lady** (✉ *410 Caroline St., Key West* ☎ *877/747-2718* 🌐 *www.eorchidlady.com*). **The Original Ghost Tours** (✉ *430 Duval St., Key West* ☎ *305/294-9255* 🌐 *www.hauntedtours.com*).

VISITOR INFORMATION

Contacts **Gay and Lesbian Community Center of Key West** (✉ *513 Truman Ave., Key West* ☎ *305/292-3223* 🌐 *www.glcckeywest.org*). **Greater Key West Chamber of Commerce** (✉ *402 Wall St., Key West* ☎ *305/294-2587 or 800/527-8539* 🌐 *www.keywestchamber.org*). **Key West Business Guild (gay)** (✉ *513 Truman Ave.* 📫 *Box 1208, Key West* ☎ *305/294-4603 or 800/535-7797* 🌐 *www.gaykeywestfl.com*). **Key West Welcome Center** (✉ *24746 Overseas Hwy., Summerland Key* ☎ *305/296-4444 or 800/284-4482* 🌐 *www.keywestwelcomecenter.com*).

Gateways to the Keys

6

WORD OF MOUTH

"When you're in South Beach, take a quick trip to Vizcaya, just south of Miami. It's an Italian Renaissance Villa and Gardens. Just beautiful. Built around 1912. Other options are Cuban food in Little Havana and the Venetian Pool in Coral Gables. South Beach has all the restaurants, bars, and clubs you could ever hope for."

–Cimbrone

www.fodors.com/forums

ALTHOUGH IT'S POSSIBLE TO FLY INTO KEY WEST, most people don't because of the expense and because of the limited number of flights. Further, if you are visiting the Upper or Middle Keys, there is a drive regardless of which airport you fly into. This means that most visitors flying into Florida to visit the Keys will pass through Miami. In many cases, people choose to stay a while to absorb some of the new luxe hotels, hot nightlife, and stylish restaurants, not to mention the expansive beaches, which the Keys do not have in abundance. Travelers on more of a budget may want to look a bit further afield to either Homestead or Florida City, both south of Miami, the two major gateways to both the Keys and the Everglades.

See ⇨ **Florida Keys Essentials** for information on flights and car-rentals in Miami.

ABOUT THE HOTELS

If you are looking for the hot spots, then you need look no farther than Miami's South Beach, which is awash with both new high-rises and restored Art Deco gems. The choices in Homestead and Florida City are more pedestrian but also more friendly to the wallet and the budget. And given the driving distance, if you arrive late in Miami, you may just want to sleep before getting an early start to drive down to the Keys, and in that case, a basic room may be just what the travel agent ordered.

WHAT IT COSTS

¢	$	$$	$$$	$$$$
RESTAURANTS				
under $10	$10–$20	$20–$30	$30–$40	over $40
HOTELS				
under $100	$100–$150	$150–$200	$200–$250	over $250

Restaurant prices are per person for a main course at dinner. Hotel prices are for a standard double room, excluding 6%–12% sales tax (depending on the county), 1%–4% tourist tax (in the Keys), and resort taxes (in both Miami and the Keys).

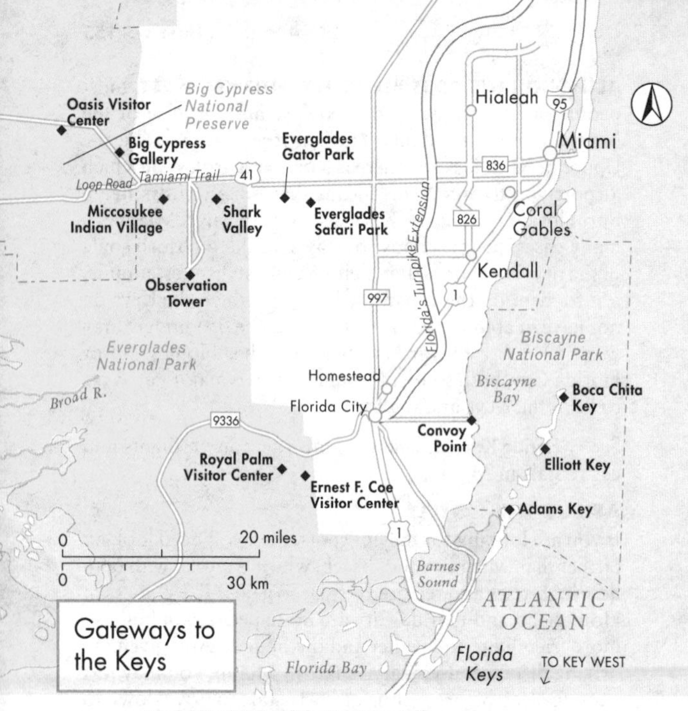

ABOUT THE RESTAURANTS

Miami has a vibrant dining scene, with prices to match, but you can still find reasonably priced local restaurants and chains, though fewer of those are in the trendy South Beach area. Most restaurants outside of Miami are small mom-and-pop establishments serving home-style food or local specialties such as alligator, fish, stone crab, frogs' legs, and fresh Florida lobster from the Keys. There are plenty of chain restaurants and fast-food establishments, especially in the Homestead and Florida City areas.

MIAMI

Updated by Julia Neyman

In the 1950s, Miami was best known for alligator wrestlers and you-pick strawberry fields or citrus groves. Well, things have changed. Miami on the mainland is South Florida's commercial hub, while its sultry sister, Miami Beach (America's Riviera), encompasses 17 islands in Biscayne Bay. Seducing winter refugees with its sunshine, beaches, palms, and nightlife, this is what most people envision when planning a trip to what they think of as Miami. If you want to do any exploring, you'll have to drive.

Numbers in the margin correspond to points of interest on the Miami map.

EXPLORING MIAMI

3 **Art Deco District Welcome Center.** Run by the Miami Design Preservation League, the center provides information about the buildings in the district. A gift shop sells 1930s–50s art deco memorabilia, posters, and books on Miami's history. Several tours—covering Lincoln Road, Española Way, North Beach, and the entire Art Deco District, among others—start here. You can rent audiotapes for a self-guided tour, join one of the regular morning (Wednesday and Friday through Sunday) or Thursday-evening walking tours, or take a bicycle tour. All of the options provide detailed histories of the art deco hotels. Don't miss the special boat tours during art deco Weekend, in early January. ✉*1001 Ocean Dr., at Barbara Capitman Way (10th St.), South Beach* ☎*305/531–3484* 🎫*Tours $20* ⏲*Sun.–Thurs. 10–7, Fri. and Sat. 10–6.*

1 **Bass Museum of Art.** The Bass, in historic Collins Park, is part of the Miami Beach Cultural Park, which includes the Miami City Ballet's Arquitectonica-designed facility and the Miami Beach Regional Library. The original building, constructed of keystone, has unique Maya-inspired carvings. The expansion designed by Japanese architect Arata Isozaki houses another wing and an outdoor sculpture garden. Special exhibitions join a diverse collection of European art. Works on permanent display include *The Holy Family,* a painting by Peter Paul Rubens; *The Tournament,* one of several 16th-century Flemish tapestries; and works by Albrecht Dürer and Henri de Toulouse-Lautrec. Special exhibits often cost a little extra. ✉*2121 Park Ave., at 21st St., South Beach* ☎*305/673–7530* 🌐*www.bassmuseum.org* 🎫*$8* ⏲*Tues.–Sat. 10–5, Sun. 11–5.*

★ Fodor'sChoice **Fairchild Tropical Botanic Garden.** With 83 acres

10 of lakes, sunken gardens, a 560-foot vine pergola, orchids, bellflowers, coral trees, bougainvillea, rare palms, and flowering trees, Fairchild is the largest tropical botanical garden in the continental United States. The tram tour highlights the best of South Florida's flora; then set off exploring on your own. A 2-acre rain-forest exhibit showcases tropical rain-forest plants from around the world complete with a waterfall and stream. The conservatory, Windows to the Tropics, houses rare tropical plants, including the Titan

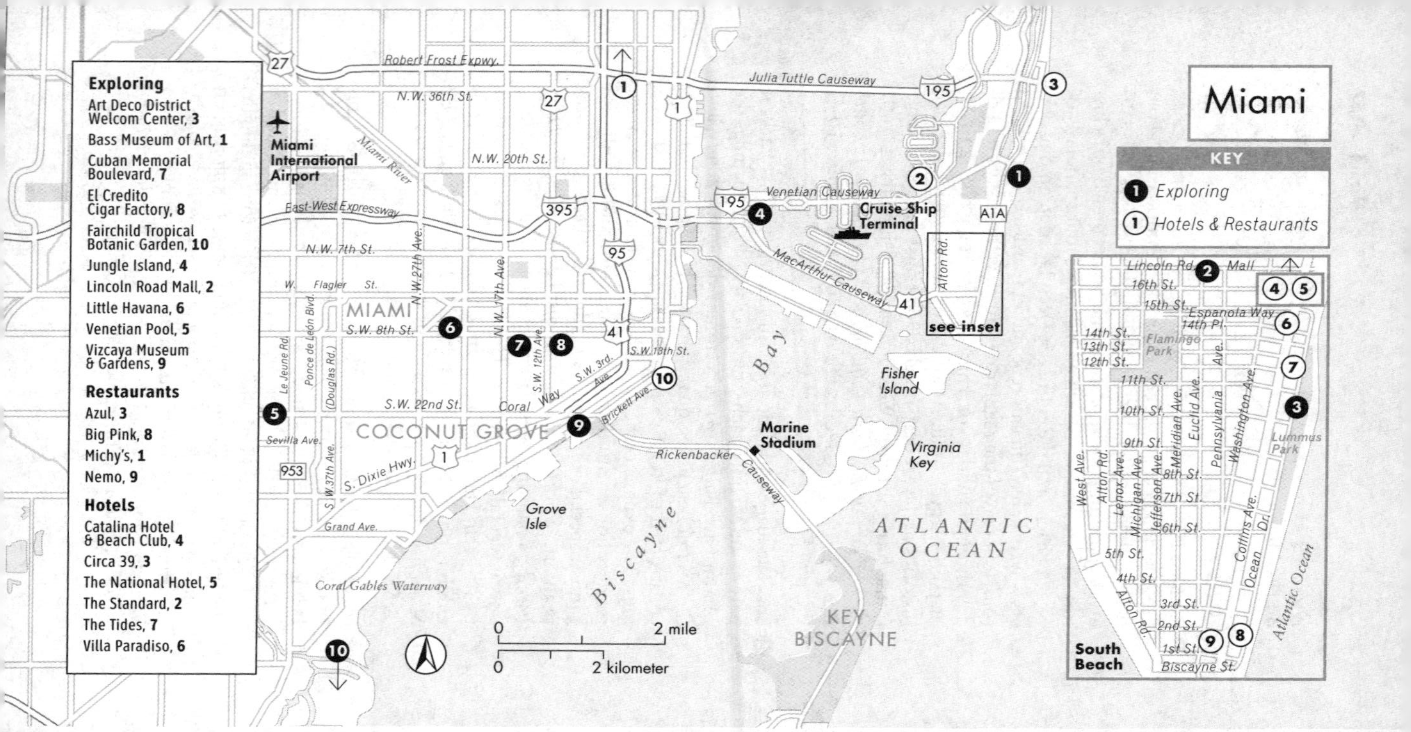
Miami
KEY
Exploring
Hotels & Restaurants
Exploring
Art Deco District Welcom Center, 3
Bass Museum of Art, 1
Cuban Memorial Boulevard, 7
El Credito Cigar Factory, 8
Fairchild Tropical Botanic Garden, 10
Jungle Island, 4
Lincoln Road Mall, 2
Little Havana, 6
Venetian Pool, 5
Vizcaya Museum & Gardens, 9
Restaurants
Azul, 3
Big Pink, 8
Michy's, 1
Nemo, 9
Hotels
Catalina Hotel & Beach Club, 4
Circa 39, 3
The National Hotel, 5
The Standard, 2
The Tides, 7
Villa Paradiso, 6
Miami International Airport
Robert Frost Expwy.
N.W. 36th St.
Julia Tuttle Causeway
Miami River
N.W. 20th St.
Venetian Causeway
Cruise Ship Terminal
East-West Expressway
N.W. 7th St.
N.W. 27th Ave.
N.W. 17th Ave.
W. Flagler St.
MIAMI
S.W. 8th St.
S.W. 12th Ave.
S.W. 3rd. Ave
S.W. 18th St.
MacArthur Causeway
Alton Rd.
see inset
Bay
Fisher Island
Le Jeune Rd.
Ponce de León Blvd.
(Douglas Rd.)
S.W. 22nd St.
Coral Way
Brickell Ave.
COCONUT GROVE
Sevilla Ave.
S.W. 37th Ave.
S. Dixie Hwy.
Marine Stadium
Rickenbacker Causeway
Virginia Key
Grove Isle
Grand Ave.
ATLANTIC OCEAN
Coral Gables Waterway
Biscayne
KEY BISCAYNE
0
2 mile
0
2 kilometer
Lincoln Rd. Mall
16th St.
15th St.
Espanola Way
14th Pl.
14th St.
13th St.
12th St.
Flamingo Park
11th St.
10th St.
9th St.
8th St.
7th St.
6th St.
5th St.
4th St.
3rd St.
2nd St.
1st St.
Biscayne St.
West Ave.
Alton Rd.
Lenox Ave.
Michigan Ave.
Jefferson Ave.
Meridian Ave.
Euclid Ave.
Pennsylvania Ave.
Washington Ave.
Collins Ave.
Ocean Dr.
Lummus Park
Atlantic Ocean
South Beach

Arum (*Amorphophallus titanum*), a fast-growing variety that attracted thousands of visitors when it bloomed in 1998. (It was only the sixth documented bloom in this country in the 20th century.) The Keys Coastal Habitat, created in a marsh and mangrove area in 1995 with assistance from the Tropical Audubon Society, provides food and shelter to resident and migratory birds. Check out the Montgomery Botanical Center, a research facility devoted to palms and cycads. Spicing up Fairchild's calendar are plant sales, afternoon teas, and genuinely special events year-round, such as the International Mango Festival the second weekend in July. The excellent bookstore–gift shop carries books on gardening and horticulture, and the Garden Café serves sandwiches and, seasonally, smoothies made from the garden's own crop of tropical fruits. ✉*10901 Old Cutler Rd., Coral Gables* ☎*305/667–1651* 🌐*www.fairchildgarden.org* 🎟*$20* ⏲*Daily 9:30–5.*

❹ **Jungle Island.** South Florida's original tourist attraction—it opened in 1936 in South Miami—closed in 2002 but reopened in 2003 on an island between Miami and Miami Beach. The park is home to more than 1,100 exotic birds, a few orangutans and snakes, a squadron of flamingos, a rare albino alligator, a liger (lion and tiger mix) and a 28-foot long "crocosaur," plus amazing orchids and other flowering plants. There's also the Hippo, but in this case, it's a three-story waterslide open on weekends. Kids enjoy the hands-on (make that wings-on) experience of having parrots perch on their shoulders. The Japanese garden that once stood on this site is next door—it's open on weekends and free to enter. **TIP→ You can eat at the indoor-outdoor lakeside café, overlooking the Caribbean flamingos, without paying the park's admission fee.** ✉*1111 Parrot Jungle Trail, off MacArthur Causeway (I–395), Watson Island, Miami* ☎*305/400–7000* 🌐*www.parrotjungle.com* 🎟*$22.95 plus $7 parking* ⏲*Daily 10–6.*

★ Fodor's Choice **Lincoln Road Mall.** A playful 1990s redesign

❷ spruced up this open-air pedestrian mall, adding a grove of 20 towering date palms, five linear pools, and colorful broken-tile mosaics to the futuristic 1950s vision of Fontainebleau designer Morris Lapidus. Some of the shops are owner-operated boutiques with a delightful variety of clothing, furnishings, garden supplies, and decorative design. Others are the typical chain stores of American malls. Remnants of tired old Lincoln Road—beauty-supply and discount electronics stores on the Collins end of the

6

strip—somehow fit nicely into the mix. The new Lincoln Road is fun, lively, and friendly for people old, young, gay, and straight—and their dogs. Folks skate, scoot, bike, or jog here. The best times to hit the road are during Sunday morning farmers' markets and on weekend evenings, when cafés bustle, art galleries open shows, street performers make the sidewalk their stage, and stores stay open late.

Two of the landmarks worth checking out at the eastern end of Lincoln Road are the massive 1940s keystone building at 420 Lincoln Road, which has a 1945 Leo Birchanky mural in the lobby, and the 1921 mission-style Miami Beach Community Church, at Drexel Avenue. The Lincoln Theatre (No. 541–545), at Pennsylvania Avenue, is a classical four-story art deco gem with friezes. The New World Symphony, a national advanced-training orchestra led by Michael Tilson Thomas, rehearses and performs here, and concerts are often broadcast via loudspeakers, to the delight of visitors. Just west, facing Pennsylvania, a fabulous Cadillac dealership sign was discovered underneath the facade of the Lincoln Road Millennium Building, on the south side of the mall. At Euclid Avenue there's a monument to Lapidus, who in his 90s watched the renaissance of his whimsical creation. At Lenox Avenue, a black-and-white art deco movie house with a Mediterranean barrel-tile roof is now the Colony Theater (No. 1040), where live theater and experimental films are presented. ✉*Lincoln Rd., between Collins Ave. and Alton Rd., South Beach.*

❻ **Little Havana.** First settled en masse by Cubans in the early 1960s, after that country's Communist revolution, Little Havana is a predominantly working-class area and the core of Miami's Hispanic community. Spanish is the language that predominates, but don't be surprised if the cadence is less Cuban and more Salvadoran or Nicaraguan. The main commercial zone is bounded by Northwest 1st Street, Southwest 9th Street, Ronald Reagan Avenue (Southwest 12th Avenue), and Teddy Roosevelt Boulevard (Southwest 17th Avenue). Calle Ocho (Southwest 8th Street) is the axis of the neighborhood.

Some of the restaurants host traditional flamenco performances and Sevillaña *tablaos* (dances performed on a wood-plank stage, using castanets), and some clubs feature recently arrived Cuban acts. Intimate neighborhood theaters host top-notch productions ranging from Spanish classics to contemporary satire. Throughout the year a variety of festivals commemorate Miami's Hispanic heritage, and residents from no fewer than five countries celebrate their homeland's independence days in Little Havana. On the last Friday of every month Little Havana takes its culture to the streets for Cultural Fridays, between 6:30 and 11 PM on 8th Street from 14th to 17th avenues. Art expositions, music, and avant-garde street performances bring a young, hip crowd to the neighborhood.

7 **Cuban Memorial Boulevard,** two blocks in the heart of Little Havana, are filled with monuments to Cuba's freedom fighters. Among the memorials are the *Eternal Torch of the Brigade 2506,* commemorating those who were killed in the failed Bay of Pigs invasion of 1961; a bust of 19th-century hero Antonio Maceo; and a bas-relief map of Cuba depicting each of its *municipios.* There's also a bronze statue in honor of Tony Izquierdo, who participated in the Bay of Pigs invasion, served in Nicaragua's Somozan forces, and interestingly enough was also on the CIA payroll. ✉ *S.W. 13th Ave., south of S.W. 8th St., Little Havana.*

8 Through the giant storefront windows of **El Credito Cigar Factory,** you can see cigars being rolled. Many of the workers at this family business dating back three generations learned their trade in prerevolutionary Cuba. Today the tobacco leaf they use comes primarily from the Dominican Republic and Mexico, and the wrappers from Connecticut, making theirs a truly multinational product. A walk-in humidor has more than 40 brands favored by customers such as Arnold Schwarzenegger, Bill Clinton, Robert De Niro, and Bill Cosby. ✉ *1106 S.W. 8th St., near S.W. 11th Ave., Little Havana* ☎ *305/858–4162* ⏲ *Mon.–Sat. 9–4. Factory closed Sat.*

★ Fodor'sChoice **Venetian Pool.** Sculpted from a rock quarry

5 in 1923 and fed by artesian wells, this 825,000-gallon municipal pool remains quite popular because of its themed architecture—a fantasized version of a waterfront Italian village—created by Denman Fink. The pool has earned a place on the National Register of Historic Places and showcases a nice collection of vintage photos depicting 1920s beauty pageants and swank soirees held long ago. Paul Whiteman played here, Johnny Weissmuller and Esther Williams swam here, and you should, too (but no kids under three). A snack bar, lockers, and showers make this must-see user-friendly as well. ✉ *2701 De Soto Blvd., at Toledo St., Coral Gables* ☎ *305/460–5356* 🌐 *www.venetianpool.com* 🎟 *Apr.–Oct., $10; Nov.–Mar., $6.75, free parking across De Soto Blvd.* ⏲ *June–Aug., weekdays 11–7:30,*

weekends 10–4:30; Sept. and Oct., Apr. and May, Tues.–Fri. 11–5:30, weekends 10–4:30; Nov.–Mar., Tues.–Fri. 10–4:30, weekends 10–4:30.

★ Fodor'sChoice **Vizcaya Museum & Gardens.** Of the 10,000 people living in Miami between 1912 and 1916, about 1,000 of them were gainfully employed by Chicago industrialist James Deering to build this Italian Renaissance–style winter residence. Once comprising 180 acres, the grounds now occupy a 30-acre tract that includes a native hammock and more than 10 acres of formal gardens with fountains overlooking Biscayne Bay. The house, open to the public, contains 70 rooms, 34 of which are filled with paintings, sculpture, antique furniture, and other fine and decorative arts. The pieces date from the 15th through the 19th century and represent the Renaissance, baroque, rococo, and neoclassical movements. So unusual and impressive is Vizcaya that visitors have included many major heads of state. Guided tours are available. Moonlight tours, in particular, offer a unique look at the gardens; call for reservations. *3251 S. Miami Ave., Coconut Grove 305/250–9133 www.vizcayamuseum.org $12 Daily 9:30–4:30.*

WHERE TO EAT

At many of the hottest spots, you'll need a reservation to avoid a long wait for a table. And when you get your check, note whether a gratuity is already included; most restaurants add between 15% and 18% (ostensibly for the convenience of, and protection from, the many Latin-American and European tourists who are used to this practice in their homelands), but reduce or supplement it depending on your opinion of the service.

For price categories, see ⇨ About the Restaurants at the beginning of this chapter.

★ Fodor'sChoice ✕ **Azul.** Azul has sumptuously conquered the devil in the details, from chef Clay Conley's exotically rendered Asian-Mediterranean cuisine to the thoughtful service staff who graciously anticipate your broader dining needs. Does your sleeveless blouse leave you too cold to properly appreciate the Moroccan lamb and seared red snapper? Ask for one of the house pashminas, available in a variety of fashionable colors. Forgot your reading glasses and can't decipher the hanger steak with foie-gras sauce? Request a pair from the host. Want to see how the other half lives? Descend the interior staircase to Cafe Sambal, the all-day casual restaurant

$$–$$$$

downstairs. ✉ *Mandarin Oriental Hotel, 500 Brickell Key Dr., Brickell Key* ☎ *305/913–8288* ⚠ *Reservations essential* ▭ *AE, MC, V* ⊗ *Closed Sun. No lunch weekends.*

★ FodorsChoice ✕ **Big Pink.** The decor in this innovative diner may remind you of a roller-skating rink—everything is pink Lucite, stainless steel, and campy (think sports lockers as decorative touches). And the menu is a virtual book, complete with table of contents. But the food is solidly all-American, with dozens of tasty sandwiches, pizzas, turkey or beef burgers, and side dishes, each and every one composed with a gourmet flair. Customers comprise club kids and real kids, who alternate, depending on the time of day—Big Pink makes a great spot for brunch—but both like to color with the complimentary crayons. ✉ *157 Collins Ave., South Beach* ☎ *305/532–4700* ▭ *AE, MC, V.*

$–$$

$$–$$$ ✕ **Michy's.** Miami's homegrown star chef Michelle Bernstein now has her own gig. The funky, blue, late 1960s–inspired dining room on the mainland's "Upper East Side" serves exquisite French- and Mediterranean-influenced seafood dishes at over-the-causeway (read: non-tourist-trap) prices. Plates come in half portions and full portions, which makes the restaurant even more of a deal. Can't-miss entrées include the blue cheese and fig croquetas, the beef short rib and the steak frite au poivre. ✉ *6927 Biscayne Blvd., Upper East Side* ☎ *305/759–2001* ▭ *AE, D, DC, MC, V.*

★ FodorsChoice ✕ **Nemo.** The SoFi (South of Fifth Street) neighborhood may have emerged as a South Beach hot spot, but Nemo's location is not why this casually comfortable restaurant receives raves. It's the menu, which often changes but always delivers, blending Caribbean, Asian, Mediterranean, and Middle Eastern influences and providing an explosion of cultures in each bite. Popular appetizers include citrus-cured salmon rolls with tobiko caviar and wasabi mayo, and crispy duck leg confit, served with lentils in a tangy pineapple sauce. Main courses might include wok-charred salmon or grilled Indian-spice pork chop. Hedy Goldsmith's funky pastries are exquisitely sinful. Bright colors and copper fixtures highlight the tree-shaded courtyard. ✉ *100 Collins Ave., South Beach* ☎ *305/532–4550* ▭ *AE, DC, MC, V.*

$$–$$$$

WHERE TO STAY

South Beach is the center of the action in Miami Beach, but it's also expensive. If you are looking for a budget hotel, then you'll almost certainly have to choose one that's a few blocks from the beach instead of being right across the street.

★ **Catalina Hotel & Beach Club.** Apparently there's value in a $$–$$$$ good hotel right on the South Beach strip that offers free drinks, airport shuttles, and bike rentals, all for south of $300 a night: The Catalina has taken over two neighboring buildings and now stretches almost a whole city block. Each of the three buildings has a distinct feel: The original Catalina (with the smallest, most inexpensive rooms) is an exercise in camp, with red shag carpets and a funky backgammon table in the lobby. The mid-range rooms are in the old Maxine Hotel, decorated in rock baroque and featuring a karaoke machine in the lobby. The newest, and most luxurious, addition is the Dorset Hotel, which now houses Catalina's biggest rooms as well as its new sushi restaurant, Kung Fu Chus. The rooms are good sized, and the extra perks—free drinks from 7 to 8, a free airport shuttle, and free bike rental until 6 PM —make this hotel the most reasonable bet on the strip. **Pros:** Free drinks, free bikes, free airport shuttle, good people-watching. **Cons:** $15 wireless fee, service not a high priority, loud. ✉*1732 Collins Ave., Miami Beach* ☎*305/674–1160* 🖷*305/674–7522* 🌐*www.catalinahotel.com* *200 rooms* *In-room: safe, refrigerator, Wi-Fi. In-hotel: restaurant, bars, pool, bicycles, laundry service, public Wi-Fi, airport shuttle, parking (fee), some pets allowed, no-smoking rooms* ▭*AE, D, DC, MC, V.*

★ Fodor'sChoice **Circa 39.** This stylish boutique combines $ the smooth management of a big-budget hotel with the quaint little details of an art deco gem. A peek around each corner reveals a new delight, from a plush lip-shaped sofa to a lush courtyard connecting the two wings of the hotel, to a bar that offers free drinks every evening. The hotel is so focused on catering to your desires that they've even created a $10 "spoil me package" which includes European-style breakfast, cocktail hour, and two lounge chairs. Don't worry about asking for the package—it's added to your room rate. Rooms have wood floors and a cool, crisp look with white furnishings dotted with pale blue pillows. An in-room "spoil me basket" has everything you may need, from potato chips to condoms. The name Circa 39? It was built in 1939 and is on 39th Street. **Pros:** Affordable, chic, and intimate. **Cons:** You can't opt out of the $10 "spoil me package." ✉*3900 Collins Ave., Mid-Beach, Miami Beach* ☎*305/538–4900 or 877/8CIRCA39* 🖷*305/538–4998* 🌐*www.circa39.com* *82 rooms* *In-*

room: safe, kitchen, refrigerator, Ethernet, Wi-Fi. In-hotel: restaurants, bar, pool, gym, concierge, public Wi-Fi, parking (fee), some pets allowed, no-smoking rooms ▭*AE, D, DC, MC, V.*

★ Fodor's Choice **The National Hotel.** Most locals have partied everywhere on Miami's hot hotel strip—except for the National Hotel. That's because this luxurious hotel serves as a bastion of calm in the sea of white on white mod decor and raucous reveling usually reserved for the beachfront masterpieces lining Collins Avenue between 15th and 20th streets. Unlike its neighbors, the National hasn't parted with its Art Deco past. Most of the chocolate and ebony hued pieces in the lobby date back to the 1930s, and the baby grand piano beckons toward a throwback D-Bar Lounge. The most spectacular feature is Miami Beach's longest pool, which stretches from the tower to a duo of tropical tiki bars, a series of comfy black and white striped cabanas and poolside tables, and then the beach. See that black-and-white striped hut on the sand? That's owned by the National as well, and staffed with runners who can bring you food from hotel restaurants. **Pros:** Stunning pool, perfect location. **Cons:** Rooms aren't stylistically impressive, $11 daily charge for Internet. ✉*1677 Collins Ave., South Beach* ☎*305/532–2311 or 800/327–8370* 🖷*305/534–1426* 🌐*www.nationalhotel.com* *143 rooms, 9 suites* *In-room: safe, DVD, VCR (some), Ethernet, Wi-Fi. In-hotel: 2 restaurants, room service, bars, pools, gym, beachfront, laundry service, concierge, public Internet, public Wi-Fi, parking (fee), some pets allowed, no-smoking rooms* ▭*AE, DC, MC, V.*

$$–$$$$

$$$ **The Standard.** An extension of André Balazs's trendy, budget hotel chain, the Standard is a Hollywood newcomer that set up shop a few minutes from South Beach on an island just over the Venetian Causeway. The message: we'll do what we please, and the cool kids will follow. The scene is trendy 30- and 40-year-olds interested in the hotel's many "do-it-yourself" spa activities, including mud bathing, scrubbing with sea salts, soaking in hot or arctic-cold waters, and yoga. An 8-foot, 103-degree cascade into a Roman hot tub is typical of the handful of adult pleasures spread around the pool deck. An informal restaurant overlooks the bay's Mediterranean-style mansions and the cigarette boats that float past. If you choose, you can go kayaking around the island. On the hotel facade you'll see the monumental signage of a bygone occupant, the Lido Spa Hotel, and the much smaller sign of its current occupant,

hung, with a wink, upside down. The rooms are small and simple, though they have thoughtful touches like a picnic basket and embroidered fabric covers for the small flat-screen TVs. First-floor rooms have outdoor soaking tubs but very limited privacy, so few take that plunge. **Pros:** Interesting island location, free bike and kayak rentals, swank pool scene, great spa, inexpensive. **Cons:** Removed from South Beach nightlife, small rooms with no views, outdoor tubs are gimmicks, mediocre service. ✉ *40 Island Ave., Belle Isle, Miami Beach* ☎ *305/673–1717* 🖷 *305/673–8181* 🌐 *www.standardhotel.com* *104 rooms, 1 suite* *In-room: safe, refrigerator, DVD, Ethernet. In-hotel: restaurant, room service, bars, pool, gym, spa, water sports, bicycles, laundry service, concierge, public Wi-Fi, parking (fee), some pets allowed, no children under 14, no-smoking rooms* 💳 *AE, D, DC, MC, V.*

★ Fodor'sChoice $$$$ **The Tides.** The newly designed Tides Hotel is fashioned after the interior of a jewelry box, and this hotel may indeed be the jewel of South Beach boutiques. Gone is the stark white-on-white minimalism, replaced with soft pinks and corals, gilded accents and marine-inspired decor. The new "Coral Bar" boasts rums from around the world, and La Marea restaurant offers delectable seafood. The Tides' main competition is Hotel Victor, but this hotel's rooms all have direct ocean views. The rooms are small, but pretty, with pink and tan accents and cool tables made of petrified stumps. **Pros:** Superior service, great beach location, and ocean views from all suites plus the terrace restaurant. **Cons:** Small rooms, tiny elevator. ✉ *1220 Ocean Dr., South Beach* ☎ *305/604–5070 or 866/438–4337* 🖷 *305/604–5180* 🌐 *www.thetideshotel.com* *45 suites* *In-room: safe, Ethernet, Wi-Fi. In-hotel: restaurant, pool, gym, beachfront, concierge, laundry service, parking (fee), no-smoking rooms* 💳 *AE, D, DC, MC, V.*

★ $–$$ **Villa Paradiso.** One of South Beach's best deals, Paradiso has huge floor-through, apartment-like rooms with kitchens, and a charming tropical courtyard with benches for hanging out at all hours. There's even another smaller courtyard on the other side of the rooms. Peeking out from a sea of tropical foliage, the hotel seems at first to be a rather unassuming piece of deco architecture. But for all its simplicity, value shines bright. Rooms have polished hardwood floors, French doors, and quirky wrought-iron furniture. They are well suited for extended visits—discounts begin at 10% off for a week's stay. **Pros:** Great hangout spot in courtyard, huge rooms with kitchens, good value, great location. **Cons:** No wireless Internet, no pool, no restaurant. ✉*1415 Collins Ave., South Beach* ☎*305/532–0616* 📠*305/673–5874* 🌐*www.villaparadiso hotel.com* *17 studios* *In-room: kitchen, refrigerator, dial-up. In-hotel: some pets allowed, no-smoking rooms* ▭*AE, D, DC, MC, V.*

NIGHTLIFE

Miami's pulse pounds with nonstop nightlife that reflects the area's potent cultural mix. On sultry, humid nights with the huge full moon rising out of the ocean and fragrant night-blooming jasmine intoxicating the senses, who can resist Cuban salsa, Jamaican reggae, and Dominican merengue, with some disco and hip-hop thrown in for good measure? To avoid the lines, decide which clubs you want to check out (consult *Ocean Drive* magazine celebrity pages if you want to be among the glitterati), and your hotel's concierge will e-mail, fax, or call your names in to the clubs so you'll be on the guest list when you arrive (tip the concierge, however). This means much easier access and usually no cover charge (which can be upward of $20) if you arrive before midnight. Dress up—casual chic is the dress code. For men this means no sneakers, no shorts, no sleeveless vests, and no shirts unbuttoned past the top button. For women, provocative and seductive is fine; overly revealing is not. At the door: don't name-drop—no one takes it seriously. Don't be pushy while trying to get the doorman's attention. With the right dress and the right attitude, you'll be on the dance floor rubbing shoulders with South Beach's finest clubbers in no time.

BEACHES

Almost every side street in Miami Beach dead-ends at the ocean. Sandy shores also stretch along the southern side of the Rickenbacker Causeway to Key Biscayne, where you'll find more popular beaches. Greater Miami is best known for its ocean beaches, but there's freshwater swimming here, too, in pools and lakes. Below are the highlights for the get-wet set.

The stretch of beach along **Ocean Drive**—primarily the 10-block stretch from 5th to 15th streets—is one of the most talked-about beachfronts in America. The beach is wide, white, and bathed by warm aquamarine waves. Separating the sand from the traffic of Ocean Drive is palm-fringed Lummus Park, with its volleyball nets and chickee huts for shade. The beach also plays host to some of the funkiest lifeguard stands you'll ever see, pop stars shooting music videos, and visitors from all over the world. The beach at 12th Street is popular with gays. Locals hang out on 3rd Street beach, where they watch fit Brazilians play foot volley, a variation of volleyball that uses everything but the hands! Because much of South Beach has an adult flavor—women are often casually topless—many families prefer Mid- and North Beach. Unless you're parking south of 3rd Street, metered spaces near the waterfront are rarely empty. Instead, opt for a public garage and walk; you'll have lots of fun people-watching, too. ✉*Ocean Dr., between 1st and 22nd Sts., South Beach, Miami Beach* ☎*305/673–7714*.

SHOPPING

If you're over the climate-controlled slickness of shopping malls and can't face one more food-court "meal," you've got choices in Miami. Head out into the sunshine and shop the city streets, where you'll find big-name retailers and local boutiques alike. Take a break at a sidewalk café to power up on some Cuban coffee or fresh-squeezed OJ and enjoy the tropical breezes.

Give your plastic a workout in shopping the many high-profile tenants on this densely packed two-block stretch of **Collins Avenue** between 5th and 10th streets. Think Club Monaco, MAC, Kenneth Cole, Barney's Co-Op, and A/X Armani Exchange. Sprinkled amid the upscale vendors are hair salons, spas, cafés, and such familiar stores as the Gap, Urban Outfitters, and Banana Republic. Be sure to head over one street east and west to catch the shopping on Ocean Drive and Washington Avenue.

This eight-block-long **Lincoln Road Mall** is the trendiest place on Miami Beach. Home to more than 150 shops, 20-plus art galleries and nightclubs, about 50 restaurants and cafés, and the renovated Colony Theatre, Lincoln Road is like the larger, more sophisticated cousin of Ocean Drive. The "see and be scene" theme is furthered by outdoor seating at every restaurant, where well-heeled patrons lounge and discuss the people (and pet) parade passing by. An 18-screen movie theater anchors the west end of the street, which is where most of the worthwhile shops are; the far east end is mostly discount and electronic shops. Sure, there's a Pottery Barn, a Gap, and a Williams-Sonoma, but the emphasis is on emporiums with unique personalities, like En Avance, Chroma, Base, and Jonathan Adler.

HOMESTEAD

30 mi southwest of Miami.

Updated by Chelle Koster Walton

In recent years, the Homestead area has redefined itself as a destination for tropical agro- and ecotourism. The emphasis is on "tropical," because as you cross Quail Roost Trail along north Krome Avenue (Route 997), you actually cross latitudes into the tropical zone. Seated at the juncture between Miami and the Keys as well as Everglades National Park and Biscayne National Park, it has the added dimension of shopping centers, residential development, hotel chains, and the Homestead Miami Speedway—when car races are scheduled there, hotels increase rates and have minimum stays. The historic downtown area has become a preservation-driven Main Street. Krome Avenue, where it cuts through the city's heart, is lined with restaurants, an arts complex, antiques shops, and low-budget, but sometimes undesirable, accommodations. West of north–south Krome Avenue, miles of fields grow fresh fruits and vegetables. Some are harvested commercially, and others have U-PICK signs, inviting you to harvest your own. Stands selling farm-fresh produce and nurseries that grow and sell orchids and tropical plants abound. In addition to its agricultural legacy, the town has an eclectic flavor, attributable to its population mix: descendants of pioneer Crackers, Hispanic growers and farm workers, professionals escaping Miami's hustle and bustle, and latter-day northern retirees.

With a saltwater atoll pool that's flushed by tidal action, **Homestead Bayfront Park,** adjacent to Biscayne National Park, is popular among local families as well as anglers and boaters. Facilities include a sandy beach with lifeguards, a playground, ramps for people with disabilities (including a ramp that leads into the swimming area), and a picnic pavilion with grills, showers, and restrooms. ✉ *9698 S.W. 328th St.* ☎ *305/230–3034* 🎫 *$4 per passenger vehicle, $10 per vehicle with boat, $12 per RV* ⊙ *Daily sunrise–sunset.*

★ Because it officially qualifies for tropical status, **Fruit & Spice Park,** in Homestead's Redland historic agricultural district, is the only public garden of its type in the United States. More than 500 varieties of herbs, spices, citrus, and nuts typically grow in the 35-acre park, but it is most famous for its exotic fruits, such as pomelo, carambola, sugar apple, and monstera. There are 70 varieties of bananas alone, plus 70 varieties of avocado, and 140 of mangos. Tours and tastings are available three times daily. ✉*24801 S.W. 187th Ave.* ☎*305/247–5727* 🌐*www.fruitandspicepark.org* *$6* *Daily 10–5; guided tours at 11, 1:30, and 3.*

Enjoy Homestead's fruity bounty in liquid form at **Schnebly Redland's Winery.** Opened to the public in 2005, it began producing fruit wines as a way to avoid wasting thousands of pounds of fruit from the family groves each year, fruit not quite perfect enough for shipping. In 2008, the winery expanded with a spacious reception/tasting indoor area that serves snacks and a lush plaza picnic area framed in coral rock, tropical plants, and waterfalls—topped with an Indian thatched chickee roof. Five bucks buys you a taste of six varieties of surprisingly tasty fruit wines, from the oaky carambola wine to the slightly sweet and acidic passion fruit. For another $5 you can taste the three new sparkling wines. You get to keep your souvenir wineglass and can bring it back anytime for free refills. ✉*30205 S.W. 217th Ave.* ☎*305/242–1224 or 888/717–9463* 🌐*www.schneblywinery.com* *$5* *Weekdays 10–5, Sat. 10–6, Sun. noon–5.*

Driven by unrequited love, 100-pound immigrant Ed Leedskalnin built **Coral Castle** in the early 1900s out of massive slabs of coral rock, a feat likened to the building of the pyramids. Visitors can learn how he peopled his fantasy world with his imaginary wife and three children, studied astronomy, and built his simple home and elaborate courtyard with no engineering education and tools he mostly fashioned himself. Highlights of the National Register of Historic Places site include the Polaris telescope built to spot the North Star, a working sundial, a 5,000-pound heart-shape table featured in Ripley's *Believe It or Not,* a banquet table in the shape of Florida, and a playground Ed named "Grotto of the Three Bears." ✉*28655 S. Dixie Hwy.* ☎*305/248–6345* 🌐*www.coralcastle.com* *$9.75* *Sun.–Thurs. 8–6, Fri. and Sat. 8–9.*

This groundbreaking project centers on a 3½-acre complex, **ArtSouth,** which includes the historic First Baptist Church, 45 artist studios, galleries, workshops, sculpture garden, and stage. Watch artists at work, take classes, and enjoy concert performances. Check Second Saturdays opening exhibits, which include live entertainment, hands-on art demonstrations, self-guided tours, and refreshments served from 3 to 7 PM. ✉*20 N. Krome Ave.* ☎*305/247–9406* 🌐*www.artsouthhomestead.org* *Free* ⏲*Tues.–Fri. 10–6, weekends noon–6.*

WITNESS PROTECTION PROGRAM. Fifteen federally protected threatened and endangered creatures survive within the protection of Everglades National Park, including manatees, crocodiles, snail kites, and sea turtles.

WHERE TO EAT

★ ¢ ✕ **El Toro Taco.** This simple, saltillo-tiled family-run favorite gets high marks for its generous portions, homemade tortilla chips (sometimes a little greasy), and friendly service. Selections include tasty fajitas, enchiladas, and burritos, and other traditional Mexican dishes such as *mole de pollo,* which combines unsweetened chocolate and Mexican spices with chicken. Order spicing from mild to tongue-challenging. And if you're tired of the same old morning fare, consider stopping here for breakfast, available 10 AM–noon. ✉*1 S. Krome Ave.* ☎*305/245–8182* *AE, D, MC, V* *BYOB* ⏲*Closed Mon.*

¢ ✕ **NicaMex.** Among the local Latin population, this is a favorite and the lowest priced. It helps if you speak Spanish, but there's usually staffers who speak English, and the menu is bilingual. Although they term it *comidas rapidas* (fast food), the cuisine is not Americanized. You can get authentic huevos rancheros or *chilaquiles* (corn tortillas cooked in red-pepper sauce) for breakfast, and specialties such as *chicharron en salsa verde* (fried pork skin in hot green-tomato sauce) and shrimp in garlic all day. Seafood and beef soups are best sellers and have generous amounts of vegetables and seafood or meat. Choose a domestic or imported beer, pop a coin into the Wurlitzer jukebox, select a Latin tune, and escape to a foreign land. ✉*32 N.W. 1st St., across from Krome Ave. bandstand* ☎*305/246–8300* *AE, D, MC, V.*

¢ ✕ **Sam's Country Kitchen.** For good old Southern-style home cooking, Sam's is the choice of the local population. Burgers, sandwiches, and dinners—including chicken livers, country-fried chicken, and fried clams—come with fresh-baked corn bread and a daily selection of sides such as okra with tomatoes, turnip greens, pickled beets, or onion rings. Don't miss out on the changing selection of homemade soups and desserts. All this goodness comes cheaply, but at

6

the expense of an anything-but-glamorous dining area and often slow service. ✉ *1320 N. Krome Ave.* ☎ *305/246–2990* ▭ *MC, V* ⊗ *Closed for dinner Sun.*

WHERE TO STAY

★ ¢ **Grove Inn Country Guesthouse.** Away from downtown but close to Homestead's agricultural attractions, Grove Inn derives much of its personality from co-owner Paul, a former showman. The garden is lush with organic, tropical fruit trees and native plants (instead of a guest book there's a live autograph tree in the courtyard, where people sign the leaves) and the rooms are decorated fussily with antique furnishings and table settings. The owners go out of their way to pamper you, starting with a country breakfast using local produce, served family-style in a dining room done in deep Victorian florals. They offer behind-the-scenes tours of orchid nurseries and farms not otherwise open to the public. A vending machine dispenses complimentary cold drinks. **Pros:** Fresh fruit, privacy, delicious breakfast, rural location. **Cons:** Far from downtown and national parks, no restaurants nearby, not suited to families. ✉ *22540 S.W. Krome Ave., 6 mi north of downtown* ☎ *305/247–6572 or 877/247–6572* 🌐 *www.groveinn.com* *13 rooms, 1 2-bedroom suite, 1 cottage* *In-room: kitchen (some), refrigerator, dial-up. In-hotel: pool, laundry facilities, some pets allowed, no-smoking rooms* ▭ *AE, D, MC, V* *BP.*

★ ¢–$ **Redland Hotel.** Of downtown Homestead's smattering of mom-and-pop motels, this is the most desirable and has the most character. When it opened in 1904, the inn was the town's first hotel. It later became the first mercantile store, the first post office, the first library, and the first boardinghouse. Today, each room has a different layout and furnishings, and some have access to a shared balcony. The style is Victorian, with lots of pastels and reproduction antique furniture. The pub is popular with locals, and there are good restaurants and antiques shops nearby. A coffee shop–Internet café with free Wi-Fi connections was added in 2006. **Pros:** Historic character, convenient to downtown, well maintained. **Cons:** Traffic noise, small rooms, ugly street location. ✉ *5 S. Flagler Ave.* ☎ *305/246–1904 or 800/595–1904* 🌐 *www.redlandhotel.com* *13 rooms* *In-room: VCR, Ethernet, dial-up. In-hotel: restaurant, room service, bar, public Wi-Fi, no-smoking rooms* ▭ *AE, D, MC, V.*

SPORTS & THE OUTDOORS

AUTO RACING

The **Homestead Miami Speedway** (✉*1 Speedway Blvd.* ☎*305/230–7223* 🌐*www.homesteadmiamispeedway.com*) is a state-of-the-art facility with 65,000 grandstand seats and two tracks: a 2.21-mi continuous road course and a 1.5-mi oval. There's a schedule of year-round manufacturer and race-team testing, club racing, and other national events.

BOATING

Boaters give high ratings to the facilities at **Homestead Bayfront Park.** The 174-slip marina has a ramp, dock, bait-and-tackle shop, fuel station, ice, dry storage, and boat hoist, which can handle vessels up to 50 feet long if they have lifting rings. The park also has a tidal swimming area. ✉*9698 S.W. 328th St.* ☎*305/230–3033* 🎫*$4 per passenger vehicle, $10 per vehicle with boat, $10 per RV, $10 hoist* ⏲*Daily sunrise–sunset.*

SHOPPING

In addition to Homestead Boulevard (U.S. 1) and Campbell Drive (Southwest 312th Street and Northeast 8th Street), **Krome Avenue** is popular for shopping. In the heart of old Homestead, it has a brick sidewalk, art galleries, and antiques stores. The **Antique Mall** contains six dealer shops plus a café.

FLORIDA CITY

2 mi southwest of Homestead.

Updated by Chelle Koster Walton

The Florida Turnpike ends in this southernmost town on the peninsula, spilling thousands onto U.S. 1 and eventually west to Everglades National Park, east to Biscayne National Park, or south to the Florida Keys. Florida City and Homestead run into each other, but the difference couldn't be more noticeable. As the last outpost before 18 mi of mangroves and water, this stretch of U.S. 1 is lined with fast-food eateries, service stations, hotels, bars, dive shops, and restaurants. Hotel rates increase significantly during NASCAR races at the nearby Homestead Miami Speedway. Like Homestead, Florida City is rooted in agriculture, with hundreds of acres of farmland west of Krome Avenue and a huge farmers' market that processes produce shipped nationwide.

WHERE TO EAT

$ ✕ **Capri Restaurant.** Locals have been coming here for affordable Italian food in a wide selection since 1958. Outside it's a rock-walled building with a big parking lot that fills up nightly. The interior has dark-wood paneling with redbrick accents and heavy wooden furniture. A pleasant courtyard affords outdoor dining. The tasty fare ranges from pizza with a light, crunchy crust and ample toppings to spaghetti 16 different ways, and broiled steaks and seafood-pasta classics. This is traditional Italian-American cuisine with no surprises and little flourish. Bargain hunters have two choices: the daily early-bird entrées, 4:30 to 6:30 for $12 to $14, which include soup or salad and potato or spaghetti, and the Tuesday family night (after 4 PM), which has all-you-can-eat pasta with salad or soup for $6.95. Specialty martinis and fruity cocktails supplement the international wine list. ✉ *935 N. Krome Ave.* ☎ *305/247–1542* 🌐 *www.the-capri.com* ▭ *AE, D, MC, V* ⊗ *Closed for lunch Sun.*

$ ✕ **Captain's Restaurant and Seafood Market.** A comfortable place where the chef knows how to do seafood with flair, this is one of the town's best bets. Locals and visitors alike gather in the cozy dining room or outdoors on the patio. Blackboards describe a varied menu of sandwiches, pasta, seafood, steak, and nightly specials. Inventive offerings include lobster Reuben sandwich, crawfish pasta, and pan-seared tuna topped with balsamic onions and shallots. ✉ *404 S.E. 1st Ave.* ☎ *305/247–9456* ▭ *AE, MC, V.*

★ $ ✕ **Farmers' Market Restaurant.** Although it's in the farmers' market and serves fresh vegetables, seafood figures prominently on the menu of home-cooked specialties. A family of fishermen runs the place, so fish and shellfish are only hours from the sea. Catering to the fishing and farming crowd, it opens at 5:30 AM, serving pancakes, jumbo eggs, and fluffy omelets with home fries or grits in a pleasant dining room with checkered tablecloths on the edge of town. The lunch and dinner menus have fried shrimp, seafood pasta, country-fried steak, roast turkey, and fried conch, as well as burgers, salads, and sandwiches. ✉ *300 N. Krome Ave.* ☎ *305/242–0008* ▭ *MC, V.*

$ ✕ **Gusto's Grill & Bar.** This fun and friendly place is mostly about drinking and watching sports on TV, yet it's also good for catching a reasonably priced meal, especially during happy hour (4 to 7 PM), when there's a free buffet (with a two-drink minimum). Sit indoors or out (televisions are situated throughout) to order your honey garlic wings, shrimp corn chowder, pasta, burgers, pizza, steak, cashew salmon, and crab cakes from the extensive menu. Shoot pool and sip a Razzeberri Mojito while you wait. ✉*326 S.E. 1st Ave.* ☎*786/243–9800* ▭*AE, D, MC, V.*

$$ ✕ **Mutineer Restaurant.** Families and older couples prefer the quirky yet well-dressed setting of this roadside steak-and-seafood restaurant with an indoor-outdoor fish-and-duck pond. It was built to look like a ship in 1980, back when Florida City was barely on the map. Etched glass divides the bi-level dining rooms, with velvet upholstered chairs, an aquarium, and nautical antiques. The big menu has 12 seafood entrées, including stuffed grouper (a favorite), Florida lobster tails, and snapper Oscar, plus another half dozen daily seafood specials, as well as poultry, ribs, and steaks. At lunch, there are burgers and seafood sandwiches and a happy hour buffet all day until 7 PM in the lounge for $2.25 and the purchase of a drink. Friday and Saturday are dance nights with live entertainment. ✉*11 S.E. 1st Ave. (U.S. 1), at Palm Dr.* ☎*305/245–3377* ⊕*www.mutineer.biz* ▭*AE, D, DC, MC, V.*

6

★ ¢ ✕ **Rosita's Restaurante.** With its population of immigrant farm workers, this area can boast the real thing in Mexican, a flavor you just don't get in the Tex-Mex chains. Order à la carte specialties or dinners and combos with beans and rice, and salad. Forty-three breakfast, lunch, and dinner entrées are served all day and range from Mexican eggs, enchiladas, and taco salad to stewed beef, shrimp rancheros style, and fried pork chop. The food is on the spicy side, and if you like more fire, each table comes prepared with fresh-tasting salsa, pickled jalapeños, and bottled habanero sauce. Clean (with lingering faint whiffs of bleach to prove it) and pleasant, with an open kitchen, take-out counter, and Formica tables, it's a favorite with locals and budget-minded guests at the hostel across the street. ✉*199 W. Palm Dr.* ☎*305/246–3114* ▭*AE, MC, V.*

WHERE TO STAY

$ **Best Western Gateway to the Keys.** If you want easy access to Everglades and Biscayne national parks as well as the Florida Keys, you'll be well placed at this pretty, modern, two-story motel two blocks off the Florida Turnpike. Standard rooms, done in tropical colors, have two queen-size beds or one king-size bed. Rooms around the lushly landscaped pool cost the most. There's high-speed Internet access available in the rooms, plus wireless access in the lobby. All rooms are no-smoking. **Pros:** Convenient to national parks and Keys, business services, pretty pool area. **Cons:** Traffic noise, generic rooms, fills up fast during high season. ✉ *411 S. Krome Ave.* ☎ *305/246–5100 or 888/981—5100* 🖷 *305/242–0056* 🌐 *www.bestwestern.com/gatewaytothekeys* *114 rooms* *In-room: refrigerator, Ethernet, dial-up. In-hotel: pool, no elevator, laundry facilities, public Wi-Fi, no-smoking rooms* *AE, D, DC, MC, V* *CP.*

$ **Comfort Inn.** Rooms are large, have contemporary tropical furnishings, and are on one of two floors (there's no elevator). They're outfitted with irons, hair dryers, and coffeemakers. Continental breakfast and newspapers are free. In-room Internet connections are high speed. It's in an asphalt complex of hotels, gas stations, and restaurants just off U.S. 1. **Pros:** Free continental breakfast, close to restaurants and services, in-room conveniences. **Cons:** No elevator, noisy location, nondescript rooms. ✉ *333 S.E. 1st Ave.* ☎ *305/248–4009 or 888/352–2489* 🖷 *305/248–7935* 🌐 *www.comfortinn.com* *124 rooms* *In-room: safe, refrigerator, Ethernet, dial-up. In-hotel: pool, no elevator, laundry facilities, public Wi-Fi, no-smoking rooms* *AE, D, DC, MC, V* *CP.*

¢–$ **Econo Lodge.** Close to the Florida Turnpike and with access to the Keys, this is a good pullover spot for an overnight. The rooms are uncramped, with attractive bedspreads, and have coffeemakers and data ports. The pool sits in the middle of the parking lot but tall ficus hedges separate it from busy Highway 1. There's a $1 daily charge to use the refrigerators that are in the rooms. **Pros:** Convenient location, business services, microwaves and refrigerators for rent. **Cons:** Urban-ugly location, noisy, lack of character. ✉ *553 N.E. 1st Ave.* ☎ *305/248–9300 or 800/553–2666* 🖷 *305/245–2753* 🌐 *www.econolodge.com* *42 rooms* *In-room: refrigerator, dial-up, Wi-Fi. In-hotel: pool, no elevator, laundry facilities, public Internet, public Wi-Fi, no-smoking rooms* *AE, D, DC, MC, V* *CP.*

¢ **Everglades Hostel.** Stay in clean and spacious private or dorm-style rooms (generally six to a room; bring your own linen); relax in indoor and outdoor quiet areas; watch videos or TV on a big screen; and take affordable airboat, hiking, biking, and sightseeing tours. This HI-AYH facility is in a minimally restored art deco building on a lush, private acre between Everglades and Biscayne national parks, 20 mi north of Key Largo. At mealtime, enjoy a free all-you-can-make pancake breakfast in the communal kitchen, pitch in for a communal dinner (according to demand, $5 each), or walk to a nearby restaurant. Pets are welcome. You can make free domestic long-distance calls from the phone in the lobby. **Pros:** Affordability, Everglades tours, free services. **Cons:** Communal living, no elevator, old structure. ✉*20 S.W. 2nd Ave.* ☎*305/248–1122 or 800/372–3874* 🖷*305/245–7622* 🌐*www.evergladeshostel.com* *46 beds in dorm-style rooms with shared bath, 2 private rooms with shared bath* *In-room: no a/c (some), no phone, no TV. In-hotel: water sports, bicycles, no elevator, laundry facilities, public Internet, public Wi-Fi, some pets allowed, no-smoking rooms* *MC, V.*

¢–$ **Fairway Inn.** Two stories high with a waterfall pool, this motel has some of the area's lowest chain rates, and it's next to the chamber of commerce. Rooms, with either one king-size bed or two doubles, have tiled bathroom and closet areas. **Pros:** Affordability; convenient to restaurants, parks, and raceway; free wireless connections in room. **Cons:** No character, plain rooms, small rooms. ✉*100 S.E. 1st Ave.* ☎*305/248–4202 or 888/340–4734* 🖷*786/217–6318* *160 rooms* *In-room: refrigerator, dial-up, Wi-Fi. In-hotel: pool, laundry facilities, no-smoking rooms* *AE, D, MC, V* *CP.*

★ ¢ **Ramada Inn.** Racing fans can hear the engines roar from this two-story motel next to an outlet mall and within 15 minutes of the raceway and Everglades and Biscayne national parks. If you're looking for an upgrade from the other chains, this one offers more amenities and comfort, such as 37-inch plasma TVs, closed closets, and stylish furnishings. Carpeted rooms are bright and clean and have upholstered chairs, a coffeemaker, and an iron and ironing board. Included are a Continental breakfast with some hot items and local calls. **Pros:** Extra room amenities, business clientele perks, convenient location. **Cons:** Busy location, chain anonymity, no sense of place. ✉*124 E. Palm Dr.* ☎*305/247–8833 or 800/426–7866* 🌐*www.hotelfloridacity.com* *123 rooms* *In-room: refrigerator (some), dial-up, Wi-Fi. In-hotel: pool, no elevator, laundry service, public Internet, no-smoking rooms* *AE, D, DC, MC, V* *CP.*

¢–$$ **Travelodge.** This bargain motor lodge is close to the Florida Turnpike, Everglades and Biscayne national parks, the Florida Keys, and the Homestead Miami Speedway. In fact, most of the racers stay here, which makes it difficult to get a room when any track events are scheduled. Clean and colorful rooms are smallish, but they have more amenities than usually found in this price range, including complimentary breakfast and newspaper, coffeemaker, hair dryer, iron with ironing board, high-speed Internet access, and voice mail. Fast-food and chain eateries, gas stations, and a visitor's bureau are within walking distance. **Pros:** In-room refrigerator and microwave, convenience to U.S. 1, complimentary breakfast. **Cons:** Lack of character, small rooms, busy location. ✉*409 S.E. 1st Ave.* ☎*305/248–9777 or 800/758–0618* 📠*305/248–9750* 🌐*www.tlflcity.com* *88 rooms* *In-room: safe, refrigerator, Ethernet, dial-up, Wi-Fi. In-hotel: pool, laundry facilities* 💳*AE, D, DC, MC, V* *CP.*

SHOPPING

Prime Outlets—Florida City (✉*250 E. Palm Dr.* ☎*888/545–1798* 🌐*www.primeoutlets.com*) has nearly 50 discount stores plus a small food court.

Divers Supply (✉*402 S.E. 1st Ave.* ☎*305/247–3483* 🌐*www.divers-supply.com*). For good deals on diving equipment before you get to the Keys' more costly shops, stop here. It carries everything from snorkels to dive kayaks.

★ **Robert Is Here** (✉*19200 Palm Dr. [S.W. 344th St.]* ☎*305/246–1592* 🌐*www.robertishere.com*), a remarkable fruit stand, sells vegetables, fresh-fruit milk shakes (the key lime shake is fabulous), 10 flavors of honey, more than 100 flavors of jams and jellies, fresh juices, salad dressings, and some 30 kinds of tropical fruits, including (in season) carambola, lychee, egg fruit, monstera, sapodilla, dragonfruit, genipa, sugar apple, and tamarind. The stand started in 1960, when seven-year-old Robert sat at this spot selling his father's bumper crop of cucumbers. Now Robert ships around the world, and everything is first quality. Seconds are given to needy area families. An odd assortment of animals out back—from goats to emus—adds to the entertainment value. The stand opens at 8 and never closes earlier than 7. It does shut down, however, during September and October.

Florida Keys Essentials

PLANNING TOOLS, EXPERT INSIGHT, GREAT CONTACTS

There are planners and there are those who, excuse the pun, fly by the seat of their pants. We happily place ourselves among the planners. Our writers and editors try to anticipate all the issues you may face before and during any journey, and then they do their research. This section is the product of their efforts. Use it to get excited about your trip to Florida Keys, to inform your travel planning, or to guide you on the road should the seat of your pants start to feel threadbare.

www.fodors.com/forums

GETTING STARTED

We're really proud of our Web site: Fodors.com is a great place to begin any journey. Scan Travel Wire for suggested itineraries, travel deals, restaurant and hotel openings, and other up-to-the-minute info. Check out Booking to research prices and book plane tickets, hotel rooms, rental cars, and vacation packages. Head to Talk for on-the-ground pointers from travelers who frequent our message boards. You can also link to loads of other travel-related resources.

WORD OF MOUTH

After your trip, be sure to rate the places you visited and share your experiences and travel tips with us and other Fodorites in Travel Ratings and Talk on www.fodors.com.

RESOURCES

ONLINE TRAVEL TOOLS

The National Park Web site has information on all the system's parks, so this is a good place to start looking for information on Dry Tortugas National Park and Everglades National Park. Likewise, the U.S. Fish & Wildlife Service Web site has information on all its refuges; look here for advice on visiting National Key Deer Refuge, Crocodile Lake National Wildlife Refuge, Great White Heron NWR, and Key West NWR.

The Florida Keys Council of the Arts' Web site has a calendar of events and directories of theaters, museums, art galleries, artists, music festivals, literature, and more in the Keys. For information on gay-related services and activities in Key West, refer to the Key West Business Guild's Web site. Historic Tours of America's Web site carries information on a number of Key West attractions and sells tickets at discounted prices.

All About the Florida Keys **Florida Keys Council of the Arts** (www.keysarts.org). **Historic Tours of America** (www.historictours.com/keywest). **Key West Business Guild** (www.gaykeywestfl.com). **National Park Service** (www.nps.gov). **U.S. Fish & Wildlife Service** (www.fws.gov).

Safety **Transportation Security Administration** (TSA www.tsa.gov).

Time Zones **Timeanddate.com** (www.timeanddate.com/worldclock) can help you figure out the correct time anywhere.

Weather **Accuweather.com** (www.accuweather.com) is an independent weather-forecasting service with good coverage of hurricanes. **Weather.com** (www.weather.com) is the Web site for the Weather Channel.

Other Resources **CIA World Factbook** (www.odci.gov/cia/publications/factbook/index.html) has profiles of every country in the

Trip Insurance Resources

INSURANCE COMPARISON SITES		
Insure My Trip.com	800/487-4722	www.insuremytrip.com.
Square Mouth.com	800/240-0369 or 727/490-5803	www.squaremouth.com.
COMPREHENSIVE TRAVEL INSURERS		
Access America	800/729-6021	www.accessamerica.com.
CSA Travel Protection	800/873-9855	www.csatravelprotection.com.
HTH Worldwide	610/254-8700	www.hthworldwide.com.
Travelex Insurance	800/228-9792	www.travelex-insurance.com.
AIG Travel Guard	800/826-4919	www.travelguard.com.
Travel Insured International	800/243-3174	www.travelinsured.com.
MEDICAL-ONLY INSURERS		
International Medical Group	800/628-4664	www.imglobal.com.
International SOS		www.internationalsos.com.
Wallach & Company	800/237-6615 or 540/687-3166	www.wallach.com.

world. It's a good source if you need some quick facts and figures.

VISITOR INFORMATION

The Web site for the Florida Keys & Key West, the official tourism agency, gives a comprehensive overview of the destination, complete with maps, videos, and easy navigation.

Contacts The Florida Keys & Key West (✉402 Wall St., Box 1146, Key West, ☎800/352-5397 🌐www.fla-keys.com).

THINGS TO CONSIDER

TRIP INSURANCE

What kind of coverage do you honestly need? Do you need trip insurance at all? Take a deep breath and read on.

We believe that comprehensive trip insurance is especially valuable if you're booking a very expensive or complicated trip (particularly to an isolated region) or if you're booking far in advance. Who knows what could happen six months down the road? But whether or not you get insurance has more to do with how comfortable you are assuming all that risk yourself.

Comprehensive travel policies typically cover trip-cancellation and interruption, letting you cancel or cut your trip short because of a personal emergency, illness, or, in some cases, acts of terrorism in your destination. Such policies also cover evacuation and medical care. Some also cover you for trip delays because of bad weather or mechanical problems as well as for lost or delayed baggage. Another type of coverage to look for is financial default—that is, when your trip is disrupted because a tour operator, airline, or cruise line goes out of business. Generally you must buy this when you book your trip or shortly thereafter, and it's only available to you if your operator isn't on a list of excluded companies.

If you're going abroad, consider buying medical-only coverage at the very least. Neither Medicare nor some private insurers cover medical expenses anywhere outside of the United States (including time aboard a cruise ship, even if it leaves from a U.S. port). Medical-only policies typically reimburse you for medical care (excluding that related to preexisting conditions) and hospitalization abroad, and provide for evacuation. You still have to pay the bills and await reimbursement from the insurer, though.

Expect comprehensive travel insurance policies to cost about 4% to 7% or 8% of the total price of your trip (it's more like 8%–12% if you're over age 70). A medical-only policy may or may not be cheaper than a comprehensive policy. Always read the fine print of your policy to make sure that you are covered for the risks that are of most concern to you. Compare several policies to make sure you're getting the best price and range of coverage available.

■ TIP→ **OK. You know you can save a bundle on trips to warm-weather destinations by traveling in rainy season. But there's also a chance that a severe storm will disrupt your plans. The solution? Look for hotels and resorts that offer storm/hurricane guarantees. Although they rarely allow refunds, most guarantees do let you rebook later if a storm strikes.**

BOOKING YOUR TRIP

Unless your cousin is a travel agent, you're probably among the millions of people who make most of their travel arrangements online.

But have you ever wondered just what the differences are between an online travel agent (a Web site through which you make reservations instead of going directly to the airline, hotel, or car-rental company), a discounter (a firm that does a high volume of business with a hotel chain or airline and accordingly gets good prices), a wholesaler (one that makes cheap reservations in bulk and then re-sells them to people like you), and an aggregator (one that compares all the offerings so you don't have to)?

Is it truly better to book directly on an airline or hotel Web site? And when does a real live travel agent come in handy?

ONLINE

You really have to shop around. A travel wholesaler such as Hotels.com or HotelClub.net can be a source of good rates, as can discounters such as Hotwire or Priceline, particularly if you can bid for your hotel room or airfare. Indeed, such sites sometimes have deals that are unavailable elsewhere. They do, however, tend to work only with hotel chains (which makes them just plain useless for getting hotel reservations outside of major cities) or big airlines (so that often leaves out upstarts like jetBlue and some foreign carriers like Air India).

Also, with discounters and wholesalers you must generally prepay, and everything is nonrefundable. And before you fork over the dough, be sure to check the terms and conditions, so you know what a given company will do for you if there's a problem and what you'll have to deal with on your own.

TIP→ **To be absolutely sure everything was processed correctly, confirm reservations made through online travel agents, discounters, and wholesalers directly with your hotel before leaving home.**

Booking engines like Expedia, Travelocity, and Orbitz are actually travel agents, albeit high-volume, online ones. And airline travel packagers like American Airlines Vacations and Virgin Vacations—well, they're travel agents, too. But they may still not work with all the world's hotels.

An aggregator site will search many sites and pull the best prices for airfares, hotels, and rental cars from them. Most aggregators compare the major travel-booking sites such as Expedia, Travelocity, and Orbitz; some also look at airline Web sites, though rarely the sites of smaller budget airlines. Some aggregators also compare other travel products, including complex packages—a good thing, as you can sometimes get the best

Online Booking Resources

AGGREGATORS		
Kayak	www.kayak.com	looks at cruises and vacation packages.
Mobissimo	www.mobissimo.com	examines airfare, hotels, cars, and tons of activities.
Qixo	www.qixo.com	compares cruises, vacation packages, and even travel insurance.
Sidestep	www.sidestep.com	compares vacation packages and lists travel deals and some activities.
BOOKING ENGINES		
Expedia	www.expedia.com	large online agency that charges a booking fee for airline tickets.
Hotwire	www.hotwire.com	discounter.
Orbitz	www.orbitz.com	charges a booking fee for airline tickets, but gives a clear breakdown of fees and taxes before you book.
Travelocity	www.travelocity.com	charges a booking fee for airline tickets, but promises good problem resolution.
ONLINE ACCOMMODATIONS		
Hotelbook.com	www.hotelbook.com	focuses on independent hotels worldwide.
Hotels.com	www.hotels.com	big Expedia-owned wholesaler that offers rooms in hotels all over the world.
Quikbook	www.quikbook.com	offers "pay when you stay" reservations that allow you to settle your bill when you check out, not when you book; best for trips to U.S. and Canadian cities.

overall deal by booking an air-and-hotel package.

WITH A TRAVEL AGENT

If you use an agent—brick-and-mortar or virtual—you'll pay a fee for the service, especially for domestic travel. And know that the service you get from some online agents isn't comprehensive. For example Expedia and Travelocity don't search for prices on budget airlines like jetBlue, Southwest, or small foreign carriers. That said, some agents (online or not) *do* have access to fares that are difficult to find otherwise, and the savings can more than make up for any surcharge.

A knowledgeable brick-and-mortar travel agent can be a godsend if you're booking a cruise, a package trip that's not available to you directly, an air pass, or a complicated itinerary including several overseas flights. What's more, travel agents that specialize in a destination may have exclusive access to certain deals and insider information on things such as charter flights. Agents who specialize in types of travelers (senior citizens, gays and lesbians, naturists) or types of trips (cruises, luxury travel, safaris) can also be invaluable.

TIP→ **Remember that Expedia, Travelocity, and Orbitz are travel agents, not just booking engines. To resolve any problems with a reservation made through these companies, contact them first.**

Complain about the surcharges all you like, but when things don't work out the way you'd hoped, it's nice to have an agent to put things right.

Agent Resources **American Society of Travel Agents** (☎703/739-2782 🌐www.travelsense.org).

ACCOMMODATIONS

The most characteristic type of lodging in the Keys is a small, family-owned place, whether it be a guesthouse in Key West or a dive lodge in Key Largo. The islands do have their share of franchised operations and big destination resorts, but intimate lodging is still quite easy to find throughout the Keys. This is particularly true in Key West's Old Town, where many of the historic Victorian homes have been transformed into B&Bs. Most serve only Continental breakfast (a restaurant license is required to serve hot food).

CATEGORY	COST
$$$$	over $250
$$$	$200–$250
$$	$150–$200
$	$100–$150
¢	under $100

All prices are for a double room in high season, based on the European Plan (EP) and excluding 11.5% tax made up of 7.5% sales, 3% tourist, 1% tourist impact.

Most hotels and other lodgings require you to give your credit-card details before they will confirm your reservation. If you don't feel comfortable e-mailing this information, ask if you can fax it (some places even prefer faxes). However you book, get confirmation in writing and have a copy of it handy when you check in.

Be sure you understand the hotel's cancellation policy. Some places allow you to cancel without any kind of penalty—even if you prepaid to secure a discounted rate—if you cancel at least 24 hours in advance. Others require you to cancel a week in advance or penalize you the cost of one night. Small inns and B&Bs are most likely to require you to cancel far in advance. Most hotels allow children under a certain age to stay in their parents' room at no extra charge, but others charge for them as extra adults; find out the cutoff age for discounts.

TIP→ **Assume that hotels operate on the European Plan (EP, no meals) unless we specify that they use the Breakfast Plan (BP, with full breakfast), Continental Plan (CP, Continental breakfast), Full American Plan (FAP, all meals), Modified American Plan (MAP, breakfast and dinner) or are all-inclusive (AI, all meals and most activities).**

APARTMENT & HOUSE RENTALS

Although short-term rentals are available throughout the Keys, Key West has the largest inventory, and several rental companies can hook you up.

Contacts **Forgetaway** (www.forgetaway.weather.com). **Home Away** (512/493–0382 www.homeaway.com). **Interhome** (954/791–8282 or 800/882–6864 www.interhome.us). **Villas International** (415/499–9490 or 800/221–2260 www.villasintl.com).

AIRLINE TICKETS

Most domestic airline tickets are electronic. With an e-ticket the only thing you receive is an e-mailed receipt citing your itinerary and reservation and ticket numbers.

The greatest advantage of an e-ticket is that if you lose your receipt, you can simply print out another copy or ask the airline to do it for you at check-in. You usually pay a surcharge (up to $50) to get a paper ticket, if you can get one at all.

The sole advantage of a paper ticket is that it may be easier to endorse over to another airline if your flight is canceled and the airline with which you booked can't accommodate you on another flight.

TIP→ **Discount air passes that let you travel economically in a country or region must often be purchased before you leave home. In some cases you can only get them through a travel agent.**

RENTAL CARS

When you reserve a car, ask about cancellation penalties, taxes, drop-off charges (if you're planning to pick up the car in one city and leave it in another), and surcharges (for being under or over a certain age, for additional drivers, or for driving across state or country borders or beyond a specific distance from your point of rental). All these things can add substantially to your costs. Request car seats and extras such as GPS when you book.

Rates are sometimes—but not always—better if you book in advance or reserve through a rental agency's Web site. There are other reasons to book ahead, though: for popular destinations, during busy times of the year, or to ensure that you get certain types of cars (vans, SUVs, exotic sports cars).

TIP→ **Make sure that a confirmed reservation guarantees you a car. Agencies sometimes overbook, par-**

Car Rental Resources

AUTOMOBILE ASSOCIATIONS		
U.S.: American Automobile Association (AAA)	315/797-5000	www.aaa.com; most contact with the organization is through state and regional members.
National Automobile Club	650/294-7000	www.thenac.com; membership is open to California residents only.
LOCAL AGENCIES		
Key West Cruisers	☎305/294-4724 or 888/800-8802	
MAJOR AGENCIES		
Alamo	800/462-5266	www.alamo.com.
Avis	800/331-1212	www.avis.com.
Budget	800/527-0700	www.budget.com.
Hertz	800/654-3131	www.hertz.com.
National Car Rental	800/227-7368	www.nationalcar.com.

ticularly for busy weekends and holiday periods.

Unless you fly into Key West and decide to stay in Old Town for your entire vacation—perhaps with a bus trip to another Key or some water sports excursions—you will need a car. Rentals of all makes and models are available at the Miami International Airport, Key West International Airport, and rental agencies throughout the Keys. Reserve your car early during big events such as Homestead Miami Speedway races (Key Largo is often affected), October's FantasyFest in Key West, and the Christmas and Easter holidays.

CAR-RENTAL INSURANCE

Everyone who rents a car wonders whether the insurance that the rental companies offer is worth the expense. No one—including us—has a simple answer. It all depends on how much regular insurance you have, how comfortable you are with risk, and whether or not money is an issue.

If you own a car and carry comprehensive car insurance for both collision and liability, your personal auto insurance will probably cover a rental, but read your policy's fine print to be sure. If you don't have auto insurance, then you should probably buy the collision- or loss-damage waiver (CDW or LDW) from the rental company. This eliminates your liability for damage to the car.

Some credit cards offer CDW coverage, but it's usually supplemental to your own insurance and rarely covers SUVs, minivans, luxury models, and the like. If your coverage is secondary, you may still be liable for loss-of-use costs from the car-rental company (again, read the fine print). But no credit-card insurance is valid unless you use that card for *all* transactions, from reserving to paying the final bill.

TIP→ **Diners Club offers primary CDW coverage on all rentals reserved and paid for with the card. This means that Diners Club's company—not your own car insurance—pays in case of an accident. It *doesn't* mean that your car-insurance company won't raise your rates once it discovers you had an accident.**

You may also be offered supplemental liability coverage; the car-rental company is required to carry a minimal level of liability coverage insuring all renters, but it's rarely enough to cover claims in a really serious accident if you're at fault. Your own auto-insurance policy will protect you if you own a car; if you don't, you have to decide whether you are willing to take the risk.

U.S. rental companies sell CDWs and LDWs for about $15 to $25 a day; supplemental liability is usually more than $10 a day. The car-rental company may offer you all sorts of other policies, but they're rarely worth the cost. Personal accident insurance, which is basic hospitalization coverage, is an especially egregious rip-off if you already have health insurance.

TIP→ **You can decline the insurance from the rental company and purchase it through a third-party provider such as Travel Guard (*www.travelguard.com*)—$9 per day for $35,000 of coverage. That's sometimes just under half the price of the CDW offered by some car-rental companies.**

TIP→ **You can decline the insurance from the rental company and purchase it through a third-party provider such as Travel Guard (*www.travelguard.com*)—$9 per day for $35,000 of coverage. That's sometimes just under half the price of the CDW offered by some car-rental companies.**

VACATION PACKAGES

Packages *are not* guided excursions. Packages combine airfare, accommodations, and perhaps a rental car or other extras (theater tickets, guided excursions, boat trips, reserved entry to popular museums, transit passes), but they let you do your own thing. During busy periods packages may be your only option, as flights and rooms may be sold out otherwise.

Packages will definitely save you time. They can also save you money, particularly in peak seasons, but—and this is a really big "but"—you should price each part of the package separately to be sure. And be aware that prices advertised on Web sites and in newspapers rarely include service charges or taxes, which can up your costs by hundreds of dollars.

TIP→ **Some packages and cruises are sold only through travel agents. Don't always assume that you can get the best deal by booking everything yourself.**

Each year consumers are stranded or lose their money when packagers—even large ones with excellent reputations—go out of business. How can you protect yourself?

First, always pay with a credit card; if you have a problem, your credit-card company may help you resolve it. Second, buy trip insurance that covers default. Third, choose a company that belongs to the United States Tour Operators Association, whose members must set aside funds to cover defaults. Finally, choose a company that also participates in the Tour Operator Program of the American Society of Travel Agents (ASTA), which will act as mediator in any disputes.

You can also check on the tour operator's reputation among travelers by posting an inquiry on one of the Fodors.com forums.

If you have a specific interest to pursue in the Keys—diving or dolphin interaction, for instance—a package may be the best way to go to insure the best use of your time without the hassle of planning and setting up excursions. Otherwise, unless you don't have time to plan or want to make the most of the time you have in the Keys, the Keys is the kind of destination best experienced at your own pace and by getting off the beaten path.

Organizations **American Society of Travel Agents** (ASTA ☎703/739–2782 or 800/965–2782 🌐www.astanet.com). **United States Tour Operators Association** (USTOA ☎212/599–6599 🌐www.ustoa.com). ■ TIP→ **Local tourism boards can provide information about lesser-known and small-niche operators that sell packages to only a few destinations.**

TRANSPORTATION

Key West International Airport is the only airport in the Keys that accommodates commercial flights, and only four commuter airlines serve the airport. Most visitors fly into Miami International Airport and either drive to their destination in the Keys or take an air shuttle to Key West. The drive is long and slow. It can be done in a half-day, but it's better to break up the drive and spend some time exploring the Keys outside of Key West.

TIP→ Ask the local tourist board about hotel and local transportation packages that include tickets to major museum exhibits or other special events.

BY AIR

Most visitors fly into Miami and drive to the Florida Keys; however Key West International Airport serves about a half-million passengers annually. Up to 100 commercial flights—including arrivals and departures—are scheduled daily, operated by five commercial carriers and two commuter airlines.

TIP→ If you travel frequently, look into the TSA's Registered Traveler program. The program, which is still being tested in several U.S. airports, is designed to cut down on gridlock at security checkpoints by allowing prescreened travelers to pass quickly through kiosks that scan an iris and/or a fingerprint. How sci-fi is that?

Airlines & Airports **Airline and Airport Links.com** (www.airlineandairportlinks.com) has links to many of the world's airlines and airports.

Airline Security Issues **Transportation Security Administration** (www.tsa.gov) has answers for almost every question that might come up.

AIRPORTS

The fittingly tiny, laid-back Key West International Airport (EYW) has greeted domestic passengers and overseas private planes since 1957. A new ticketing, security, and baggage complex more than doubled Key West International Airport's terminal space in 2008. The new McCoy Terminal sits atop a 475-car parking ramp.

The airport is a short drive from Old Town, so should your flight get delayed (it happens often enough), jump in a taxi and enjoy a few more hours of Key West freedom. Note that *www.keywestinternationalairport.com* is not the official airport site; it is operated by an outside travel agency.

TIP→ Long layovers don't have to be only about sitting around or shopping. These days they can be about burning off vacation calories. Check out *www.airportgyms.com* for lists of health clubs that are in or near many U.S. and Canadian airports.

Airport Information **Key West International Airport** (✉E.S. Roosevelt Blvd., Key West ☎305/296–7223 🌐www.keywestinternationalairport.com). **Miami International Airport** (☎305/876–7000 🌐www.miami-airport.com).

GROUND TRANSPORTATION

Airporter operates scheduled van and bus service from all Miami International Airport (MIA) baggage areas to wherever you want to go in Key Largo ($45) and Islamorada ($50). A group discount is given for three or more passengers. There are three departures daily, and reservations are required.

Greyhound Lines runs a special Keys shuttle two times a day (depending on the day of the week) from Miami International Airport (departing from Concourse E, lower level) and stops throughout the Keys. Fares run from around $20 for Key Largo (Howard Johnson, MM 102) to around $41 for Key West (3535 S. Roosevelt, Key West International Airport).

Keys Shuttle runs scheduled service six times a day in 15-passenger vans (nine passengers maximum) between Miami Airport and Key West with stops throughout the Keys for $70 to $90 per person.

SuperShuttle charges about $101 per passenger for trips to the Upper Keys. To go farther into the Keys, you must book an entire van (up to 11 passengers), which costs about $250 to Marathon, $350 to Key West. SuperShuttle requests 24-hour notice for transportation back to the airport.

Contacts **Airporter** (☎305/852–3413 or 800/830–3413). **Greyhound Lines** (☎800/410–5397 or 800/231–2222). **Keys Shuttle** (☎305/289–9997 or 888/765–9997 🌐www.floridakeysshuttle.com). **SuperShuttle** (☎305/871–2000 🌐www.supershuttle.com).

FLIGHTS

Service between Key West International Airport and Miami, Fort Lauderdale/Hollywood, Fort Myers, West Palm, Atlanta, Naples, Orlando, St. Petersburg, and Tampa is provided by American Eagle, Comair/Delta Connection, Gulfstream/Continental Connection, and US Airways/US Airways Express. Expect tiny planes from some of these hubs; you'll be asked your weight, and you may have to sit in the copilot's seat.

Flying time from Miami is 50 minutes, from Orlando 3½ to 4 hours, from Atlanta 4 to 5 hours.

Airline Contacts **American Airlines** (☎800/433–7300 🌐www.aa.com). **Continental Airlines** (☎800/523—3273 for U.S. and Mexico reservations, 800/231–0856 for international reservations 🌐www.continental.com). **Delta Airlines** (☎800/221–1212 for U.S. reservations, 800/241–4141 for international reservations 🌐www.delta.com). **USAirways** (☎800/428–4322 for U.S. and Canada reservations, 800/622–1015 for international reservations 🌐www.usairways.com).

BY BOAT

Boaters can travel to and along the Keys either along the Intracoastal Waterway (5-foot draft limitation) through Card, Barnes, and Blackwater sounds and into Florida Bay, or along the deeper Atlantic Ocean route through Hawk Channel, a buoyed passage. Refer to NOAA Nautical Charts Numbers 11451, 11445, and 11441. The Keys are full of marinas that welcome transient visitors, but they don't have enough slips for everyone. Make reservations in advance and ask about channel and dockage depth—many marinas are quite shallow.

For nonemergency information contact Coast Guard Group Key West; VHF-FM Channel 16. Safety and weather information is broadcast at 7 AM and 5 PM Eastern Standard Time on VHF-FM Channels 16 and 22A. There are stations in Islamorada and Marathon.

Key West Express operates seasonal air-conditioned ferries between the Key West Terminal (Caroline and Grinnell streets) and Fort Meyers Beach, Miami, and Marco Islands. For all ferries, a current, legal photo ID is required for each passenger. All bags are subject to search. Advance reservations are recommended.

The trip from Fort Myers Beach takes 3½ hours each way; ferries depart Fort Meyers Beach at 8:30 AM, with the return from Key West at 6 PM. The fare is $73 one-way, $128 round-trip.

Miami ferries depart daily at 9:30 AM (8:30 AM Sunday); the return from Key West is 6:30 PM (5:30 PM Sunday). The fare is $53 one-way, $108 round-trip. The trip takes 4 hours.

Marco Island ferries depart daily at 8:30 AM, returning from Key West at 5 PM. Fares are $54 one-way, $108 round-trip. The trip takes 4 hours.

Information **Coast Guard Group for the Florida Keys** (✉Key West ☎305/292–8856 or 800/368–5647 ✉Islamorada ☎305/664–8077 information, 305/664–4404 emergencies ✉Marathon ☎305/743–6778 information, 305/743–6388 emergencies). **Key West Express Ferry** (☎888/539–2628 or 239/463–5733 (Fort Myers Beach and Marco Island), 866/593–3779 [Miami only] ⊕www.seakeywestexpress.com).

BY BUS

The City of Key West Department of Transportation has six color-coded bus routes traversing the island from 6:30 AM to 11:30 PM. Stops have signs with the international symbol for bus. Schedules are available on buses and at hotels, visitor centers, and shops. The fare is $1 (exact change) or $3 for an all-day pass that you purchase on board.

American Coach Lines (formerly the Dade–Monroe Express) provides daily bus service from MM 50 in Marathon to the Florida City Wal-Mart Supercenter on the mainland. The bus stops at major shopping centers as well as on-demand anywhere along the route during daily round-trips on the hour from 6 AM to 9:55 PM. The cost is $1.85 one-way, exact change required.

The Lower Keys Shuttle bus runs from Marathon to Key West ($2 one-way), with scheduled and on-demand stops along the way.

Bus Information City of Key West Department of Transportation (☎305/809–3910). American Coach Lines (☎305/770–3131). Lower Keys Shuttle (☎305/809–3910 🌐www.monroecounty-fl.gov).

BY CAR

From MIA, follow signs to Coral Gables and Key West, which put you on Lejeune Road, then Route 836 west. Take the Homestead Extension of Florida's Turnpike south (toll road), which ends at Florida City and connects to U.S. 1. Tolls from the airport run approximately $2.25. The alternative from Florida City is Card Sound Road (Route 905A), which has a bridge toll of $1. Continue to the only stop sign and turn right on Route 905, which rejoins U.S. 1 31 mi south of Florida City.

Except in Key West, a car is essential for visiting the Keys. The best Keys road map, published by the Homestead–Florida City Chamber of Commerce, can be obtained for $5.50 from the Tropical Everglades Visitor Center.

Avis, Budget, and Enterprise serve Marathon Airport. Avis, Alamo, Budget, Dollar, and Hertz serve Key West's airport. Enterprise has offices in Key Largo, Marathon, and Key West. Thrifty Car Rental has an office in Tavernier.

TIP→ Avoid flying into Key West and driving back to Miami; there could be substantial drop-off charges for leaving a Key West car there.

GASOLINE

The deeper you go into the Keys, the higher the pump price goes. Gas stations in Homestead and Florida City have some of the most affordable prices in South Florida, so fill your tank in Miami and top it off in Florida City.

PARKING

The only place in the Keys where parking is a problem is in Old Town Key West. There are public parking lots that charge by the day (some hotels and B&Bs provide parking or discounts at municipal lots). If you arrive early, you can sometimes find spots on side streets off of Duval and Whitehead, where you can park for free—just be sure it's not marked for residential parking only. Your best bet is to bike or take the trolley around town if you don't want to walk. The trolleys and Conch Train allow you to disembark and reboard at will.

ROAD CONDITIONS

Most of the Overseas Highway is narrow and crowded (especially on weekends and in high season). Expect delays behind RVs, trucks, cars towing boats, and rubbernecking tourists. The section of highway that travels from mainland to Key Largo is particularly slow and congested. Occasional passing lanes allow you to get past slow-moving trucks. Currently crews are working at four-laning the route, so construction delays aggravate the situation. The project is supposed to be completed by 2012. The completion of a high-span bridge into Key Largo to replace the drawbridge, expected in 2009, should relieve some of the problem.

The quality of local roads in Key West is good, though some side streets are narrow. Traffic in the historic district often becomes congested throughout the day and night.

BY TAXI

Serving the Keys from Ocean Reef to Key West, Luxury Limousine has luxury sedans and limos that seat up to eight passengers, as well as vans and buses. It'll pick up from any airport in South Florida. Florida Keys Taxi Dispatch (also called Five Sixes Taxi) operates around the clock in Key West. The fare for two or more from the Key West airport to Old Town or New Town is $7.50 per person. Otherwise meters register $2.75 to start, 60¢ for each 1/5 mi, and 60¢ for every 50 seconds of waiting time. Their pink taxis all have bike racks.

Taxi Companies **Florida Keys Taxi Dispatch** (Five Sixes Taxi ☎305/296-6666 or 305/296-1800 ⊕www.keywesttaxi.com). **Luxury Limousine** (☎305/367-2329 or 800/664-0124).

ON THE GROUND

COMMUNICATIONS

INTERNET

Internet access is the norm in the smaller guesthouses, lodges, motels, and resorts. Typically it's Wi-Fi and often free, although not always available in every room, especially in older concrete-block or tin-roof structures. The larger resorts often charge for the service.

Contacts **Cybercafes** (🌐www.cybercafes.com) lists more than 4,000 Internet cafés worldwide.

EATING OUT

The variety of restaurants in the Keys is vast, but if you were to ask a visitor what is typical, you would probably hear about the colorful seaside fish houses, some with more character than others. Seafood comes so fresh you'll be spoiled for life. Pay special attention to local catches—especially snapper, mahimahi, grouper, lobster, and stone crab. Florida spiny lobster is local and fresh from August to March and stone crabs from mid-October to mid-May.

Also keep an eye out for authentic Key lime pie. The real McCoy has yellow filling in a graham-cracker crust and tastes pleasantly tart. (If it's green, just say "no.") Cuban and Bahamian styles influence local cuisine, so be sure to sample some black beans and rice and conch fritters.

Restaurants may close for a two- to four-week vacation during the slow season—between mid-September and mid-November.

MEALS & MEALTIMES

Unless otherwise noted, the restaurants listed in this guide are open daily for lunch and dinner.

PAYING

Most restaurants accept the major credit cards. Some of the small, family-owned operations do not.

For guidelines on tipping see Tipping below.

CATEGORY	COST
$$$$	over $40
$$$	$30–$40
$$	$20–$30
$	$10–$20
¢	under $10

All prices are the median cost per person for a main course at dinner (or lunch, if dinner is not served) excluding 6% tax.

RESERVATIONS & DRESS

Regardless of where you are, it's a good idea to make a reservation if you can. In some places (Hong Kong, for example), it's expected. We only mention them specifically when reservations are essential (there's no other way you'll ever get a table) or when they are not accepted. For popular restaurants, book as far ahead as you can (often 30 days), and reconfirm as soon as you arrive. (Large parties should always call ahead to check the reservations policy.) We mention dress only when men are required to wear a jacket or a jacket and tie.

Online reservation services make it easy to book a table before you even leave home. OpenTable covers most states, including a few restaurants in the Keys.

Contacts **OpenTable** (www.opentable.com).

WORD OF MOUTH

Was the service stellar or not up to snuff? Did the food give you shivers of delight or leave you cold? Did the prices and portions make you happy or sad? Rate restaurants and write your own reviews in Travel Ratings or start a discussion about your favorite places in Travel Talk on www.fodors.com. Your comments might even appear in our books. Yes, you, too, can be a correspondent!

WINES, BEER & SPIRITS

If the Keys have a representative tipple, it is the margarita. Kelly's Caribbean Bar & Brewery in Key West is the Keys' only microbrewery, and it sells bottled product.

EMERGENCIES

Keys Hotline provides information and emergency assistance in six languages. Florida Marine Patrol maintains a 24-hour telephone service to handle reports of boating emergencies and natural-resource violations. The Keys have no 24-hour pharmacies. Hospital pharmacists will help with emergencies after regular retail business hours. Fishermen's Hospital, Lower Florida Keys Health System, and Mariners Hospital have 24-hour emergency rooms.

Contacts Emergencies (911). Fishermen's Hospital (MM 48.7, OS, Marathon, 305/743–5533 www.fishermenshospital.com). Florida Marine Patrol/Fish and Wildlife Conservation Commission (MM 48, BS, 2796 Overseas Hwy., Suite 100, State Regional Service Center, Marathon, 305/289–2320, 800/342–5392 after 5 PM www.myfwc.com). Lower Florida Keys Health System (MM 5, BS, 5900 College Rd., Stock Island, 305/294–5531). Mariners Hospital (MM 91.5, BS, Tavernier, 305/434–3000 www.baptisthealth.net).

MONEY

ATMs are common throughout the Keys if you need to get cash, so there's no need to carry a large amount of money on your person.

CREDIT CARDS

Throughout this guide, the following abbreviations are used: **AE**, American Express; **D**, Discover; **DC**, Diners Club; **MC**, MasterCard; and **V**, Visa.

It's a good idea to inform your credit-card company before you travel, especially if you're going abroad and don't travel internationally very often. Otherwise, the credit-card company might put a hold on your card owing to unusual activity—not a good thing halfway through your trip. Record all your credit-card numbers—as well as the phone numbers to call if your cards are lost or stolen—in a safe place, so you're prepared should something go wrong. Both MasterCard and Visa have general numbers you can call (collect if you're abroad) if your card is lost, but you're better off calling the number of your issuing bank, since MasterCard and Visa usually just transfer you to your bank; your bank's number is usually printed on your card.

Reporting Lost Cards **American Express** (☎800/528-4800 in U.S., 336/393-1111 collect from abroad 🌐www.americanexpress.com). **Diners Club** (☎800/234-6377 in U.S., 303/799-1504 collect from abroad 🌐www.dinersclub.com). **Discover** (☎800/347-2683 in U.S., 801/902-3100 collect from abroad 🌐www.discovercard.com). **MasterCard** (☎800/627-8372 in U.S., 636/722-7111 collect from abroad 🌐www.mastercard.com). **Visa** (☎800/847-2911 in U.S., 410/581-9994 collect from abroad 🌐www.visa.com).

TIME

The Florida Keys are in the Eastern Time Zone. The Dry Tortugas lie in the Central Time Zone, but the ferry boats and seaplanes run according to Eastern time. During daylight saving time, some operations stay open later.

TIPPING

Tip at restaurants (15% is sufficient except at the most fancy, expensive places, where a larger tip of around 18% is more common). It's common courtesy to leave a dollar or two for the housekeeper at your hotel (unless you are staying at a B&B that's run by the owners); leave the money each morning before your room is cleaned.

INDEX

D

E

F

NOTES

NOTES

NOTES

ABOUT OUR WRITERS

Chelle Koster Walton admits she's a "fair-weather writer"—her specialty is travel and cuisine in Florida, the Caribbean, and other tropical locales. She has written for such publications as *FamilyFun, Bridal Guide,* the *St. Petersburg Times, National Geographic Traveler, USA Today,* and the *Miami Herald.* A resident of Sanibel Island, Florida, for 25 years, she is the author of several Florida guidebooks, including The Sarasota, Sanibel Island & Naples Book; Fun with the Family in Florida; and *Adventure Guide to Tampa Bay & Florida's West Coast.* Walton also contributes annually to Fodor's Florida and Bahamas guidebooks and is the Regional Getaways producer for WGCU Public Television. Her love affair with the Florida Keys began more than 20 years ago, when she and her husband Rob began their diving-camping trips to Long Key State Park. More recently, Walton introduced her teenage son Aaron to Key West, and they coauthored a teen-travel article about their visit to the island and the Dry Tortugas.

Julia Neyman updated the Miami chapter of *Fodor's Florida 2009,* from which material is excerpted in "Gateways to the Keys."

ACKNOWLEDGMENTS

Chelle wishes to express her appreciation to her mindful editors, Douglas Stalling and Mark Sullivan, and to the following Keys residents and experts whose spirit and knowledge helped her infuse this book with that indefinable Keys flavor: Josie Gulliksen, Carol Shaughnessy, Keely Baribeau, Captain Victoria Rose Impallomeni and her wild friends, Mary Stella, Tiffany Boeckman, Joe and Ronnie Harris, and Maureen Lamarra. Final thanks to Robert and Aaron Walton for their forbearance during the completion of this project and for their shared love of the Florida Keys.